Barefoot Britain
by Anna McNuff

Book design by Sally & Kim from Off Grid

@somewhereoffgrid

somewhereoffgrid.com

If you're from a book club, corporate, business or school and would like to place a bulk order for copies of this book, substantial discounts are available. Drop an email to **hello@annamcnuff.com** for more details.

Other books by Anna McNuff:

For adults:

The Pants of Perspective

The United States of Adventure

Llama Drama

Bedtime Adventure Stories for Grown Ups

For Kids:

100 Adventures to Have Before You Grow Up

Find Anna on Social Media:

@AnnaMcNuff

Join her mailing list:

AnnaMcNuff.com/McNewsletter

ANNA MCNUFF

BEFORE YOU GET STUCK IN

Barefoot Britain is a true story and these pages feature real events and real people. There are a few occasions when an event has been shifted slightly to help the story flow better, and a few character names which have been changed – either because there are only so many people called Jennie/Jenny you can have in one book or because that particular person moonlights as 007 on the side. Other than that. . . This is the truth, the whole truth and nuffin' but the truth.

For all the runners who joined me on Barefoot Britain:
You are made of sweat and magic.

Contents

The Route

Start

Finish!

Prologue

It's April 2019 and I'm standing on the start line of the London Marathon. I'm a bag of nerves and my legs feel like jelly. I look down at my feet and am reminded that I'm not wearing any shoes. What the heck have you got yourself into, Anna? Part of me wants nothing more than for a giant hole to open up in the universe and swallow me into it. Then I wouldn't have to go through with this ridiculous idea, an idea I've told everyone about. And yet, beneath the nerves, there's excitement. Adrenaline courses through my veins. It's addictive, and I like it. And so it continues. A flood of worries. A rush of excitement. The perfect pre-run cocktail.

I hop around on the spot in a bid to disperse the nerves, and turn my attention to the day ahead. A total of 26.2 miles, from Blackheath to Buckingham Palace, with no shoes on. I've only ever run 17 miles barefoot before, so the plan is to make it to mile 17 and then. . . hope for the best. It's foolproof.

Somehow, in a crowd of 42,000 people I find some friends in the starting pen, and – thanks to social media — we're joined by others I've never met before but who recognise my pink hair and come over to say hello.

'Blimey, so you're really doing it,' says one of them.

'I really am,' I reply.

I'm just wondering whether I need yet another wee when the runners ahead of me surge forwards and. . . we are off! I'm skipping on air for the first mile. The tarmac beneath my feet feels cool on my soles. I scan the road ahead, looking for any potential hazards — glass, grit, other debris — but I find none. I soon realise that running in the road is a lot easier than on the pavements and trails I've been training on. There are no edges of paving slabs to contend with, no curbs — the surface is good and smooth. My nerves have settled and the streets are lined with people — cheering, clapping, shouting from megaphones, ringing bells and waving banners. It's hard not to get carried away but I settle into a steady rhythm and allow myself just to be carried along instead. Three miles in and I feel greeeaaat. Really great, in fact. Do I feel too great? Chill out. No use running too hard early on and blowing up, I tell myself.

At the 5-mile marker there's a drag queen dressed like Tina Turner belting out hits from a balcony above a pub. Her voice is booming from speakers close to the edge of the road and the bass makes my belly rumble. She's partway through the chorus of 'Simply the Best' and calls out as I pass, 'Here. . . Pinky! Pinky! You look FAAABBBBULOUS!' And I, for that moment, let myself believe that I am, like Tina, just a little bit fabulous.

Seven miles in and an Irishwoman appears by my side.

'Would you be in bare feet?' she says, and I'm unsure if it's a statement or question.

'I would,' I reply.

2

'Oh no,' she shakes her head and, this time, it's definitely a statement. From that moment on, the concerned Irishwoman appoints herself as my chief safety officer. She's convinced that someone will step on my toes and so runs around me in circles as we move down the course, shouting, 'BEWARE! BAREFOOT RUNNER! BEWARE!' After half a mile, the Irish lady has gathered enough evidence to believe that my feet and I are able to stay out of harm's way and bounds off ahead, back to her own race.

At mile 11, I'm overtaken by a man dressed as a toilet. I take it on the chin and forge on.

When I reach the iconic Tower Bridge at mile 13, a Bon Jovi classic is blaring out from speakers over a sea of bobbing runners and he's telling me we're halfway there. There's a steel band going for it at the side of the road and the noise is deafening. It's a welcome boost and I cruise on, through to mile 17.

It's only at mile 20 that the wheels begin to fall off. The balls of my feet are burning, my legs ache and my right hip is threatening to cramp. I seek out easier surfaces where I can, tiptoeing along smooth, painted white lines in the middle of the road, and take great joy when I pass a bus lane (because the lines on the outside of them are double width and offer extra relief).

At the aid station, where gels and sports drinks are being handed out, my soles stick to the pavement. Moving over the ground sounds like pulling Velcro apart. It takes more energy than I have to give. But then come the water stations. . .

sanctuaries of cool, wet tarmac, where I get a much-needed foot bath and shuffle on.

Mile by mile, my legs get heavier, and the crowds lining the road thicken. The lines of support are 10 people deep at Embankment and I can see that the running styles of those around me are becoming increasingly jerky, and their breathing ragged. I know they're suffering. I'm suffering too. Twenty-four miles down and my soles are on fire, but there's not far to go now. Just a few more steps, Anna, just a few more steps. I play the words like a record on repeat.

At last, the pink tarmac of the Mall comes into view. I turn a sharp right and look down the final 100 metres of the course. The crowds here are louder still and I can barely hear my own thoughts, but my legs take over. I stretch them out in front of me, taking long strides and breathing hard. I look up at Buckingham Palace and then down at my feet, now covered in a layer of grime from the city streets. My chest swells with pride and as I cross the finish line, I am head over heels in love — with London, with the supporters, and with my body and its ability to keep going.

One barefoot marathon down, 99 to go.

1

Barefoot or Bust

I love my feet. Really, I do. They are slender and elegant and strong. I like my high arch. I love the tiny mole on the outside of my right little toe (which I think would be used to identify me if I were ever to end up as one of those bodies on the TV show Silent Witness). It's a happy mole. It looks happy to be there. Come to think of it, most of my other toes look happy too. I love the tattoo on my right foot — Art Deco swirls and stars. I love that I can clearly see the veins on my feet. Veins that run thick and proud over the top, close to the surface.

Yes, my feet have their oddities. My big toes have tufts of blonde hair on them which make them each look like the lead singer of a punk rock band, for starters. And my second toes don't play by the rules. They both demonstrate a flagrant disregard for toe-length etiquette by being longer than their neighbouring big toe. Each one juts out, a good half a centimetre past the biggun, basking in the glory of being the most extended part of my tootsie kingdom. I've never considered how my big toes feel about being second in line, but now I wonder whether the fact that one of my second toes slants ever

5

so slightly is because of a falling out they had with the big toe about who should be longer.

Of course, it occurs to me that not everyone does love their feet, which is sad. Because feet are amazing. There are 26 bones, 33 joints, 19 muscles and 107 ligaments in each foot, and more than 200,000 nerve endings — which makes it the most sensitive part of your body. More sensitive than your fingertips or your face. More sensitive than your nipples, even (just sayin'). Our feet support us, all day, every day. They carry us on adventures, transport us to new places, play footsie with people we fancy, they let us dance all night and (unless wearing stilettos) they rarely complain.

Over the years, I have used my feet for many of those things. But mostly I have used them for running. And despite not ever feeling like a 'runner', I really do love to run. When I turned 30, I ran the length of the Te Araroa trail in New Zealand, carrying all of my gubbins on my back. It was a 2,000-mile journey that had me dancing over mountains and scampering along the fragile ridge line that straddles possibility and stupidity. It was, as the Kiwis say, hard yakka, and I solemnly declared at the end of that trip that I would never do anything quite so difficult ever again. But time is a great healer, or rather, I have a terrible memory, and a few years later, I was toying with the idea of doing another long-distance running journey.

One Sunday morning in spring, I was sitting on the sofa in the living room with my boyfriend Jamie, and I decided it was time to reveal the next big idea to him. Sunday Brunch was on in the background, a full cafetière was on the table in front of us and we had reached the 'King of the Tin' segment in the show — where the celebrity guests share their favourite and least favourite UK biscuit. A musician had just put a Bourbon at the bottom of their list and therefore placed it in the 'Crumb Dungeon' (which hurt my soul), and now we were witnessing a long and heated debate about whether a Jaffa Cake is a cake or a biscuit. I longed to get drawn into settling the all-important issue (it's a cake for crying out loud), but I had something else on my mind.

'J. . .'

'Mmm hmm?'

'I've got an idea for the next adventure. . .'

'Have you?' Jamie picked up the remote and put the TV on pause. He turned to face me on the sofa.

'I'm thinking about doing another big run.'

'Oooh — how big we talking?'

'Well, I was thinking it'd take at least a couple of months.'

'Okay.'

'It'd be in Britain. . .'

'Of course.'

'And I'd do it for Girlguiding.'

'That makes sense,' Jamie nodded.

'And I'm going to do it barefoot,' I added as quickly as I

could — as if skimming over the fact made it seem less of a mad idea, somehow.

'Barefoot? What, you mean in those monkey shoes?'

'No, no monkey shoes — barefoot-barefoot.'

'Bloody Nora. I love it.'

'Yeah, so. . .' I took a deep breath. Here goes, I thought. I was going to put it out there for the first time. 'I'm going to run the distance of fifty marathons. In bare feet,' I exhaled and my stomach did a flip. That was over 1,300 miles with no shoes on. It was a bloody long way.

'I like it.' Jamie took another sip of coffee and pressed play on the TV.

'You do?'

'Yeah. It's nails,' he smiled, patting my leg and turning his attention back to Sunday Brunch.

I breathed a sigh of relief. It felt good to have put the idea out in the ether. And especially to have shared it with someone I love and knew would support me. I could now relax into Sunday and get back to the Jaffa Cake vs Jaffa Biscuit debate. I turned my attention back to the TV and raised my coffee cup to my lips.

'One hundred barefoot marathons sounds better though,' said Jamie, nonchalantly.

Bugger.

He was right.

Even thinking about covering the distance of 100 marathons — 2,620 miles — in bare feet felt like someone had emptied a dumper truck of popping candy into my blood stream. Jamie had planted the seed, and I couldn't let it go. It now had to be that 100-marathon distance. Barefoot or bust.

Upping the distance was a change in plan, but the idea to do a long run for Girlguiding had been rolling around in my brain for a few weeks before I'd shared it with Jamie. I'd recently been made the UK ambassador for the charity, and it was my job to help them support and encourage young women to be their brilliant selves — whether that meant going off on adventures, taking up sport or anything else they wanted to do in life — science, maths, engineering, politics — anything. I was on hand to say, 'YES! That thing you love, do it, chase it until you catch it, and then cling on for the ride.'

The ambassador role suited me perfectly and it came at the right time in my life. When I'd started doing adventures, almost a decade before, it was purely to satisfy personal curiosity, but now, with a few expeditions under my belt, my motivation had shifted. I wanted another reason to put myself through the wringer. Something that would impact more lives than just my own. So, I decided from the off that I'd use the Barefoot Britain run as a means to show the young women of Britain the marvellous and messy reality of taking on big ideas. During the run, I planned to visit as many Girlguiding units as I could throughout the country and share tall tales from wild adventures, past and present. I would encourage them to be brave and take on things just beyond their reach, but I would also be open with the girls. I would be honest. I wouldn't for one minute pretend that I knew what I was doing.

As for the barefoot part, well, barefoot running had always intrigued me. The idea of moving over the land with nothing between your soles and the earth seemed wildly appealing and refreshingly simple. But in truth, I was drawn to the idea of running in bare feet because it felt tantalisingly close to the impossible. I've always been obsessed with seeing how far the human body — well, my body — can go. It may have some-thing to do with the fact that my parents are both Olympians — pushing myself physically and mentally is in my blood. And if I took on another long run in trainers I knew, deep down inside, that I could do it. Even if it was a tiny voice that whis-pered from the pit of my stomach that I could. But without shoes? That was a whole other ball game. There was a large chance I would fall flat on my face and fail spectacularly. And if I was going to be encouraging the girls to reach further than they thought possible, then I had to be on that journey too. Uncomfortable as it was going to be, I had to walk the walk (or, rather, run the run).

After getting used to the idea of a 100-marathon distance, I decided I was going to run from the tippy-top of the Shet-land Islands to where I was born and raised in South West London. The route would be very (very) wiggly, and I'd visit all the places I'd yet to make time to see, like the Scottish High-lands, the Isle of Man, Northern Ireland and even the Chan-nel Islands. I planned to approach an adventure through Brit-ain like a hunt for hidden treasure — exploring secret beauty spots, vibrant cities and meeting the people who brought those places to life. As an added bonus, being on home turf meant that if anything went tits up, I could turn up as a weepy mess on my mum's doorstep, begging for a cup of tea and a chat.

I did as much research as I could on the kind of terrain I'd be moving over as I wiggled across the country. I pored over maps of trails and minor back roads, zooming in on places I could potentially stop for the night. I then did some loose spreadsheet-ing (this is totally a word) and, factoring in rest days and extra days to visit cool cities en route, I figured I could cover the distance in just under six months — which was perfect because it would mean starting in June and finishing in November, just before winter kicked in.

It was February 2018 when I began proper training. I say 'proper' because I had already read lots of books on barefoot running by that point. I'd adored getting stuck into Christopher McDougall's Born to Run, but other more practical 'how to' books were full of words like 'shod' and 'gait' and were, in short, very dull. It would be like reading a book about eating a chocolate cake (it's probably best to just eat the chocolate cake and see if you like it or not). It wasn't long before I realised that the best way to learn how to run barefoot is to actually go out and run in bare feet. Who knew?

For my first training session, I decided I would aim for a 20-minute barefoot jaunt. One cold winter's evening, I drove to a section of the Cotswold Way that I knew well and parked my car at the bottom of Leckhampton Hill, on the outskirts of

Cheltenham. It was just starting to get dark and there were a few dog walkers milling around in the car park. I didn't want them to see me taking my shoes off, in case they thought I was weird. So I hung around for the following 10 minutes, trying to look 'busy' — opening and shutting my car doors, sitting and staring out of the window and, in short, looking weird. The only thing stopping me from appearing as if I was in the car park for some dogging action was flashing my lights on and off. Eventually, the other doggers, I mean dog walkers, got in their cars and left. I was alone.

I slipped off my shoes, then my socks, and a stiff wind blew across the tops of my toes. Crikey, it was cold! It had snowed the night before and the ground was still dusted with white, but I wasn't going to let that put me off. I could come up against snow and ice during the run, after all — it'd be good for me to go in at the deep end, harden myself up, I thought. I started the timer on my watch for 20 minutes and set off up the hill, eager to embrace my first steps into the bold barefoot unknown.

Right from the off, being able to feel everything beneath my feet was all-encompassing. It was as if my feet had just woken up from a 100-year slumber. Rough stone, a gnarled tree root, a patch of cold, dank mud. Everything felt strangely therapeutic. This is brilliant, I thought. I am going to love being barefoot, always.

It wasn't long before my toes got cold. They began to sear with pain, like a hand left out too long from a glove on a cold winter's night. But I continued to push on up the hill, trying to ignore the fact that my feet were screaming at me to stop this madness, immediately, and plunge them into some fleecy socks. Instead, I focused on my breathing — blowing out lungfuls of warm air, creating a mist around my face as I moved over more tree roots and fallen leaves. On and on I went, pounding through the pain, which had now extended from my toes and into the soles of my feet.

When I hit the top of the hill, I was tempted to look at my watch. But I resisted. Not yet. Not until I was sure I had got close to the 10-minute halfway point. I turned right and ran along the ridge. There was even more snow on the ground up there and it was difficult to stay upright, but I reminded myself that it was a good thing to be challenged. What a way to train my feet to cope with anything. A baptism of fire, or rather of snow! Finally, I allowed myself to check my watch. Four minutes and 46 seconds. What the hell?! Oh, sod this, I thought. I turned around, slid back down the hill, got in the car and went home for a hot bath.

If I learned anything from my first disastrous training run, it's that I had no idea what I was doing. I needed help. I'd taken a slapdash approach to adventures in the past, but once I stood on that start line in Shetland, there would be nowhere to hide. Not only did I need to get my body used to running long distances again, I'd also have to undo everything I'd learnt by running in shoes over the past 30+ years. This time, I had to take physical preparation for the journey seriously. So I sought the advice of a running gait specialist, a strength and conditioning expert and a podiatrist. They all told me, in a kind way, that I was off my rocker but that the way I ran, my body type and foot shape could potentially allow me to cope with barefoot running. Whether I could cope for 100 marathons was still an unknown, but I felt better equipped having chatted things out with them. After gathering as much advice as I felt was needed for a confidence boost, I resolved to spend the next 18 months building up the miles, slowly, in minimalist trainers. I would get my ligaments, tendons and muscles used to what was to come and look out for any signs of weakness or potential injury and then gradually, very gradually, transition to bare feet.

By the autumn of 2018, I'd built up to running 10¬–15 miles in my minimalist shoes and was doing some miles in socks or completely barefoot. As a result, my legs had started to look racehorse-like. Or, to put it in runner's terms, they looked like the legs of the world famous ultrarunner Dean Karnazes. If a little less hairy. Since putting my clumpy shoes away, everything from my waist down looked leaner. It was as if transitioning out of supported shoes had made the lower half of my body stand to attention.

'Calves and Quads reporting for duty, Corporal McNuff! Pumped and ready to flex at a moment's notice. . . Hup! Hup! Hup!'

My feet looked stronger too. The tendons were more defined, and I could wiggle my toes in all sorts of new directions. It was a sad day when I had to give my favourite hard-soled, pointy-toed cowboy boots a kiss and tuck them away in a box in the closet. I'd bought them with my very first paycheque from my very first grown-up job in Carnaby Street in Soho, but my toes now felt so squished and uncomfortable in them. I wasn't sure when I'd wear them again, if ever. Even if they did make me feel like I could round up some cattle and ride off into the sunset on a mustang.

***

With over a year of steady training under my belt, in the April of 2019, I ran the London Marathon, in aid of Girlguiding. It was the first real test for my barefoot running. By this point, I was two months away from starting the main journey up in Shetland, and I'd told everyone about my plans. The social media post of me holding a marathon finisher medal, with my feet covered in London street-grime was shared far and wide. Clare Balding gave me a shout out on the BBC during the race, I appeared on CBBC's Operation Ouch! and media attention for the run gathered pace.

At first, that gave me confidence, but I soon discovered that hype before you've even started a challenge is a double-edged sword. The more interviews I gave, the more pressure I felt. I just wanted to start in Shetland ever so quietly, and to only talk about the run once I knew it was possible. Which, of course, wouldn't be until I'd done it. The growing attention now felt like a wave building offshore. I could surf it. Or I could slip under, into the pounding space beneath the waves, and be crushed. I flitted between the two.

In the month before starting the run, I barely slept. My body was all over the place on account of trips back and forth to visit Jamie — who was on his own adventure running 5,000 miles across America. The jetlag and subsequent lack of sleep left me feeling overwhelmed and anxious. I'd dread going to bed because the moment my head hit that pillow everything from the day would flood my mind. The rational part of my brain knew that there was nothing to worry about, but the irrational side had yet to get that memo. When my mind was racing like that, I took big belly breaths in and out and focused only on those breaths.

There were some nights when I would actually manage to get to sleep, but then I'd wake at 2 a.m. with a gasp. Brain whirring, heart pounding — my mind filled with ALL OF THE THINGS I had to do before the adventure began. It was as if the weight of the journey had dragged me from my sleep. Like a bandit tied behind a runaway horse. Each evening via a call from America, Jamie reminded me that this was all part and parcel of these adventures. The feeling of accomplishment and satisfaction at the end is always worth it, but it's inevitable that we have to go through this to get there. To sit in the quiet of the night and feel our hearts beat clean out of our chests at the sheer scale of the challenge ahead.

And yet, through it all, I never once thought about backing

out. Instead, when things got too much, I reminded myself what one of my favourite writers, Elizabeth Gilbert, had once said. She has a theory about big ideas like Barefoot Britain, which she describes in her memoir Big Magic. She believes that ideas are like free spirits roaming the universe. Sometimes, they land on a person and if they aren't acted upon, taken up, grasped with both hands — if they get passed over or locked away in a drawer for many years — they will leave. They will fly off and land with someone else instead.

I have had many ideas leave me over the years because they spent too long buried under the weight of reasons why I couldn't possibly do them, or, more often than not, why they weren't quite right for me at that moment in my life. But my gut told me that everything about this run felt right. I couldn't put my finger on it. I couldn't explain it. It all just felt. . . magic. The right motivation. The right level of crapping my pants. The right levels of fear and excitement and trepidation and scepticism from others.

Do you ever have moments where you feel like you are exactly where you are supposed to be? All the riches in the world couldn't sway you from the path you're on — because it is so uniquely yours. There is a little person inside of you jumping up and down and screaming, 'YES! YES! THIS IS THE ONE! KEEP GOING!' Despite all the anxiety, the doubt, the wondering if I had gone one step too far this time, I'd had that feeling the moment I settled on the idea for the run. And that's why I knew, whatever the outcome, whether I succeeded or failed, it was going to be one heck of an adventure.

SHETLAND

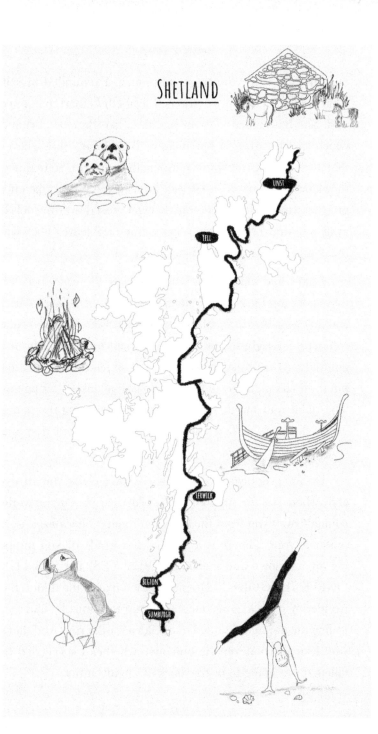

UNST

YELL

LERWICK

BIGTON

SUMBURGH

2

Here. We. Go!

It was 4.30 p.m. when my 33-seater plane touched down on the runway at Sumburgh Airport, Shetland. Out of the window, beyond a still-spinning propeller, was a cornflower-blue sky filled with marshmallow clouds. The sun was beaming down and, as the clouds drifted across the horizon, their shadows trailed over bright green hills below. It was a scene that wouldn't have looked out of place in a kid's drawing, all bold shapes and primary colours. Wowsers. If this was the kind of landscape and weather that Shetland was going to be serving up, I was in for a treat.

Truth be told, I wasn't sure what to expect from the Shetland Islands. I'd read about them in the lead up to the journey and they struck me as a mystical place. Originally given to Scotland by the King of Norway as dowry for a marriage in 1469, the islands are technically British, but their location hints otherwise. To find them on a map, head to the north coast of Scotland, way out into the North Sea and just. . . keep going north. And I mean, a long way north — until you're in line with Greenland and within sniffing distance of Norway.

It's that close proximity and historic connection with Norway which makes the islands so unique. A lot of their language includes terms rooted in old Norse, and Viking history is widely celebrated there. It all seemed so otherworldly. Just by tracing my finger over the dozens of dots of land on the map, I had a feeling I was going to leave this tiny place in the North Sea having barely scratched the surface.

After hauling my kit bag off the baggage belt in the airport terminal, I went to check the bus timetables. I needed to make my way up to the northern tip of the islands, to Skaw Beach, which was a three-hour bus ride and two ferries away from where the plane had landed at Sumburgh. From Skaw, I'd take a straight shot south, running the length of Unst (population 650), Yell (population 1,000) and then Mainland Shetland (population 23,00), home to the capital city of Lerwick.

After much squinting at the timetable and double-checking with a passer-by, I worked out that the next bus north wasn't leaving for another two hours, so I settled down at a surprisingly stylish Art Deco coffee shop, inside the terminal. With a coffee in hand, I flicked open my laptop and turned my attention to some last-minute arrangements for the following 10 days on Shetland.

Since coming up with the idea for the run, it had grown legs and run away with itself. I'd decided that the best way to get to know Britain on the journey was going to be through the people. Not only would I be giving talks to Girlguiding units en route, but I would also have 'open' running stages, where members of the general public could join me for the day. I didn't have a support crew, so thanks to a combination of locals and the Girlguiding network, my main kit bag was going to be passed through the country like a giant baton, from one kind soul to the next. Needless to say, this adventure had more moving parts than a Meccano model.

Even though I was self-funding the adventure, I'd decided to employ someone to take care of the day-to-day logistics. It would make a big dent in my bank balance, but it meant I could really focus on the running. And if I could focus on the running, then there was more of a chance I'd make it to all the Girlguiding units I'd promised to visit, and I'd cover the 100-marathon distance. So, I found a woman who was up for the job, told her she could pick her own job title and Abby the Barefoot Britain 'Adventure Logistics Queen' was born.

When I'd shared the plans for the adventure online and posted details of my route, I'd always hoped I'd get a handful of keen beans who might be up for helping out by having me stay with them for a night along the way. But shortly after the adventure announcement went live, my inbox was flooded with offers from local hosts.

'Errrr, Anna — I've just had two hundred messages come in over the past hour! They're all offering up places to stay. Were you expecting that many?' Abby squealed down the phone.

Of course, I wasn't. It was overwhelming to say the least. I'd experienced generosity on past adventures but nothing like this. I'd put a mad idea out there, and the general public had responded with offers of bed and board. How lovely was that?

In that first wave of emails was a message from a friend in New Zealand, Jacqs Manson. Jacqs was born on the Shetland Islands and she said that much of her family were still there. She worked like a trooper to hook me up with her cousins, aunties, uncles and other relatives on the islands (I lost track of the sprawling family tree), all of whom had agreed to take in a barefooted stranger from the south. Thanks to Jacqs' fine networking and the generosity of what I was now calling the 'Manson Massive', I was sorted for hosts along much of the route in Shetland. The only place I didn't have a host was near the start, on Unst. Even the Manson Massive hadn't been able to think of anyone they knew up there.

I'd been sat at my laptop for 10 minutes and just booked into a hostel on Unst when I noticed an email from a woman called Jane:

Hi Anna, I've been trying to get in touch over the past week — my name's Jane. I live very close to where you plan to start your Barefoot Britain run, in Unst. I'm a leader with our local Brownie group. You're very welcome to stay with me, and we would love to have you speak to our lasses about your adventures.

Jane had included a mobile number in her message. I sat back in my chair and thought. Could I call this woman up and ask to stay? I felt a wave of familiar discomfort rise up. I hated the idea of being a burden, of putting another person out. But I had promised myself that this was part of the challenge of the journey. To let others help where it was offered, because. . . surely they wouldn't offer it unless they wanted to? I took a deep breath and I hit dial.

'Hello. Is that Jane?'

'Hi, yes.'

'Hi Jane. This is Anna. Err, the barefoot runner. I've just picked up your message which says you might be willing to help me out while I'm on Shetland?'

'Of course, of course! How many nights will you be wanting to stay?'

I told her that I was sorted for tonight and that I'd be staying in Lerwick on the way north, but then I paused. I bit my lip. In response to her question, I really wanted to say 'for as many nights as possible' because I wasn't going to be running huge distances over the first few days. It'd be lovely to go back to the same place each night and have a start-line base camp. But equally, I felt like that was asking too much.

'Oh, well, I've booked into a hostel for some nights, so one night would be fine.'

I already realised how ridiculous that sounded as the words came out of my mouth. As if I was some kind of shady criminal who didn't want to let anyone too close to my dodgy barefoot dealings.

23

'A hostel? Oh, no, why would you do that? You can stay with me for as long as you want.'

'Are you sure?'

'Absolutely. Anna, we're very excited to have you here, and I can't wait to meet you.'

'Brilliant. And you too, Jane. In that case, I'll see you sometime tomorrow, before the sun goes down.'

'Wonderful.'

'Oh, Jane. . .?'

'Yes?

'Could you text me the address of your house, please? A postcode or something?'

'I can tell you it now.'

'Ah okay. . . go ahead. . .' I said, rummaging around in my bag for a pen.

'When you get off the second ferry, if you tell the bus driver, Connor he's called — he's a lovely man. . .'

'Connor. . . got it.'

'If you tell Connor that you're staying with Jane, then he'll drop you off at the end of my road.'

'Right.'

'Walk down the road and you'll see a bungalow with a red roof. You'll know the house by the dandelions.'

'Bungalow. Red roof. Dandelions. Got it,' I repeated, scribbling down the directions.

'Oh, I'm SO pleased you're coming to stay. I'll make you up a room and get some fresh sheets out drying in the sun. See you tomorrow now, bye bye.'

The conversation with Jane was like a warm embrace. In the space of three minutes, she'd dispelled any belief that Shetlanders would think me crazy for taking on this run and choosing their islands as the starting place. If Jane's reaction was anything to go by, I was being welcomed with open arms.

After a night stopover in Lerwick at the Manson Massive HQ, I made the journey north, changing buses twice and taking two ferries until I reached the most northerly island of Unst. Just as Jane had said, Connor was driving the final bus which took me onto the island and he wasn't in the slightest bit surprised that she'd offered to take me in. He dropped me off at the end of her road, and from the moment I crossed the threshold of the red-roofed bungalow with the dandelions out the front, I felt at ease.

'You made it! Welcome, welcome,' said Jane, ushering me inside. In her mid-sixties, with short curly reddish-brown hair, she was wearing a blue fleece with a black gilet over the top. She looked warm, cosy, but ready for action at a moment's notice and she wasted no time in making me feel at home. Jane showed me to the guest bedroom, which she said I was to treat as my sanctuary for the following few days, including strict instructions to sleep as long as I wanted to. She then led me into an open-plan living room which had an adjoining wooden farmhouse-style kitchen.

'Okay then, our runner from the south, what would you like to do first? A shower? Some tea? Or do you just want to sit for a while?' Jane clasped her hands and flashed me a big smile. All three of those options sounded fantastic, but I was well-rested and eager to get stuck into understanding Shetland life.

'Tea sounds lovely, thank you. I want to hear all about what it's like to live here. In this place,' I said, looking out the window.

'I hoped you might say that.' Jane smiled then turned to put the kettle on. 'And likewise. . . I want to hear all about this mad run of yours. I've made shortbread. Do you like short-bread?'

'I do. Who doesn't like shortbread?'

'Well, I wasn't sure if you'd be one of those healthy types . . . on a strict diet for the run.'

'My diet consists of anything that's delicious, and short-bread ticks the box.'

'Good, good, in that case. . . I've got strawberries and cream to go along with it,' she grinned.

'Well, that's one of my five-a-day right there.' I smiled.

Jane's home was a warm place, and I mean that not just in that it offered respite from the wind and rain that were now lashing at the windows, but it had a warmth to it. Her shortbread was still warm too; fresh from the oven, it was buttery, crumbly and melted in my mouth. And, on account of the spell cast by its crumbly, buttery, melty goodness, I had more pieces than I should have done. All of which was washed down with several cups of tea as we sat at the kitchen table for an hour and I collected the details of Jane's life on Shetland. As someone who knew nothing about me until a week or so ago, Jane was equally eager to learn about my life, and so the conversation flowed easily, each of us trying to build a picture of the whens, wheres and whys of one another's lives.

Mostly, Jane and I bonded over a shared love of travel. She had a large world map on the wall in the hallway, and the brightly painted walls of her home were adorned with photos and souvenirs from her travels around the globe — masks from Africa, paintings from Greece, carvings from South America. It was while inspecting a plate from Morocco that I realised I'd made an assumption that, because Jane lived on a tiny remote island in the North Sea, that was where she would stay.

'Ah, but what you have to understand, Anna, is that we may be a tiny island but that means our horizons are big,' said Jane, and I thought that was quite lovely — the idea that a remote place, surrounded by the sea, offered a better vantage point from which to view the rest of the world.

A mother of three, Jane had travelled all over the world with her family, and some of her kids and grandkids were now living on other continents, so she had good reason to leave the island often. But she also went on to explain that, in the 30 years she'd lived on Unst, the world had come to her door. Although, I suspected that the world had not arrived at Jane's bungalow by chance but, instead, had been sought out and invited there.

There was no doubt that Jane was an adventurer at heart. Her stories were peppered with one-liners that made me laugh out loud. She'd throw in the odd comment, like 'I had a dream to swim across Canada once. . .', in between talking about sailing adventures and hiking up mountains. We also chatted about travels closer to home, to nearby Fair Isle, a place that's 3 miles long and home to 65 people and a bird sanctuary.

'Oooo, I got stuck on Fair Isle once,' Jane said. 'The fog rolled in and we were marooned for five whole days.'

'Oh no!' I replied, thinking it would be an inconvenience to be stuck on a tiny island in the North Sea in the fog.

'Oh, yes. It was fantastic!' she beamed.

Having ploughed our way through a couple of pots of tea, the conversation slowed. I curled my fingers around the still-warm mug in my hand and looked out of the kitchen window. It was still raining outside and down the hill I could see a white stone house. A wind turbine next to the house was going at a rate of knots, and a blue and white Shetland flag was flapping wildly on a pole next to it. Jane was right; the horizon was big on Shetland — you could see for miles and miles from her home, across wind-ravaged fields which tumbled towards the North Sea. I also noticed that I couldn't see any trees and, come to think of it, I hadn't seen any on the journey up to Unst either. There would be no shelter for a lone runner out there, that was for sure.

The thought of running in such an exposed part of the country should have added even more nerves to the start of the journey, but instead, it felt exciting. It felt wild. There was nowhere to hide from the elements on Shetland and, after a couple of nights settling in at Jane's home, I had nowhere left to hide from the adventure either. It was time to start the run.

***

I exhaled a long deep breath and looked out at the North Sea. Wriggling my toes, I burrowed them into the cool, damp, golden sand of Skaw Beach. It was an overcast June day, gloomy even. The sky and sea all seemed as one — a mass of blueish-grey, the horizon was interrupted only by the white-tinged crests of waves breaking offshore.

I zoomed out in my mind's eye and thought about where I was in the world. I was a speck of a human, on a speck of land, on the most tippy-top part of Britain. I shut my eyes for a moment and felt the sea spray land on my cheeks. I let out another breath. My teeth were chattering and this time the air stuttered as it left my lungs. My hands were shaking too. I was a bundle of nerves, but I didn't mind. I was used to this feeling by now. I'd come to know it like an old friend. I knew

ANNA MCNUFF

that all of these things were a tell-tale sign that something truly magical was about to unfold.

Further down the beach, where the sand met the road, Jane had gathered a modest band of merry humans to wave me off: a local photographer, the couple who owned the most northerly house in Britain and a pair of male cycle tourists, who had foil Viking horns attached to their cycle helmets and just so happened to be finishing their length-of-Great-Britain bike ride on the beach that day. To top things off, Jane had also roped in some passing bird watchers, who'd agreed to witness the migration of a rare, pink-haired, 5-foot, 10-inch, barefooted bird, flying south to London ahead of the winter.

'Ready?' I called to Jane across the sand.

'Ready!' she shouted back, and the little crowd gave a little cheer.

'Ten. . . nine. . . eight. . . seven. . .' I said, beginning my own countdown. It felt ridiculous to give myself a countdown, but I wasn't sure how else to begin a 100-marathon run — just shouting 'GO!' seemed awfully unceremonious.

'Six. . . five. . . four. . .'

Beyond the sound of breaking waves and wind swirling around the nearby granite cliffs, I could hear the bystanders now joining in too.

'Three. . . two. . . one. Wahooooooo! Here. We. Gooooo! Two thousand, six hundred and twenty miles from Shetland to London. . . in my bare feeeeet!' I hollered, throwing my arms

into the air and taking the first few steps across the sand —
legs pumping, heart pounding, and a mass of limbs and Lycra
tumbling across the beach.

The mini-crowd clapped and cheered as I passed, and
one of the cycle tourists let out a blood-curdling Viking roar. I
waved and cheered back, marvelling at the absurdity of it all.
Who needed a mass send-off when I had a gaggle of locals,
some bird watchers and an overexcitable man in a tin-foil Viking helmet?

After leaving the small gravel car park, I started up a hill,
away from the beach, and within 30 seconds, the sound of the
claps and cheers had faded away. I was alone. I blew out my
cheeks and looked down at my hands. They were still shaking.
Holy hell! I thought. This was it. I was off! Just me, the open
road and my bare feet. Britain was my oyster. There was no
one and nothing that could stand in my way. Except — oh,
crap. I needed a wee. In all the pre-start excitement, I'd neglected to take the time to empty my bladder. The adrenaline
and the many cups of tea drunk that morning at Jane's house
had caught up with me, and now it felt as if I was running with
a watermelon attached to my front.

I glanced back down the road. I could still see the start-line
supporters chatting at the edge of the beach. They spotted me
looking back towards them and waved. I waved back, then
waited for them to return to chatting amongst themselves before ducking off the road and crouching in a nearby peat bog.
Ahhh. The sweet relief of a wild wee. Mid-stream, I realised

ANNA MCNUFF

it was quite possibly the most northerly wee I would ever take in Britain. A quarter of a mile down. . . just 2,619 and three quarters of a mile to go.

Without a bladder the size of a watermelon, I was able to run more comfortably, and I did my best to settle into a rhythm. But my mind was all over the place, hopping from one thing to the next: logistics to sort, how I would thank Jane for her hospitality, what the weather would be like tomorrow. Anything and everything to do with the journey ahead piled into my consciousness and ran amok like a bull in a china shop.

I knew that any extra energy expended in the first week of the run was going to be energy I'd need later down the line. Fun as it was to be so excited, I couldn't stay so wired all day long — that was a sure-fire way to crash and burn. So I took a few more deep breaths and tried to calm down. I switched my focus to the road beneath me and concentrated on watching my pink feet move over its blackness. And the road was very black. Blacker than the roads in the south. It also seemed to be made of a different type of rock too — sharper than I was used to underfoot — as if rock chips had been loosely sprayed over a layer of tar. 'Naughty tarmac,' I muttered, telling it off for having the gall to be so spiky, and on my first day too.

I spent the following 30 minutes flitting between running on the 'naughty tarmac' and giving my soles a break by scampering along the grassy verge at the edge, which was spongy and moss-like. I got a glimpse of some of the roadside hazards I'd need to dodge in the coming months, including broken, razor-sharp mussel shells and a giant dollop of dog poo. I took extra care to avoid both, thinking it probably wasn't wise to cut my foot and coat it in turd so early on. I was sure I would have plenty of time to do that as the run progressed.

Eventually, I managed to get my heart rate down to a manageable level and I surrendered to the adventure. I settled into a rhythm, enjoying long stretches of solitude, where I was alone with my just my thoughts, with the sea to my left and the greens of the Unst hills to the right. Jane drove by every now and then, tooting her horn and waving as she went, and groups of locals appeared at various points along the route: in car parks, on clifftops, clapping and cheering as I passed. When that happened, it felt like I was in an organised running event — except the finish line was a long way off and I was the only entrant in the race.

On one section, I was joined by a group of 10 local Brown-ies. They met me as I passed a full-scale replica of a Viking long boat and ran up a steep hill by my side, asking me all kinds of questions as we ran.

'Are you really running to London?' said one.

'Do you ever wear shoes?' asked another.

'Are you going to come back and live in Shetland when you're done?' said a third.

I finished the day buzzing. I'd only run 7 miles, but at least I was out of the starting gate and on my way.

The following morning, after a 12-hour sleep, Jane

dropped me back to where I'd finished my first day of running. Before I started running, I gave her a link to my GPS tracker. The tracker was a neat bit of kit I'd used on past adventures for safety, although, on this run it was less about safety and more about encouraging the general public to come out and find me if they wanted to — to join in or for a fly-by hug. I told Jane she could use the link to see exactly where I was so that she'd have an idea of where and when to collect me at the end of the day.

On account of how spiky the tarmac was, my soles became sore, so I decided to stay off the road as much as possible, choosing instead to run over grass-covered clifftops and follow the coastline. Although I had a schedule to stick to for the overall journey, I was in no rush for the time being. The softer surface was gentler on my soles, so I explored every nook and cranny of the coast as I ran, soaking up the salty air and watching seabirds dance above the water.

Later that morning, I was running around a small inlet, when I saw a flash of brown moving over the grass on top of one of the sections of rock. I watched as an otter scampered up from the water's edge and paused to flop over and dry its back on a grassy tuft. I'd never seen an otter in the wild before and I was dumbstruck. To a gal who grew up in the suburbs of London, otters only exist in far-off places, on TV documentaries or in children's books (where they went on adventures with water voles). The otter stopped its shimmy on the grass and looked at me. I looked back at it. Then it was gone in a flash — a blur of brown disappearing over the crest of the cliff, leaving me wondering if I'd imagined the whole thing.

Much as I was enjoying getting to know the local wildlife, the downside to the clifftop scampering was that it was always windy, and so the miles were hard-won. I battled against gusts which encased me like mini tornados and, at times, the wind was so strong that it stopped me in my tracks — especially when I rounded a headland and was met with a new wall of wind that I'd been unknowingly sheltered from just a few steps beforehand.

In a bid to distract myself from the wind, I often put headphones in and listened to music — notably Olly Murs' greatest hits. The cheeky chappy from Essex and his instructions to be a 'Troublemaker' had me skipping along from one headland to the next. When the Murs album moved on to my favourite song, 'Dance with Me Tonight', I couldn't resist. I hadn't seen anyone since Jane had dropped me off that morning, and the likelihood of bumping into anyone out there was slim, but even that didn't matter. I stopped, looked out over the sea, made sure that I was a sufficient distance from the cliff edge (in case I got carried away) and threw my hands in the air. I wiggled my hips, and moved my legs and my bare feet, shuffling and sliding from one spot to the next, singing along over the wind to words I knew so well. I made that patch of salt-spattered grass my own private dance floor. . . and I let the music engulf me.

At lunchtime, I took shelter behind large boulders on one of the many white sandy beaches, spying on seals who poked their heads up between the crest of waves and listening to the squawk of orange-beaked oystercatchers as they tip-toed, double-time, across the sand in front of me. I ran on through a sea of lilac wildflowers, which would only be in bloom for a few weeks of the summer, and scampered around jagged headlands, exploring every inch of them as the icy swell of the North Sea slammed mercilessly into the great fangs of rocks below.

Overall, the running on Unst was tough, but the surrounding landscape more than made up for any physical hardship. I continued to weave along grass-covered clifftops on terrain that was easy underfoot, dodging clusters of broken cockleshells brought inland by seagulls. Every hour or so, the remains of a croft house, often just a shell of one, would appear on the horizon. A lone building, close to the cliff edge, walls made from chunky grey stones that must have taken some effort to haul into place, especially so far from the road. With the fresh sea air battering at my cheeks, the warm earth beneath my feet and blue sky above my head, I felt wild and free. As if there was nowhere else on earth I would rather be.

At the end of each day, Jane collected me at a pre-agreed meeting point and transported me home to the red-roofed bungalow. She enveloped me in the warmth of her home and made sure I was dry, relaxed and well-fed. In the evening, my soles prickled while I ate dinner, but I took this as their way of adjusting to the task at hand. I got into a neat pre-bedtime routine of giving my feet a good scrub, checking for any small cuts and then slathering them in a cocoa butter-based moisturiser to keep any newly formed hard skin supple. My feet were everything on this journey, so I figured that giving them a little spa treatment each night would keep me on top of any potential issues from the off. With well-scrubbed feet, I slept like a baby in Jane's spare room and continued to rack up 12-hour sleeps. No matter how much I was enjoying the Shetland scenery, my body was taking its time to adapt to a new daily routine and sleep was a huge help.

It was clear that Jane led a full and vibrant life on Unst, and she always seemed to be doing something to contribute to the local community. Every time I came out of the bedroom, there was a new smell wafting from the kitchen. Carrot cake, fish pie, lasagne, quiche, more shortbread; on one occasion, she'd spent the afternoon making sugary Scottish tablet to be sold in the local shop.

Just like the surroundings she lived in, Jane was a force of nature who was always on the go and always plotting something. As it was midsummer, we had plenty of daylight — 22 hours of it each day to be precise — for extra exploring after the runs. Jane wanted to show me as much of the island as she could, and I could tell she was proud to live there. As we drove around the winding, windswept roads, Jane casually pointed out Shetland ponies with new foals, which are quite possibly the most adorable things on planet Earth. Imagine an already small horse with stumpy legs that gives birth to an even smaller horse the size of a dog. . . with even stumpier legs, a rotund belly and a beautiful mane fluttering in the wind. My cup of cuteness runneth over.

At the end of my last day on Unst, Jane met me with my main kit bag at the Belmont Ferry Terminal to wave me off. She said she was terrible with goodbyes so we only had a brief hug, but just before getting into her car she stopped and spun back around.

'You will send me your adventurous friends, won't you, Anna?' she said, and I laughed.

'Jane, I've got a lot of adventurous friends. I'm not sure you want them all turning up at your door.'

'I absolutely do — please, send them my way.'

As I boarded the ferry to Yell, I thought back over the past week. Jane, her home and the community of Unst as a whole had been a safety net. They had made me feel secure in the wildest of places, even amid the wildness of my mind. And in the moment of silence that followed after Jane's car tyres rumbled off up the road, I felt a new wave of nerves threatening to rise. Without my safety net on Unst, it was as if I was starting the run all over again.

3

Toemageddon
(and Other Dramas)

It felt like hitting a brick wall. One minute I was moving forwards at light speed (or my version of it), bounding along, soft ground underfoot, enjoying the views across the North Sea, and the next. . . WHAM! Suddenly, I was no longer moving at all. The only view I had was of the bog. My left big toe had sunk through the sun-scorched layer of shrub on the surface of the bog and into the dank, dark earth below. And there it had stayed — dropped like a tootsie-anchor into the depths of a boggy sea as the rest of my body attempted to motor on. I felt a sharp tug across the tendon on the top of the toe and a bolt of pain shot across my foot.

It had been an eventful day for my toes. Since starting Barefoot Britain, I'd gradually upped the daily mileage, progressing from 7 miles on day one to 13 miles on day two, and now, on my first day on the island of Yell, I was midway through a lung-busting 18 miles. I knew it was still early days, but I had expected things to get easier by this point. I'd hoped my body would adapt and that, each day, the running would be less arduous. But that wasn't the case at all.

The chunky, quartz-laden, naughty tarmac continued on Yell (I could only conclude that the naughtiness had been spread Shetland-wide), so I would desperately look for somewhere else, anywhere else, to run. That led to me tiptoeing along the grass verge at the edge of the road or traversing a peat bog. Sometimes, the bog running was wildly satisfying; I felt like an Amazonian (of Wonder Woman fame), the stomp, stomp, stomp of my still-soft feet over rich earth, inhaling lungfuls of fresh air as I went. Well, it was mostly fresh: a mixture of wood shavings, garden pond and a compost bin left out in the sun too long. Quite the nostril cocktail. But, other times, progress was slow and frustrating. And, so far, bog running had resulted in three minor cuts from sharp pieces of heather and now, a 'toe-wrenching'.

I had read much about boggy peatlands since arriving in Shetland and discovered that 20% of all of the world's bogs are located in Great Britain and Northern Ireland. I'd also learned that, despite being a challenging place for barefoot running, bogs are fantastic for the environment. Not only do they help minimise flooding risk, but they are masters of carbon dioxide storage. In fact, there's more carbon stored in peatlands across the world every year than in all other types of plant and tree put together.

In short, we all need a bit more bog in our lives. Although, on Yell, I wished there was less bog in mine. Or rather, that it had stuck to attempting to store carbon dioxide and not my toe.

Still sat on my bum in the bog, I let out a sigh and rubbed the toe tendon. Jeepers, it was sore. I took the toe between my thumb and forefinger and waggled it back and forth, thinking that if I could keep my toe mobile, it was less likely to seize up. I decided the best thing to do was to carry on running on it. Use it or lose it, I thought. So I got to my feet, instructed all of my toes to do their best to keep up with the rest of my body from now on and took off again.

Thankfully, in between my many toe mishaps, there was still plenty going on to distract me. My run of good luck with hosts continued, and I was taken in by a lovely local family, the Hauxwells. I bonded with mum Kim over a mutual love of the prince of pop Olly Murs and spent a couple of days dancing around her kitchen, chatting with her two home-schooled kids, Brynn and Faith, and eating freshly baked carrot cake.

Kim ran the local Girlguiding unit and had arranged for me to give a talk to her girls, who were aged between seven and sixteen. Many of them had been following the build-up to the journey on social media, so they were excited about my arrival at their Guide hut after another day of bog-battling. The girls made a small campfire outside, and we roasted marshmallows while snuggled up in blankets. It took me right back to being a youngster and enjoying campfires with friends. I remember that I always took great joy in hunting for the perfect stick to lance my marshmallow with. I had learned that marshmallow roasting was an art that needed many years (and lots of practice) to perfect. And I was happy to put in the work.

As excited as the girls were to see me, I was equally excited to see them. But at this stage of Barefoot Britain, I was still fine-tuning what I wanted to say to them. I had all my adventure stories down pat — from New Zealand and the USA to South America and Europe — but it was the in-between bits I needed to finesse. The messy stuff that happened inside my head when on these adventures and in the lead-up was equally, if not more, important than the razzle-dazzle stories of derring-do. When all else failed, I imagined I was talking to a younger version of myself. I thought about what I would say to her and said it. I also asked the girls a lot of questions. Challenge is relative, after all, and they were the masters of their own destiny; I was just there to shine a light on what was possible if they let their heads follow where their hearts wanted to lead them.

One of the older girls, Lily, had a guitar. So, as the sun dipped lower in the sky and my stories came to an end, we pulled the blankets tighter around our shoulders and listened to her play. Despite it being a long while before the sun set, the hills around the hut had begun to glow rose-gold. The wind had dropped to a gentle breeze, and there was a nip in the air. Sitting around the fire, my hair infused with smoke, made the hardship of the days of running seem a world away. Any worries about the journey ahead were carried off on the wind with the wisps of smoke. When the final song came to an end, Kim stood up.

'Anna, the girls have got you a present,' she said.

'Have they?' I looked around the group, and they all nodded in reply.

'Lily, do you want to give it to her?' said Kim, and Lily laid her guitar down by the side of the fire. She then got to her feet and rummaged around in her pocket.

'Yes. So. We all made a bit of this,' she said, holding out a bracelet with blocks of brightly coloured threads running around it. 'We took it in turns, to choose the colours, I mean. And we thought, well, you could wear it on the run, all the way to London. Because it's not heavy. And then you could think of us and remember that you came to Yell.'

I took the bracelet from Lily's palm and looked down at the band of brightly coloured threads.

'Will you tie it on for me?' I asked, holding out my bare wrist. Lily nodded. I was so touched by the gift, and the thought that had gone into it. The very idea that this bracelet would make it all the way to London still seemed ludicrous. But the girls believed that it would and, therefore, so did I.

Kim's hospitality and the bracelet put a spring in my step, but both of those things weren't enough to stave off the slow creep of physical exhaustion. As I left Yell and continued onto Mainland Shetland, I started to do battle with a weary body and a muddled mind. I had hoped by now that the aches and pains from the start of the run would have settled down, but the soles of my feet were still painful to the touch. They would tingle at nighttime as I tried to get the all-important hours of sleep, and, worse still, an alarming patchwork of red and purple bruising had developed under the balls of my feet.

The aftermath of Toemageddon was also in full swing and the tendon over the top of the toe was puffy, red and filled with fluid — it looked all kinds of angry, and I didn't blame it. All in all, my feet looked like they'd gone 10 rounds with Tyson Fury.

I was just so frustrated — with my feet, with my brain, with the speed at which both were adapting to the task at hand. I had spent over a year training for this run and now I was impatient. By the time I made it to Shona Manson's house in the city of Lerwick on Mainland Shetland, I had run 82 barefoot miles. . . and I was a wreck.

'So, chick — how ye doin'?' Shona asked over a stack of breakfast pancakes. Or 'Panekaka' as she called them. Shona, chief-in-charge of the Manson Massive, was a starburst of a woman, with dyed orange-red hair cut into a snazzy shoulder-length bob. She was all heart, passion and bright colours, and when I'd stopped overnight in Lerwick on my way up to Unst, we'd hit it off immediately. She spoke quickly in a strong Shetland accent and took a straightforward yet laid-back approach to life. We had invested a good chunk of time discussing our mutual love of brightly coloured sports gear (leggings especially), and her home was a reflection of her personality — brightly coloured cushions, rugs and fairy lights dominated the living room. Shona had also installed a hot tub on the decking in her back garden. 'Because life is too short not to sit in a hot tub and drink wine,' she said. Shona was the kind of person who would see through a false veneer in an instant, so when she asked me how I was doing, I knew couldn't lie.

'Umm. . . honestly, Shona. . . not great,' I said, pushing a piece of pancake around on my plate. I had to fess up. I was doing terribly.

'Och. Really? I'm sorry to hear that.'

'Mmm,' I mumbled, wondering if she thought me soft. I thought back to how I'd arrived at her door the previous week, on the way north from the airport. Back then, I'd been full of excitement — so naive. Oozing with a confidence that was now nowhere to be seen. I could only conclude I'd lost it in a peat bog somewhere. That, or it had been ground down by the spiky tarmac on the roads.

'Well, I've got to be getting to work, but you know what, Anna. . .' Shona stood up and began clearing the plates.

'What?'

'You do these things — these adventures — because not everybody can. If it was easy, everyone would be doing it.'

'Mmm hmm.'

'Now, there's more Panekaka there if you want them, 'kay? I'll see you later.' She smiled, turned on her heels and left.

Shona reminded me a lot of her Kiwi cousin, Jacqs, who had sorted me out staying with her in the first place. The 'ahh she'll be right, mate' Kiwi mentality had a lot of merit to it, but there was a kindness to the sentiment too. Her words were comforting.

With a belly full of pancakes, I went upstairs to the bedroom. I flopped onto the bed and stared at the ceiling. I felt a lump in my throat. Tears collected in the corners of my eyes and rolled down my cheeks. I was supposed to be running 10 miles that day, but I could think of nothing worse.

I had to accept that the shiny new-adventure excitement had well and truly worn off and, while staring at that ceiling, I was staring down the barrel of its reality. Bloody hell, it looked ugly. It dawned on me that this run was going to be far harder than I had imagined. I was one to grit my teeth and muscle through anything. That approach is fine for a day or two, a few weeks even, but it isn't fun.

Did I expect this run to always be fun? I wondered. I couldn't remember. What if the run never gets easier? What if it's going to be this hard for months on end and zero fun at all? I thought. I didn't want to give up, but equally, I didn't want to be miserable — life was too short for that. I felt trapped. I pulled my camera out and started filming. I was making a YouTube series about the run, mostly for the young girls following the journey. Filming added a layer of complexity, but if I wanted the documenting of the adventure to be real and raw, video was the best way to do that. I knew it was precisely when I didn't want to record and share how I was feeling that I had to.

'How on earth am I going to do this. It's just so hard. . . I mean, I knew it would be tough, just not this tough.' I let out a sigh and then paused. 'And the thing is. . . of course, I don't want to tell you all how hard it is because the second that comes out of my mouth, then that means I actually have to acknowledge it. And that's not a nice feeling.'

I turned off the camera and set it down beside me on the bed. I stared at the ceiling again and tried to pin down one of my wayward thoughts so I could get a closer look at it. What was scaring me more than anything was that something about this adventure felt different. I was used to battling through the bumpy first few weeks of a challenge. There was always a period of adjustment — a transition from 'normal life' to life on the road. But in past adventures, I had never for one moment thought I wouldn't want to carry on. When stopping isn't an option, then the carrying on was easier to do. But lying on the bed thinking about all the months ahead, my mind kept straying to the idea of packing it all in. They were only thoughts, but they were terrifying. Plus, I was only a week into the journey, for goodness' sake. This was pathetic. I was pathetic.

I called Jamie to talk things through. He was the best person to turn to in an adventure-related crisis. Or in any crisis, really. Not only was he a fantastic listener (and sometimes, all you need is someone who will listen) but, given his own adventure credentials, he would get it. Just before leaving for the barefoot run, I'd watched Jamie break a world record on the treadmill — running the furthest anyone ever had over seven days — a total of 524 miles. I had witnessed how he'd almost thrown the towel in on day two of that challenge. And again on day five. As far as gruelling experiences went, Jamie was more than qualified to understand how I felt.

'Hello, my love, have you got time to chat?' I asked.

'I've always got time for you, my dear. Talk to me.'

'It's weird, J. Something feels off. It's just so hard, I mean, harder than I thought it would be, and I'm exhausted. I'm sure it's too early to be this exhausted. My feet hurt. I can't even think straight. I'm not getting that buzz, you know, the buzz of running? I'm not getting that. And I'm slipping behind schedule already, but I can't go any faster. . . I mean, my body won't let me. . . and it's just. . .' I felt the lump rise in my throat again. 'I'm not sure if I can do it, J. I think I've gone too far this time.'

There was silence on the end of the line.

'Anna. How long have you got to make it to London?' Jamie asked, even though he knew the answer.

'Err, five-ish months. . .'

'Five months! And you're a week in. Why don't you take a few days off? Take a whole week off if you want!'

'But I can't. . .'

'Anna. How far have you run?

'Eighty-two miles.'

'Right, so you've just run the furthest you've run in a long time. . . with no shoes on.'

'I know. But I've got the schedule. I've got talks with the girls, I've got people waiting to run with me. There's people expecting me to be there. On time.'

'I'm sure they'll understand. You always said this would be a suck-it-and-see kind of thing. Didn't you warn them of that? I'm sure Abby's been letting them know.'

'Yeah. . . I did. I said I'd do my best, but that things could change. . .'

'Well then, they'll understand.'

'Maybe. . .'

'Take your time. Relax. And get Abby to do some logistics magic — that's what she's there for.'

I hung up the phone and immediately felt better. Jamie was right. I'd convinced myself that I only had two options: to stop or to carry on. But in reality, there are always many more options than the two you think you have. I could take a few days off and see how I felt for starters. It was all well and good trying to stick to a schedule, but if it ground me to a halt entirely then what good was that? The most important thing was making the 100-marathon distance — how I did that was far from set in stone.

I took the following two days off and, instead of pounding the Shetland streets in my bare feet, I spent the time hanging out at Shona's house with her pets Tom (the largest ginger cat known to humankind) and Max the wonder dog. Max was a wonder dog because he didn't care if I carried on the run or not. He wagged his tail anyway. In between conversations with the animals, I slept, I ate and did what I often do when things feel overwhelming — I wrote. Uncomfortable as it made me feel, I wrote an account of the first week of the adventure and, alongside the video I'd taken, shared it with everyone following the journey. Because if there was one thing I had promised I would do, besides run the distance I said I would, it was that I would be honest.

One evening, I joined Shona and a friend of hers for dinner in Lerwick. My eyelids began to droop at 9 p.m., and the girls were still going strong, so I offered to take Max the dog for a walk on my way home before heading to bed. It was a serene stroll through the small alleyways of town, over the sandy-coloured paving stones of Main Street and south towards Shona's house. The midsummer sun was just beginning to set. Peach-fringed clouds hung low over Bressay Sound. White and grey cottages on the surrounding hills glowed scarlet, partly obscured by folds of green. Eider ducks bobbed along the surface of the water. Arctic terns swooped and shrilled. The lights of offshore oil ships twinkled, and the air was still.

I sat on the shore with Max, watching the sun dip below the horizon until the water in the sound turned violet. It was so peaceful and so beautiful that it made me wonder how many other parts of Britain there were that were equally as beautiful that I had yet to see. And suddenly, I had the clarity I needed. The road ahead had the potential to be dark and difficult. So my head was screaming at me to stop. But my heart was begging me to carry on.

4

Totties and
Tammie Norries

'Hello, everybody, it's eight a.m., and this is the Chris Evans Breakfast Show. . . You've got a very special guest lined up for us today, haven't you, Vassos?'

'I have, Chris. It's a goody, I'm really excited about this one. A woman called Anna McNuff is running the length of Great Britain for Girlguiding. And she's doing it in bare feet.'

'She's what?'

'Bare feet. No shoes. Nada.'

'Wowsers. And I think we've got her on the line for a chat. . . Anna, are you there?'

'Hi, Chris! Hi, Vassos! I'm here,' I chirped.

'Fantastic. So, Anna, where are you right now, and how many miles have you done so far?'

'I'm on Shetland, and I've just hit one hundred miles, Chris. . . just this morning, in fact.'

'One hundred miles! With no shoes on?'

'Yep.'

Saying it out loud still felt strange, especially to two people I'd been a big fan of for a long time. I knew Vassos had always been a runner, but Chris had come to embrace it as a hobby more recently too. I was dead chuffed that they'd heard about the barefoot adventure.

'And how are your feet?' Vassos asked.

'Err. . . they're okay. A bit of a mess, but they're adapting,' I added quickly.

Which was true. My feet were now doing 'okay': not great, not terrible. Just okay. I was picking up tiny cuts here and there, but I could see and feel that the skin on my soles was beginning to get thicker and harden up. We chatted for a few minutes more — I talked to them about the kind of surfaces I'd come across so far — grass, mud, spiky tarmac and all of the luscious sandy beaches — then I explained I was having to keep a keen eye out for bits of broken glass and stray cockle-shells. Vassos shared stories of his own attempts at minimalist running, and Chris said he was actually wearing minimalist 'monkey shoes' right that very moment. They seemed to get the idea of the Barefoot Britain challenge, at least, and were super supportive.

'And so, tell us a bit about the Girlguiding connection. I know you're giving talks to young girls along the way,' said Vassos.

'I am indeed. I figure that if I stand in front of the girls in my smelly, dirty bare feet, and I'm in the middle of an adventure myself, then they might see that doing this kind of stuff, the messy stuff, I mean, well, that's for girls too.'

'Absolutely. I love that. And you're running to. . . London is it?' asked Chris.

'Yep. London. But I'm taking it one day at a time.'

'I bet you are. Well. . . keep in touch, won't you, Anna? Let us know how you're getting on?'

'That'd be ace, thanks, Chris. I will.'

I hung up from the show and sat back in my chair. It felt surreal to know that five million people had just listened to me give the young girls of Britain a shout-out and declare my intentions for the run live on the air, when 24 hours earlier I'd been moping into my pancakes about how difficult it all was. But sometimes, you need a force outside of yourself to propel you forward. Sometimes, you need to get out of your own way. Which is exactly what happened after I left Shona's house. I stepped aside and let the adventure take the lead.

As well as the interview with Virgin Radio, one of Scotland's main TV stations — STV — came out to do a video piece and put me on the evening news, as did BBC Shetland. With more attention from the media came more attention on the roads. I started to get beeped and honked by passing traffic. Through a combination of support from local hosts, those following online and in person at the roadside, gradually, my mood began to lift. The running didn't necessarily get any easier, but I was in a better frame of mind. Rather than refusing the reality of it being tough, I had accepted that every day would be difficult — that way, anything other than 'bloomin' tough' was a bonus.

I also realised that my brain was crumbling because I was thinking about the journey as a whole. My thoughts kept going round and round in circles, and the recurring question was always: If I am this tired, 100 miles in, then how in the world am I going to make it 2,620 miles to London? My thoughts were getting stuck, like loose clothing snagged on a rose thorn.

It was clear that thinking beyond next week wasn't working, so I decided not to think that far ahead. In fact, I wouldn't think about making it to London at all. Instead, I would find something that felt more manageable. If I could cover 500 miles, then that would get me as far as Aberdeen, on Scotland's east coast. And I liked the sound of that. So, from then on, I told myself I was only running 500 miles. I could work the rest out later on.

Another huge help in raising my spirits was being joined by local ultrarunner Charlotte for my first day back on the road. Charlotte helped skip the miles along with talk of running, adventures further afield and her experiences as a mum of six. Motherhood was no walk in the park, that much I knew, but if Charlotte took managing six kids in her stride (which she very much did), then I could take a bit of rough tarmac in mine. And besides, that day, the surface underfoot was smooth. My feet were still sore, but come the end of the run, I had. . . really enjoyed myself! Wonders would never cease.

I overdid it with the gratitude by delivering a rib-crushing hug to Charlotte. I was overcome with relief and could see twinkles of light in the dark road ahead. From that moment on, I was able to appreciate what I was doing rather than just wishing the miles away. Now, rather than get upset about the tarmac and view its incessant spiky-ness as a personal attack, I did my best to become at one with it. I couldn't control the surface beneath my feet, after all. It was what it was.

A day later, I was having a cup of coffee in Sandwick, feeling smug about my new Zen-like state, when I got a message from Charlotte:

Anna, I'm so sorry. You're not going to believe this. . . but you know that naughty tarmac you hate so much? Well. . . the local council are just a day ahead of you, and they're re-chipping the road. Laying down fresh rocks over the tar. I pulled over and asked them if they could hold off for a day because there was a barefoot runner coming through. . . but I don't think they got it. No luck! Thought you better know!

Wowsers. Not just naughty tarmac, but freshly laid, spiky-as-it-comes naughty tarmac. I had to laugh, or I would have cried.

Doing my best to avoid the newly laid rock chips where I could, I continued to inch closer to the southern tip of Shetland. I carried on staying with local hosts, many of whom were Mansons or friends of the family. I then took a detour to follow a network of small roads which skirted the west coast of the island, and it wasn't long before the fresh chippings Charlotte had warned me about had disappeared. The roads became smooth again, and the traffic died down to next to nothing.

When I made the tiny village of Bigton, I popped in for lunch and a cuppa with Yvonne, one of Shona's sisters. She welcomed me into her old farmhouse, nestled in a green valley just outside town, and cooked up butternut squash soup with a side of freshly baked Turkish bread, which was crispy on top and doughy in the middle (just the way it should be) and sprinkled with rosemary and rock salt. Yvonne didn't seem to mind that I had two bowls of soup, ate half of the loaf of bread and slathered it with a truck ton of butter.

'Have you got time to see the beach?' Yvonne asked as she cleared the table.

'I absolutely have time to see the beach!' I said, washing down the last mouthful of bread with a swig of tea. There was no way I was going to miss out on a visit to St Ninian's. The beach was the reason I'd chosen to take such a wiggly route south from Lerwick in the first place.

St Ninian's was one of the only places I'd read about before coming to Shetland. It's a tombolo beach, which, much to my disappointment, has nothing to do with pulling balls out of a machine at a village fete and winning crap prizes. Instead, tombolo describes a stretch of sand with the sea on both sides — where the waves lapping at the shore create two beautifully symmetrical sandy crescents. At low tide, St Ninian's is 70 metres wide and 500 metres long. It's covered in the whitest of white sand, and the pictures I'd found online made it look like something out of a Caribbean holiday brochure. I also knew it had once been voted by Lonely Planet as one of the most beautiful beaches in the world. At one end of the beach are the grassy dunes of Mainland Shetland, and at the other end is an island — with steep, grey, grass-topped cliffs rising from the sea and the remains of a neolithic chapel perched on top.

It was a windy day when Yvonne and I took a post-lunch stroll along the beach, so I put the hood of my duffel coat up and pulled the cord tight around my head as we walked, or rather battled from one side of St Ninian's to the other. The sun was doing its best to break through the clouds and it caught the white sand in places, making the beach sparkle.

The sand whipped across my bare lower legs and grains of it got lodged in my eyebrows. The wind-sand combo was just the wrong side of painful, but exhilarating all the same — it carried with it a feeling of everything being wild and raw. I was exposed to the elements, and I liked it. Although, I was grateful for the amount of food in my belly, weighing me down and stopping me from being blown away entirely. In spite of the wind and at the risk of sand finding its way into every orifice, I decided to channel my gratitude for the superb surroundings into some cartwheels. Because, well, adults should cartwheel more often. Yvonne embraced my excitement. Although she passed on the cartwheeling.

Sand gymnastics complete, I hugged Yvonne goodbye and took one last look at the beach, trying to hold a snapshot of it in my mind. With a belly full of soup, a body coated in a fine layer of sparkly sand and a buzzy mind, I ran back up the hill and re-joined the main road heading south.

The magic of St Ninian's must have followed me out of the bay because the route from Bigton to Dunrossness was a dream. There wasn't a whiff of naughty tarmac in sight, and the ground beneath my soles was as smooth as a baby's bottom. The road was narrow, with enough room for just one car at a time, but there were very few of those, so I had it all to myself, floating south on a silky ribbon of grey — green fields to my left, the North Atlantic to my right. I was running in a postcard. Albeit a very windswept one.

As I padded along the ribbon road, I realised that if this journey was going to be a success, each day couldn't be determined by how easy the running was. It had to be about more than that. It had to be about the distractions, the interruptions, the bits in between — beaches like St Ninian's and the chance to get to know a corner of my own country just that little bit better. Above all, it had to be about the people. If I could rely on them (and their tea, soup and freshly baked bread) to get me from the start of one day to the next, if only as far as Aberdeen, then everything would be easier.

***

Way down in the south of Shetland, perched on a rocky outcrop at the end of a long curve of white sand on West Voe Beach is a little grey stone bungalow. Long grass sways in the front garden and wind chimes tinkle above the door. The bungalow sits in the shadow of the ancient Norse settlement of Jarlshof, whose 4,000-year-old neolithic remains are visible from the back garden. Beyond the settlement is Sumburgh Head — the most southern point on Mainland Shetland.

I'd had another cracking day of running to West Voe. The wind had continued to whip across the island, but I didn't mind because I was in high spirits. Higher still because I'd had the opportunity to run across the Shetland Airport runway. Oh, yes, you read that right, I said across the runway. The man sitting in the glass booth at the entrance to the runway seemed bemused that a barefoot runner had appeared in front of him, but he nodded and lifted the red and white safety barrier anyway. I smiled and waved at him as I passed, and he smiled and waved back, shaking his head as he did. A few paces later, I passed a big sign that read: "NO STOPPING ON THE RUNWAY. DO NOT STOP FOR ANY REASON." Noted, I thought — better keep those bare feet a-movin'.

It was only when I'd scampered across half of the airstrip that a wave of excitement hit me. I was on a freakin' runway! When do you ever get to run across the tarmac of a commercial airport runway?! I looked over my shoulder to see if the man in the booth was watching, but he'd gone back to keeping an eye on the road coming into the airport. So, I broke the rules and stopped. To my left, I could see a traffic control tower and the hangers of Sumburgh Airport. To my right, it was just a couple of hundred metres to the edge of the land, and then, the sea. Yikes, there isn't much room for a pilot to make an error here, I thought. As I broke into a run again, I felt an overwhelming urge to spread my arms out like an aeroplane. So I did. Arms outstretched, I hollered at the top of my lungs over the wind, 'McNuff Airways! Ready for take-off!' Then I ran as fast as I could across the remainder of the airstrip, hoping that perhaps, with some freak gust of wind, I might take flight.

My first-class, barefooted flight took me all the way to West Voe Beach. Just like St Ninian's, West Voe was breath-taking. Turquoise waters lapped at a white sandy shore, which curved away from my feet towards the horizon. I ran along the pristine curve, splashing into the water every now and then — enjoying the cool rush of the sea and the sand between my toes. After a few minutes of running, I slowed to a walk at the water's edge. I'd covered 16 miles that day and was due to leave Shetland the following afternoon. West Voe was the last patch of sand I'd journey along, so I wanted to savour every footstep.

Reluctantly, I made it to the end of the beach and padded up a few wooden steps onto a small slip road. I had begun my journey on Shetland being taken in by the Manson family, and my last day on the island was to be no different. Shona had sorted me out a stay with her dad's cousin, whom I hoped lived in the grey bungalow in front of me. The directions had been as basic as those Jane on Unst had given me. 'We're the house at the end of the beach' was what I was working with, so I hoped I was at the right beach and the right house. I crept down the driveway and knocked lightly at a wooden door with frosted glass panels. A white-haired man in glasses answered.

'Oh, hi! Am I in the right place?' I asked.

'Well, now, let's see — are you Anna the barefoot runner?' He looked at my feet with a wry smile.

'I think that's me. Are you Sonny?'

'I am. Welcome, welcome — come on in!'

As I stepped across the threshold, I did my best to dust off the sand from my feet on the doormat, but there were large clumps of it wedged between my toes.

'Oh, don't worry about that. We're not fussy around here. . .' said Sonny, waving his hand at my feet.

Just behind Sonny in the hall was a woman with whitish-blonde hair and a broad smile spread across her face. Without so much as a word, she flung her arms open wide and engulfed me in the warmest of hugs. It was all soft and snuggly, just how hugs should be. She smelled of cakes and summertime flowers and, based on the brief glimpse I'd caught of her face before the hug tornado began, she reminded me of my Scottish nan.

'Hello, Joyce!'

'Hello, wee Anna!'

Joyce released me from the hug and ushered me into the

kitchen, where she had a freshly baked fruit loaf on the side and a pot of tea on the go.

'Wid you laek sum cake?' she asked in a thick Shetland accent.

'I would absolutely love some cake, Joyce, thank you.'

'An' wid you laek butter on it? You're surely no one of dis fok dat dunza wirk wi butter, ir you?'

Butter on a cake? I'd never tried it before, but if Joyce was dishing up that kind of indulgent deliciousness, I was all for it.

For the following hour, I sat in Sonny and Joyce's kitchen, listening to stories about their life on Shetland and Sonny's time spent as a taxi driver on the island. Soon after, Shona arrived. She'd driven down from Lerwick to join in for my last dinner on Shetland, and kindly brought my main kit bag with her too. As Shona chatted to Joyce, the conversation moved at breakneck speed. Clipped words rattled back and forth as they discussed a family member who'd visited recently. I was soon staring intently at the two women, my mouth wide open and looking back and forth between them as if watching a game of tennis. Sonny noticed I'd gone quiet.

'Anna, ir you keeping up wi dis?' He gestured towards the women.

'Err, not really. I might need subtitles.'

'Oh, we shuld be knappin' fur you, Anna!' Shona laughed.

'What's knappin'?'

'It's da wye wi wid spik tae fok fae Lundun!' Sonny put on an even thicker Shetland accent.

'It means speaking "properly",' Joyce clarified.

I insisted that they shouldn't change any of their words on my behalf, and that it was good for me to try to work out what on earth they were talking about. The distinct accent and slang were things I had grown to love about Shetland, after all. In my 10 days on the islands, I'd learned words like peerie (small), damorn (tomorrow), dee (you) and, one I had a lot of personal experience with, spaegie (muscle soreness).

The language on Shetland really made it seem like a world apart from the Britain I knew, and so I had taken to asking my hosts whether they felt Scottish, British or Norwegian. The answer was largely the same across the board: 'We're Shetlanders,' they said. I had a lot of respect for that. There is no way to put Shetland, nor those who live there in a box. They are a breed apart.

The Shetland slang chit-chat between Joyce and Shona continued while Sonny made dinner.

'Wir haeing totties. Do you laek totties, Anna?' Joyce asked.

'Err, I think so. Hang on. . . What are totties?'

'They're potaaaatoes to you!' said Sonny, mimicking my South London accent.

And so, I had totties. Mashed totties, with breadcrumbed cod, beetroot, broccoli and peas — it was a feast fit for a queen. And I didn't mind one bit that Joyce was the kind of person who asked if you'd like to have more totties — while she was spooning them onto your plate. . .

The following morning, after a hearty breakfast, Joyce took me on a quick spin up to the Sumburgh Head Lighthouse. I had a few hours before my flight south to Orkney and, although I was stoked with the Shetland pony foals and an otter sighting, I had still yet to see a puffin while on Shetland. Joyce said that all the puffins (or 'Tammie Norries', as they're called in Shetland) had gone back out to sea a week or so ago, but we could go up and have a look, just in case.

The lighthouse was a large, white, stone building with an impressive tower, owned by the National Trust. We spent 30 minutes wandering up and down the cliff path, peering over walls, hoping to catch a glimpse of one of the elusive birds, but alas, we found none.

'Och, dats a shame, there were hundreds here last week — jus' runnin' arooond,' said Joyce.

'Well, that's my own fault for taking so long to get here then, I suppose. Never mind,' I sighed.

'Sorry, Anna,' Joyce turned around and started to head back to the car.

'Joyce!'

'Yees?'

'A puffin!'

'Where?'

'There! And another one!' I pointed to a patch of rock 5 metres away, over a stone wall.

'And one more! Oh brilliant,' Joyce said, clasping her hands together with glee.

I couldn't believe it. Three puffins, all in one place. Oh the wonder! I nearly pooped myself and hiccupped all at once.

I stood and watched the three 'Tammie Norries' go about their birdy business for a while — marvelling at the black, white, red and yellow on their bill — until all three had disappeared into their respective nests. The puffins were much smaller than I'd expected them to be, and how something so small could survive for months on end out on the waves of the cold North Sea was beyond me. What a mighty and colourful little package of determination a puffin is — I was in awe.

Seeing the puffins was a neat end to what had been a turbulent journey across Shetland. As I boarded my flight south, I couldn't even begin to make sense of everything that had happened since I'd started up in Unst. I was sad to be leaving, that much was true. I had begun the journey knowing no one on the islands and left with countless members of extended family who had looked after me like a long-lost daughter. The Shetlanders had given me warm beds, giant hugs and gigantic wodges of buttered cake. They had shared their good vibes, furry pets and pristine, secluded beaches with me, and I knew, someday, I'd be back. I'd barely scratched the surface, after all. But for now, after 112 miles of barefootin', it was time to wave goodbye to Shetland.

Orkney & The Highlands

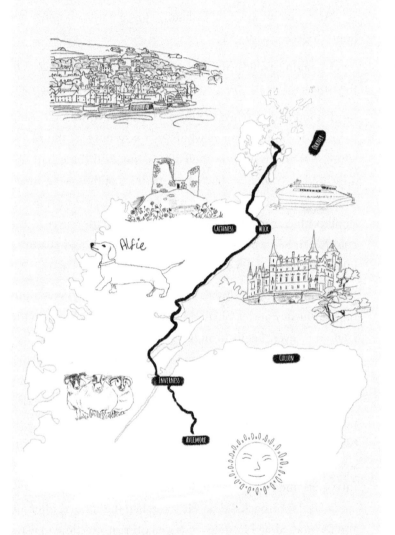

Alfie

ORKNEY

CAITHNESS

WICK

CULLEN

INVERNESS

AVIEMORE

5

Half Woman, Half Animal

It was a foggy morning on Scotland's north coast, and I was standing in a small white- brick outbuilding at Gills Bay ferry port, inspecting my toes. After leaving Shetland (full of buttered cake and totties), I'd flown to the Orkney islands and spent an all-too-brief 48 hours running south from Kirkwall, before catching a ferry to Gills Bay. The nicks and cuts collected in the Shetland island bogs had just about healed and, after a few nights of careful icing, my big toe was now back to normal size.

Eager to avoid running alongside a stream of disembarking cars (and the attention that might attract), I was delaying leaving the ferry terminal. I sucked in a lungful of musty air and blew it out again. The outbuilding smelled of cement, armpits and cigarette smoke. That alone should have been motivation to get running, and yet, there I was, still inspecting my toes.

I peered through a heavily scratched glass window and watched a muted trail of cars and taillights rumble away through the soup-like fog. Usually, that kind of weather has a negative effect on my mood — it can feel oppressive to be surrounded by so much grey. But that morning, I felt differently. I liked the fog being there. Just like the musty outbuilding, I liked that it could hide me.

While it might seem normal for an adventurer to want to bask in the glory of their expedition, my urge to stay out of sight that day was because I was still getting used to the reaction of passers-by when they saw me with no shoes on. I like to run because it allows me to transcend and to zone out. But as soon as I started going barefoot, I realised I couldn't just blend in and run on by; everyone noticed my bare tootsies, whether I wanted them to or not. Teenagers would shout, 'You've got no shoes on!' as if it were breaking news. Little kids would ask, 'Mummy. . . where have that lady's shoesies gone?' And older, wiser adults would mutter: 'Oh, no, no, no! No shoes? Terrible idea.'

Despite some better days on the road, I had to be honest — my mindset was still fragile. Although I had just about managed to convince myself that I was running to Aberdeen (and then, maybe London), I couldn't risk any passers-by questioning whether what I was doing was a good idea. So, in the fog, I felt safe — like the run could remain a secret between the landscape and me. And that, under its protection, I could creep, stealth-like, through the Highlands, building up speed, stamina and confidence as I went.

Once all the cars had gone from the ferry port, I ran away from the outbuilding, up a hill and darted across the main road. From there, I knew I'd be able to follow a network of minor back roads for most of the 18 miles to the town of Wick, so I settled into a rhythm on those roads. Turning left, right, left, right. . . I let the thick fingers of fog wrap themselves around me as I weaved south-east. Every now and then I ran off-road, across a field or, on one occasion (when my navigational skills failed), through someone's back garden and under a line of washing, taking care not to leave with underpants on my face. Visibility was poor in the fog, and I could only ever see 50 metres ahead of me, but the sun was doing its best to break through the grey in patches. The result was that the road was lit by an ethereal yellow glow, as if I was running on the inside of a lightbulb. My own personal ball of illumination.

It was late afternoon when I ran into Wick. I'd been there once before, on a cycling journey with an ex-boyfriend many years ago. We'd arrived in the dark and left early in the morning, so I couldn't remember much about the place. Seeing it in the daylight, I found it to be a mishmash of a town. Some parts of it were quite beautiful: old stone buildings, an earthy-green river running through the centre and a church spire reaching into the clouds. But other parts were run-down: streets filled with closed shops, alleyways littered with graffiti, pavements scattered with broken glass.

I spent one night in town before tracing the meandering path of the River Wick out into the suburbs and towards the sea. After a shot of civilisation, I was eager to get back to the coast. The fog had now cleared and I had high hopes for a few days of easy, sunshine-fuelled running along the clifftops to the east.

Once out of Wick, I passed through Pulteneytown Marina which, in stark contrast to the greys and browns of the stone buildings in Wick proper, was an explosion of colour. Dozens of yachts had masts adorned with brightly coloured flags from countries all over the world, which fluttered like petals in the breeze. Fishing boats and dinghies of all shapes and sizes were moored off the stone walls of the marina, their bows painted in bright greens, pale yellow and tangerine. Fluorescent buoys bobbed in the navy water and ducks navigated the passages between the boats, leaving ripples in their wake. There was something about the brightness of the marina and the life contained within its sea walls that made me feel alive. The many Union Jacks tinkling on the masts also caused an unexpected swell of patriotic pride. I could only imagine the adventures the boats in the harbour had been on so far, and the journeys yet to come. I ran off feeling recharged.

At the crumbling ruins of the Castle of Old Wick, I turned southwards and picked up signs for the John O'Groats trail — a 147-mile coastal route I could follow all the way to Inverness, avoiding the busy A9. I made easy progress for the following few hours on the trail, through long grass along the clifftops. Purple and white wildflowers were scattered here and there, like confetti over the expanse of green. The coastline to my left was jagged, and every half a mile or so I'd pass a small headland which jutted out into the sea. Sometimes, the headland had been eroded by the water, transformed into a fully separated stack or an intricate archway of rock with a mass of foaming sea clawing at the base. All along the coast, the cliff edge dropped away steeply, and so, given my ability to fall over while running (quite the talent), I took great care not to run too close to the edge. But I did pass close enough to marvel at the hundreds of seagulls making their nests on tiny ledges above the crashing waves.

All in all, the first day on the John O'Groats trail was a treat. The terrain was easy underfoot, I had beautiful views, the birds and the wildness of nature was all around. I was convinced that if I just followed the trail all the way to Inverness, I'd make swift progress and be there in no time. Of course, nothing lasts forever — the good and the bad — and as the headlands became more distinct and the coastline increasingly fragmented, finding the trail became more of a challenge.

Now a long way from Wick, the path wasn't as well-trodden as it had been. Small trails were still faintly visible, but they appeared and disappeared, like snakes slithering through long grass — there one moment and gone the next. The route became increasingly overgrown, and, in turn, I became paranoid that I would pick up ticks. I know that other countries have grizzly bears and sharks and poisonous beasties to worry about, but in Great Britain we have midges that nibble on your flesh, seagulls that poop on your head (usually after stealing your lunch) and. . . ticks. Of that lot, ticks are the worst because they carry Lyme disease.

Earlier that week, I'd sent my friend Faye a picture of the

John O'Groats trail that I'd found online. She'd swiftly replied with a message that read: Beware of the ticks! I once found one hiding near my lady bits. No idea how it got there. Yikes. I didn't fancy finding a tick in my foof, or any other area of my body for that matter, so as I ran on through the long grass, I stopped to check my legs regularly for any sign of stowaways.

I did manage to stay tick-free, but there were other challenges at hand. On one occasion, I was on the trail (or at least, I think I was) when it dipped down into a small bay and led me to a secluded, stony beach. It was very picturesque and all that jazz, but there didn't seem to be any way out from the bay, and I had no idea how to get back up to the clifftops above my head. I looked around for a few minutes before deciding to scramble up a steep incline to my right. As I climbed up a close-to-vertical section, my mind began to rage. This was not the plan, I thought. Not only was clambering up cliffs painfully slow, but it took every ounce of energy I had, and I hadn't started with much in the first place.

At the top of the climb, the trail had another treat in store: stinging nettles. And not just any stinging nettles. I can solemnly declare that these were the stingiest stinging nettles I have ever encountered. In fact, these particular stinging nettles deserved a plant-based promotion, such was the efficiency of their stings. I ran for half a mile through them until my legs were on fire.

I took the lack of a clear and easy trail as a personal affront. Which was, of course, ridiculous, but that's how I felt. At one point, I got so frustrated, I began swearing at the trail. Couldn't it see I was tired? Didn't it know I had 21 miles to run that day? Couldn't it just cut me some slack and go back to being easy, like it had been near Wick? I ran on through anger, into self-pity, and ended the day at sheer delirium.

It wasn't unusual for me to behave like a grumpy teenager at some point during a long run, but I realised my outbursts that day were less about the trail and more about the fact that I was more tired than usual. In fact, my legs were leaden. I'd run 85 miles since the last time I'd taken a day of rest (at Shona's) and, on top of the dull throb of fatigue, there were some new guests at the pain party. My hip flexors were sore, and my Achilles tendons were beginning to play up too. They creaked and groaned in the mornings and took an hour to warm up before quietening their cries.

I did my best to keep my muscles in check on the run with the help of a massage therapist called Sylvia, aka the Body Goddess (this was just my name for her; it's not an official title). Sylvia had helped Jamie through his 5,000-mile run across America with her unique 'trigger-point therapy' — which is all about pressing on specific points of your body to encourage overtight muscles to release. Sylvia lived in America and was offering me self-treatment advice via video messages. Both Jamie and I liked the virtual therapy method because it relied on getting to know your own body and was something you could learn to do to yourself. Perfect for the wayward adventurer on the road.

Using the trigger-point technique was helping to keep my sore spots under control and, on the plus side, my hips and Achilles were aching evenly on both sides of my body, which told me the pain was more about general overuse, rather than a specific injury. So, I took all of this as a silver lining and whispered a promise to my weary body that I'd take it easy in the days ahead.

Aside from Sylvia's virtual support, my saving grace down the north-east coast came, once again, in the form of lovely locals. This time, my rescuers were Janet and her daughter Natalie (and Alfie the sausage dog too). Both of them were leaders at a nearby Girlguiding unit in Caithness and had arranged for me to give a talk to their girls one evening while I was staying with them for two nights. After doing battle with the coastal trail, coming 'home' to their white cottage, set back from the cliffs just south of Lybster, was a welcome relief. The view from the house across sheep-filled fields towards the sea was serene. It was a haven of calm with an uninterrupted view of the horizon. In the evenings, we chatted and ate plates of steaming fish pie. Natalie made fresh meringues and topped them with cream and strawberries. And, when Janet had to nip out one evening for a meeting, Natalie and I curled up under piles of blankets in the living room and binged on reality TV.

The disconnect between cosy evenings with hosts and the brutal days of running was stark, and I grappled with switching between the two. I would finish the day's run completely exhausted, wondering how I was going to get up and do it all again. I wanted nothing more than to go straight to bed, curl up in a ball and sleep for a thousand years. Instead, I would do my best to hold down a coherent conversation with a kind host before making my way to the bedroom, where I would lay on the bed for 10 minutes and stare at the ceiling — revelling in the first time I'd been still since setting off that morning. I'd listen to the beat of my heart, tune in to the dull ache in my legs and focus on the throb, throb, throb of the soles of my feet. I'd then haul myself into the shower and wince as watery soap moved over the cuts and scrapes from a day of bush-bashing.

Once out of the shower, in a clean set of clothes, I would feel like a new woman — transformed from feral to fine in under an hour. Sometime midway through dinnertime chat, I would wonder if I had imagined how hard the day had been. Because, in that moment, I felt fine. Was I being overly dramatic? How could this run really be that hard if I could spend the evenings eating fish pie and meringues and watching trashy TV? As a result, each night I would walk a fine line. The line between accepting how difficult the challenge was and shoving it to one side whenever I could.

***

A few days into my battle with the John O'Groats trail, I was sitting enjoying breakfast at The River Bothy cafe at Berriedale. I'll level with you — it was a second breakfast. I'd already been fed by Natalie and Janet earlier that morning but, by the time I arrived at the cafe, another 90 minutes had passed, which warranted another meal. And besides, if I needed any more convincing to go inside for some nosh, the chalk blackboard sign on the edge of the road read: 'Skinny people are easy to kidnap. Stay safe, eat cake.' Better to be safe than sorry. I was in.

I spent longer than I should have in the cafe. It was a quirky place, which sold local arts and crafts and all kinds of handmade trinkets. The coffee was next-level fantastic, so I had two of those, then some eggs on toast and a slice of walnut cake for afters. When the time came to pay the bill, the owner waved her hand and told me it was on the house. 'Really? Are you sure?' I gawped.

'Yes, of course. You gave a talk to my daughter last night — she's in the local Guide group. I promised her that I'd keep you well-fed if you came this way.'

What a woman. And what a legend. I felt guilty for having had double coffee helpings — I would have stuck to one if I'd known she was picking up the bill — so I thanked her profusely. It was a lovely gesture, one which kickstarted the day in sweet style.

Whether it was the act of kindness, the quality of the coffee or the fact that I was now protected by the power of cake, I will never know, but the John O'Groats trail got the message loud and clear that I needed some respite. Despite a steep climb from the cafe, the miles that followed were on easier terrain, through light forest, along minor back roads or across grass-covered fields. I still lost the trail often, but it was simple enough to find again by hopping over a few fences and keeping the sea on my left. It'd rained on and off for much of the morning, and the air was filled with that wonderful post-rain smell — one of damp earth and wet grass. As I ran, I looked out at rows of propellers on a wind farm and a few offshore oil rigs in the distance and, when there was a break in downpours, light beamed though the clouds and collided with the sea mist, giving the horizon a lemony glow.

As the rain started up again, the trail weaved through a thick blanket of heather and past patches of gorse. The amethyst flowers of the heather were beautiful, but gorse had become my favourite sight in Caithness — bright yellow petals exploding like a thousand stars from needles of green. It's a nightmare to run through in bare feet — the needles pierced my soles and got stuck into my upper foot — but thankfully, I could often steer clear of it, admiring the mini supernovas from afar, by following one of many rough sheep tracks which cut through the heather instead.

The heather was more forgiving to run through because the brown stalks of the plants had often already been pressed flat and into the earth by the sheep, so it was more of a massage for my soles than anything too uncomfortable. And the sheep tracks were easy to spot and follow — snagged clumps of sheep's wool were strung like a line of prayer flags all the way along the clifftops.

I'd been galloping through the heather for an hour or so, when a wide trail crossed my path, running from west to east towards the cliffs. That was strange. It looked too manicured and well-trodden to be a sheep track and so, like Alice in Wonderland, I followed it. There was a good chance it led nowhere, but there was also a chance it would lead to somewhere exciting. After a few minutes of following the trail towards the sea, it opened out onto a clearing.

There was a collection of ground trails that led away from my feet to the weather-beaten ruins of stone croft houses, and I could see more stone structures in the distance, further along the cliffs. Just as I was beginning to wonder whether I'd happened upon anything of historical interest, I found some information signs. The signs were faded in many places, but I could read the title on the first one, which said: 'Welcome to Badbea Clearance Village'. This was a village, and it really was in the past tense. There was nothing much left of it now except crumbling ruins. It seemed like the strangest place for a village to be. Why on earth would people choose to live out here? I wondered. It was miles from anywhere, on a windswept, exposed patch of land only accessible by foot, and close to steep cliffs which plunged into the freezing sea.

I read more about the village on the signs and, as it turned out, the inhabitants of Badbea hadn't chosen to live there at all. They'd been forced from their homes after local lairds began 'clearing' parts of the Highlands in the eighteenth century, so the land could be used for lucrative sheep-farming. The windswept clifftops at Badbea were one of the few places the displaced families were allowed to settle. The villagers were self-sufficient, hauling their fishing boats up and down the steep cliffs to get food, while living off the land for everything else. They kept cattle and other livestock but needed to tether them close to their homes for fear that high winds would blow them over the cliffs, into the sea.

I spent 10 more minutes investigating the ruins of Badbea and reading about village life. I couldn't imagine the hardships they'd endured — being uprooted from your home and forced to make a new one in such an inhospitable environment seemed cruel and unfair. When I began to think about all of the people who had lived there and were now gone, it felt like an eerie place. Are any of them buried beneath my feet? I wondered. A stiff gust of wind blew through the bracken and sent a shiver down my spine. I'd enjoyed the history lesson, but the place was now giving me the willies. I shuddered and took off again along the cliffs.

It must have been the spirits of Badbea whipping the weather into a frenzy because, further along the coast, the rain started up again, and this time it was full-blown torrential. I pulled the hood of my jacket up around my ears and retreated into it as far as I could, squinting through the rain as the wind rattled around me. I could see the trail turned sharply away from the coast and went inland for a short way, before dropping down a steep slope and into a stream which rushed towards the sea. On the other side of the stream, up an equally steep slope, I could see a patch of trees! How exciting. I hadn't seen more than a few trees since starting the run in Shetland

— only bushes and scrub — and it was only in seeing the trees that I realised quite how much I'd missed their presence in the landscape.

One of the downsides of barefoot running is a lack of grip on wet ground, especially on grass and mud. So, as I began the descent to the stream, I slipped and slid all over the place and spent a decent chunk of time on my arse. The trail up the other side through the trees was steeper still and just as slippery. On any other day, I'd have found all of the sliding around frustrating, but I was enjoying the challenge of it.

Going upwards was a tough slog but the ground was soft underfoot, so it was easy on my soles, and I settled into a rhythm for the climb. I began to use low hanging branches on surrounding trees to haul myself up the slippery sections, taking care to get one foot in place before reaching for a new branch. Keeping my balance wasn't easy, and it all felt like a giant game of snakes and ladders, where one false move would result in me sliding all the way down the back of a muddy snake, to the stream at the bottom.

As the rain hammered down harder still, the noise of it colliding with the surrounding leaves and the hood of my jacket was deafening. Despite the racket, I settled into a rhythm as best I could: foot in place, branch grab, heave. Next foot in place, trunk grab, heave. And on I went. Halfway up the climb my lungs were really beginning to burn, but I paused for a moment and thought about where in the world I was — I was in the Scottish Highlands, having run along a section of trail where no cars or bikes could go. I'd discovered an abandoned village, followed sheep tracks through heather, my legs were caked in mud, I was in my bare feet in a forest and feeling every piece of earth beneath them. This was the Britain I'd come in search of. This was what I'd hoped for. This was AWESOME!

It took me 20 minutes to make the top of the climb and, as the ground levelled out, I left the forest behind and took off again across open fields of bracken. The rain continued to pour and the wind picked up a notch. I was still full of adrenaline from the climb, and now I felt like Mother Nature was playing with me — she was tossing me another challenge and sitting back to watch. I turned into a feral beast, pushing my legs harder over the rough ground.

'It's a test!' I shouted out loud. 'A test!' I spread my arms wide and let out a war cry at the top of my lungs. 'Rarrrrrrr-rrr!' I was half woman, half animal, soaked to the skin and at one with the elements.

Post-war cry, the rain finally stopped, and all of the energy I had expended over the course of the morning caught up with me. By the time I made it to the town of Helmsdale, it was 4.30 p.m. What with the morning of torrential rain, the stop for a history lesson and the scrambling through the forest, progress had been slower than usual. I'd run 9 miles and still had 13 left to run to complete the full 22-mile day.

It dawned on me that I wasn't going to make the rendez-vous with my new hosts at Brora Beach on time. I pulled out my phone to check the messages we'd exchanged earlier in the week.

Hello Gill and Jim. It's Anna McNuff here, I hope you're super well. I think I'll be finishing the run at 6.30 p.m. at Brora beach on Monday. Would it be okay to get collected from there? Anna xx

Hi you beautiful human, of course we can collect you. Absolutely not a problem. You let us know when you get close to the beach and we'll be there. Woop woop! Can't wait to welcome you to our home. A big bath awaits you my friend. G&J (and Biscuit the cat) xx

The message was accompanied by a picture of a big bath with a smiling rubber duck on the edge of it. I wasn't sure I'd ever seen a duck smile, but this one definitely was. Rereading the messages made me laugh, but there was no way I could make 13 miles in two hours. Not if the terrain was anything like it had been that morning. I cursed myself for not leaving Berriedale sooner (and blamed the cake for luring me in).

Aside from regretting the time spent enjoying a leisurely second breakfast, I was now beginning to wonder if it was pushing things too far to run all the way to Brora. I had to listen to my body and my body was telling me that running 22 miles on an ordinary day was a feat, but running those miles over undulating terrain in the rain and the wind. . . it could be a stretch too far. I decided I would stop short of Brora that night. I'd just run for two more hours and see where I ended up, then get collected from there.

I messaged Gill and Jim to give them the heads-up that I wasn't sure if I'd make it the whole way and a reply came swiftly back.

Fab. There's no time limit my friend. It's all good. Look after those feet. We will find you wherever you are. We'll be the ones in a Blue Beetle.

Gill sent a picture of her bare feet, covered in henna tattoos, propped up on the Beetle dashboard. Of course they'd be in a blue Beetle. I hadn't even met these two yet and I knew that the Beetle would be a car that suited them.

Beyond Helmsdale, I followed the John O'Groats trail across some fields, through a grotty A9 underpass and began running alongside a train track, which cut back towards the coast. The miles were slow and sloggy, and I couldn't find a rhythm as I hopped between small tarmac roads, bike trails and overgrown grassy tracks, but despite that, I was in a chipper mood. Something about giving myself permission to stop short of Brora if I needed to had taken the pressure off. Instead of feeling anxious as to whether or not I'd make it, I ploughed on and just took every mile as a bonus. One mile closer to London, one mile less to run.

My new, relaxed mood didn't ward off the challenges, however, which continued to come thick and fast. In a patch of rough trail lined with brambles, I picked up a small cut on my little toe. It was bleeding, so I sat down at the side of the trail to wrap it in white micropore tape. I went overboard with the taping, and it looked like a little Egyptian mummy by the time I was done.

'Come on then, Toe-tankhamun,' I said, giving the toe a little wriggle before running off again.

Toe-tankhamun was clearly worse at navigating than I was because we then lost the trail a couple of times, ending up in a stinging-nettle gulley on one occasion. When that happened, I had a good old swear and felt a lot better.

By the time the top of Brora Beach came into view, I'd run a total of 16 miles since leaving Berriedale. I crossed a small river, then ran along flat-packed, golden sand for 10 minutes before weaving through grassy dunes at the edge of the beach. The long grass disappeared, and I scampered through a large caravan park, waving at holidaymakers enjoying early evening dinners on deck chairs on the grass outside their temporary homes on wheels.

For the first time that day, I felt like I was really moving. In fact, I was on fire! (And not just because of the stinging-nettle stings.) I was on fire from the inside out. A mix of sand and grass was one of my favourite surfaces to run on barefoot, because it was hard enough to not sink, but soft and springy too. I began to feel as if my feet were landing on mini trampolines with each step. Boing! Boing! Boing! I went, bounding from one patch of grass to the next. I also had a clear view of everything beneath my feet, so I stretched out my legs, confident of their placement with each stride.

Suddenly, it felt like my legs were spurring me onwards. I was all high knees and upwards motion, as if I was a puppet and there were strings attached to my knees, hips and arms. As a 5-fot, 10-inch woman, I have long limbs which often feel unusually heavy for running. But in the dunes, I felt weightless. I'm not sure if you've watched The BFG, but if you have, you'll remember the scene where he pops Sophie in his pocket and bounds across the earth towards the land of the giants, leaping over cliffs and bouncing off boulders. That was me in the dunes, although I hoped I looked less like the BFG and more like a graceful gazelle. We can all hope.

A few miles further on and now, with just 4 miles to go to Brora, I realised I was going to make the full 22 miles after all — albeit an hour later than intended. I didn't want to stop, but having yet to master the art of texting and running, I paused briefly to message Gill and Jim.

I'm going to make it to Brora! These feet are going for it! Steaming towards you and the finish. Eta 7.30pm!

Beaches are dreamy for barefoot running, and Brora beach was no exception. It's 2 miles long and wide too, so I was able to find that sweet spot between the soft, dry sand and the wet sand near the sea, so I could run freely without sinking in. I narrowed my eyes and squinted into the distance along the golden sand. I could see two lone figures in the middle of the beach. That must be Gill and Jim!

I took off again and began madly waving at them. I ran as fast as I could and continued the waving but quickly realised they were still a long way off. If I kept up that level of enthusiastic arm-waggling I would exhaust myself, or take off in the wind, one or the other. So I stopped waving and just ran. I ran, and I ran, and I ran, until the two people got much closer. And when they did, I resumed waving even more wildly; although then, they got really close, and I realised the people didn't look anything like the pictures I'd seen of Gill and Jim. Which made sense because it wasn't Gill and Jim at all. I moved my arms up in the air again, as if I was just stretching them out, and exchanged some awkward smiles with the strangers as I ran on by.

Some 10 minutes later, I was approaching a set of rocks at the very end of the beach when another couple came into view. One was a tall man with grey hair and a beard, and another was a woman with short brown hair. They both had bare feet. Now that has to be them, I thought, although I held off waving until right at the last minute, just in case.

'Alright!' came a call over the wind in a Scouse accent.

'Helllooo Gill, and hellooooo Jim! So sorry I'm so late,' I said, padding the last few steps towards them. 'I've had one heck of a day.'

'Honestly, McNuff, you could have pulled your finger

out,' said Gill as she engulfed me in a hug, and Jim joined in on the hug-action too.

'Come on our barefoot wanderer. Let's get you home,' he said.

As we walked away from the beach towards where Betty the Beetle was parked, I felt such a mix of things. It was only one day in the grand scheme of the run, but it had felt like such a triumph. I'd thought I was going to have to stop short of Brora and have to make up the miles on another day, and then BAM! Just when I'd believed there was nothing left in the tank, my bod had gone ahead and scooped up another bucketload of muscle magic from the depths. Despite my mind asking me to stop at so many points throughout the day, my body had grabbed the Barefoot Britain controls. It had taken over.

6

'I'll Sleep with the Kombucha'

Gill and Jim were latecomers to the Barefoot Britain party. I'd had an overwhelming response to the call for hosts in the lead-up to the start of the run, but there were still some blank lines in Abby's logistics spreadsheet of wonderment, many of which were in more remote areas of Scotland, Northern Ireland and Wales. Contrary to it being a cause for concern, I actually liked seeing the gaps. Because it's often in the space between order and certainty that wonder blooms. And I am going to class Gill and Jim of the Scottish Highlands as an unexpected, wonderful thing.

They'd found out about the run via social media after it had started and dropped me a message while I was hop-skipping my way across the Orkney Islands.

Hello lovely lady. Just wanted to offer you a warm welcome to Scotland, and also a bed for the night, bath, food etc. on your barefoot run. We're 1/2 a mile off the A9 in the Highlands, and you would be very welcome at Broomfield (our cottage). We run a micro business here and would love to meet you, and maybe run with you for a mile or two.

The couple lived just a smidge inland from my intended run route and I'd be passing them on a stretch of days when I didn't have a planned place to rest my weary head. Having looked at their Glamp 'n' Drive eco-business website, which described vegan breakfasts, homemade kombucha and Mr Biscuit (the royal ginger cat in residence), I knew they were my kind of people. And when they said I would have the option of staying in a shepherd's hut, a Norwegian log cabin, a tent, a yurt or an actual bedroom, well — that sealed the deal.

Gill was a Liverpudlian, with short, pixie-cut, brown hair, and dark-brown eyes which are full of mischief. She mostly wore black or blue dungarees with a T-shirt underneath, showing off intricate black tattoos on her arms, and she often wandered around without shoes on. She had a firecracker of a personality: all sharp wit, sarcasm and candid remarks — which made me smile right from the off.

Jim was the more laid-back of the duo; in fact, Jim is so laid-back, he's horizontal. Which takes up a lot of space because he's a tall man, with grey hair and a white-grey beard, a kind smile and a soft Glaswegian accent I could listen to all day. In fact, I had to be careful not to talk to Jim when I was feeling too tired, or he would send me off to sleep, just like Matthew McConaughey does when storytelling in his Texan drawl. There was an air of the sensible about Jim and it was clear to see that 'semi-retired chartered accountant' was a profession he was well-suited to. I'd trust Jim with my accounts for sure, even more so because beneath a more sensible exterior, I could see mischief in Jim's blue eyes. And he jumped at any chance for silliness. Sense and silliness — what a combo.

After Gill and Jim collected me at Brora Beach, we drove home in their beloved blue VW Beetle. From the moment I slipped onto the leather of the back seats of the Beetle, I was one happy girl.

'This is Betty,' Gill said, patting the dashboard of the car.

'Nice to meet you, Betty. Thanks for letting me in for the ride.'

'Yeah, you're a lucky lady. She's a bit picky, our Betty.'

'I'm honoured.'

'And I know it looks like Jim's driving right now, but really Betty's in control. She knows the way home. Jim's just for show,' Gill smiled.

'I'm the decoration,' said Jim, raising one hand to his face and doing his best impression of a pantomime dame.

Betty the Beetle smelled of a mix of oil, leather and tin, and on her back seat I was transported to being in Florrie, the 1960 Morris Minor my family had back home. Florrie has grey paintwork, red leather seats and little orange indicators that stick out from the side of the car when she wants to turn a corner. She is a marvel to behold, especially since my mum had spent years lovingly restoring her. I had spent many an early morning being driven to rowing training in Florrie, or being collected from school — watching my mum as she worked the choke on the dashboard to get her to start or prevent her from stalling at traffic lights. Florrie is used less these days, and spends a lot of time in my parents' garage, but she is called into duty for special occasions, like weddings, when the sound of her engine spluttering down the road is preceded by her loud carry-on style horn. Florrie the Morris is pure joy.

'You alright, McNuff?' Gill said, and I realised I'd been staring out of the window, reminiscing about Florrie.

'Huh? Oh, yep. Great thanks — just chilling back here.'

'Great — thought you might have fallen asleep. Which is totally groovy, by the way. Sleep if you want to.'

Have you ever met someone for the first time and there's no awkwardness, no polite dancing around introductions? You chat for a few minutes, and that's it. As if the weird and wonky parts of your own character fit neatly with the weird and wonky parts of theirs. That was how I felt within a few minutes of meeting Gill and Jim. They were off-the-wall, and I liked it. I had to be some way from the wall myself to be doing a barefoot run, so the conversation flowed easily. Running beneath the surface of their outwardly quirky characters, I could immediately feel an undercurrent of kindness too. It felt all warm and snuggly to be hanging out with them, and I wrapped that warmth around me like a blanket in the back seat of Betty the Beetle. I always wonder, when someone has the ability to make you feel that way, whether it's through something they are actively doing, or the absence of trying to do anything at all.

When we arrived at Broomfield Cottage, Jim parked up next to a VW camper van, which Gill introduced as Minto (all their vehicles had names). It was pale-green on the bottom half, white on the top half, with a silver bumper. The spare tyre on the back of the van was in a cover which was designed to look like a Tunnock's tea cake. Minto was their ride for adventures further afield, she said.

We walked past Minto, and Jim pushed open a waist-high wooden gate, then led me down a short pathway to the front door.

'Well, welcome to Broomfield,' he smiled.

Broomfield is a cosy place, just as you would expect a cottage to be. Stone slabs on the kitchen floor, exposed wooden beams, low ceilings. Chunky wooden shelves, laden with glass jars. I knew Gill and Jim were vegans and cared a great deal about the environment, and their home reflected that. Things had an old-world feel, with modern twists. Broomfield was as funky as Gill and Jim.

'Your bag's waiting for you upstairs. It's missed you,' said Gill with a grin.

I really appreciated them collecting my main kit bag — it was filled with things that made the journey a whole lot more comfortable: my laptop for all the logistics (I hated working hunched over my phone), a spare set of comfy, clean clothes, a big puffy down jacket for colder days, emergency snacks (for when I woke up starving in the middle of the night), a pair of shoes(!), a few different-sized balls to help with my trigger-point treatment and a homemade foot-care kit, comprising antiseptic wipes, a little towel and tubs of Rip Stopper — a thick balm that's used by gymnasts to stop the hard skin on their hands from cracking. I still couldn't quite believe the kit bag was managing to get passed along while I ran. I wasn't sure I'd ever get used to it, in fact. I wasn't having to stress about it too much, which was testament to Abby's planning ability and also to the back-up option I had of just throwing my overnight things in my smaller backpack and running with them for a few days if needs be.

'So, where do you fancy sleeping?' Gill asked. 'Like I said, we've got a cabin, or a shepherd's hut. . . the tent's a bit out of action at the moment but. . .'

I looked at the floor and bit my lip. I knew exactly where I wanted to sleep, but I was nervous about asking because it might go some way to dispelling the myth of me as a hardy adventurer. But I planned to spend a couple of nights staying with Gill and Jim — with them ferrying me back and forth to carry on running in between — so the sleeping arrangements were important.

'Would it be okay if. . . I mean, do you mind if I sleep inside, in the bedroom?'

'Of course! I wondered if you might go for staying indoors. You'll be sharing the room with some giant jars of homemade kombucha though. . . So long as you're okay with that?'

'Ooo, I've never slept with kombucha before — does it snore?'

'Not any worse than Jim,' Gill said.

'Brilliant. Then, I'm game.'

I was relieved. Much as I loved the outdoors, I craved being in a warm comfortable bed after spending all day running. If that made me soft, then so be it. And besides, there was something extra nice about being in the house, knowing Gill and Jim were there too. I found a comfort in that. The physicality of being closer to other people made me feel like the journey wasn't such a solo one.

The following day, Gill and Jim dropped me back at Brora Beach, and I ran a slow and sloggy 19 miles from the beach to Dornoch. I'd slept well, but each 5-mile stint felt like 10. I was hideously sleepy as I picked up the John O'Groats trail and followed it along more beaches, through fields and light forest. At one point, I was so lethargic that I lay down in the long grass, on the water's edge, just shy of Dunrobin Castle — a beautiful, white-stone building, rectangular in shape, with the large windows of its 189 rooms flanked by fairy-tale-worthy turrets. Dunrobin had gone one step further and upped the turret game by not only having main turrets, but mini ones too. It was as if the turrets had had babies. Beyond a low, grey stone wall, the meticulously maintained gardens of the castle — complete with a pond and pink and white lilies — were equally as spectacular as the building itself.

Gill had told me to look out for the castle and joked that it was their second home. So, after my nap in the grass, I pulled my phone out and dropped her a message, with a picture of Dunrobin: 'Just passing your second home.'

A reply came swiftly back: 'Awww, brilliant. You're doing

great. Sorry we couldn't put you up in it. Didn't want to over-whelm you.'

'Probably for the best. I hear the maids needed a few days off anyway. And the butler.'

'I wish the maids would nip over to Broomfield and clean the cabin here for our next guest. Mr Biscuit is trying to help but he can't hold the broom very well with his cat-thumbs.'

'Poor Mr Biscuit. Tell him to have a cat nap instead. I just had one and it was glorious.'

'Will do — run strong, and see you later for a pick up. G xx'

In between the running, during our chats in the car or over homecooked dinners, I was able to get to know Gill and Jim better. I learned that, not only do they have a set of names that tumble off the tongue, but they are also a couple who go together like (vegan) cheese and crumpets. Sure, a crumpet is great on its own, as is cheese, but put them together and woof! Things go next level. They are free-spirited souls, with the abil-ity to keep their heads in the clouds but their (sometimes bare) feet planted firmly in the earth. Gill and Jim's love is the kind of partnership that makes my heart swell — because it was clear that they are kids at heart and their spirits just love to hang out.

The more time I spent with Gill, the more I could see similarities between us. From what I could gather, she had the ability to operate at a million miles per hour and, when in that life-gear, she had the energy of a recently exploded supernova. But bright stars burn out, and I suspected, like me, she would need to lie on the sofa and watch back-to-back box sets from time to time to restoke the fire.

One night, over a delicious vegan dinner of lentil bolognese, we talked about life in the Scottish Highlands and Gill and Jim's recent trip to Nepal, and I filled them in on my struggles up in the Shetland Islands. We also chatted about guilty pleasures, and Gill and Jim said that the Aussie soap Neighbours was the only thing they turned on the TV for nowadays. I, in turn, then had to confess that I had become addicted to watching the reality TV show Love Island.

'What? No way? I wouldn't have had you down as a Love Island fan, McNuff!' said Gill.

'I know. . . there's something about it, it's so trashy that it's glorious. And it's on at nine p.m., so I'm usually in bed by then, and I use it as an hour of "decompressing" before sleep.'

While running, the days tended to feel like a tumbling mess of madness. In between the running, I was messaging Abby, replying to emails, doing social media and chatting to future and past hosts and Girlguiding units from the moment I woke up until I snuck off to bed. I even used any time I had in the bath to do 'badmin' (bath admin). So that hour before going to sleep had become precious me-time. The Love Island-watching was a routine that let my brain know the day was done, and I could relax into the arms of something altogether mindless. And besides, even though Love Island was more about lust, the premise was love. And I loved love. I was all about love.

Jamie had become addicted to the show back home too, so I explained to Gill and Jim that we would watch it at the same time each night, and then chat on the phone afterwards and dissect the conversations and behaviour of the cast members.

'Awww, that's so romantic,' said Gill.

'It is, isn't it? Some couples look up at the moon to connect them to wherever in the world they are each night. J and I watch trashy TV. We're modern romantics.'

'Well. . . in that case. . . Jim. . . whaddya say we get Love Island on tonight? It's almost nine p.m.'

'Oh no! You don't need to do that!' I said, now feeling embarrassed and wishing I hadn't made the confession.

'Look, McNuff, we can't have you missing out on your romantic connection with Jamie. You can fill us in on who in the show has been kissing who… Alright?'

'Alright, but off the bat. . . all you need to know is that everyone has pretty much kissed everyone.'

'I like this show already,' Gill smiled.

During the TV binge, Gill and Jim brought out a big bowl filled with Tunnock's tea cakes. Even though they're vegan and don't eat Tunnock's, they told me to help myself. I tried to be polite and just eat one, but that led to eating four, after which I said they really should take the bowl away or I'd make the whole lot disappear into my belly. For anyone not familiar with this Scottish delicacy, it's a layer of biscuity sponge, with a dome of soft marshmallow above it and the whole lot is then coated in chocolate. And the only acceptable way to eat a Tunnock's tea cake is to nibble off the chocolate, lick up the marshmallow then finish up with the biscuit base.

During my nights at Broomfield, sleeping with the kombucha and enjoying the smell of the fermentation, I felt truly relaxed. Almost too relaxed, in fact. I was aware that it was taking longer and longer to wake up each morning, and my days of running were consistently lacklustre. I was 260 miles into the journey and now regularly running 18–22-mile days, which was taking its toll. Since my last rest day, I'd run for eight days on the trot, and I had a suspicion that I needed to take a day off soon. But I had a Girlguiding talk lined up in the next town and a load of runners signed up to join me too, so I needed to stay on track. And as my friend Fran, a five-time Olympian, once said, 'When you're tired, it really doesn't help to think about how tired you are.' So I shoved any thoughts of being tired aside and continued to crack out the miles, running south along the coast, towards Inverness.

After a few days of using Broomfield as a base camp, it was time to say goodbye to Gill and Jim. Before agreeing, yet again, to ferry my bag along to the next host further down the coast, they packed me off on the outskirts of Dornoch with a hug, some Vego chocolate bars and yet more Tunnock's tea cakes. I'd been given the special treat of riding in Minto, and after some photos of us all by the van, Gill opened her arms wide for a hug.

'Well. . . so long, McNuff. It's been a blast. We'll miss you. Come back soon?'

'I will. I promise. I might even wear shoes next time.'

'You'd better bloody not!'

***

'Come as your brightest self.' These were the dress-code instructions sent out to anyone who had signed up to join in on one of the 80+ public running stages throughout Britain. And when I met a 15-strong group of runners outside the Novar Arms Hotel in Evanton, I was in no doubt that they had nailed the brief. In front of me was a sea of neon yellow, orange, pink and green. The group looked more set for an all-night rave than a run towards Inverness — although some of them would have been refused entry, as the group included some brightly clad teenagers, who I'd spoken to at a Girlguiding event the night before.

I'd loved visiting a community hut in Evanton Wood and spending time with 30 youngsters. They'd all painted their feet and made coloured footprints on a giant white bedsheet around the words: 'Our own barefoot challenge!' Some of the older girls were self-conscious about having their feet on show, which was sad. Because our bodies are wonderful and feet even more so. My bare feet had carried me the equivalent of 10 marathons so far — who cared what they looked like?

The girls soon forgot their worries when they realised that no one was looking at their feet. Everyone was too busy slapping brightly coloured paint on their own soles and hopping across the forest floor, doing their best to make it from the log where they sat to the art canvas (the bedsheet), without picking up any rogue twigs. Post-foot-painting, the girls and leaders sat on logs around a fire in the forest, as I darted around and told adventure stories. We ended the evening with a BBQ and a treasure hunt, looking for geocaches that had been hidden in long-forgotten hollow tree trunks in the nearby woods.

For the running stage from Evanton, the girls had decided, of their own accord, that they would like to run from the centre of town, across the A9 bridge over the Cromarty Firth. I'd never seen teenagers so excited about the prospect of running on an A-road bridge, but they were giddy. There was no holding them back when we reached the edge of the firth.

'We're on an adventure!' shouted one as we began the crossing of the bridge.

'Yeah! Let's wave at the cars as they pass!' said another.

'We're running OVER the water!' shouted a third.

The young runners were having so much fun that they convinced their chaperone (who was sensibly following on a bike) to let them carry on for a further 6 miles, past the EPIC A9 road bridge and up a steep hill to the small village of Munlochy. Needless to say, the youngsters left me for dust at the foot of the hill. I stayed at the back, chugging slowly up the incline in the late-morning sunshine with some other grown-ups. Despite the girls insisting they wanted to carry on 'Allll the way to Inverness!' and complete the full 17-mile running stage, they were reluctantly collected by their parents at the top of the hill. Most of the rest of the group called it a day there too, except one dad, called Steven, who said he'd like to carry on for the remaining miles to Inverness.

'Do you mind if my little girl joins in?' he asked, as his wife unloaded his three-year-old daughter from the family car and placed her into a running buggy.

'Not at all. She can take the prize for the youngest runner so far!'

'Great. This is Isabella,' said Steven as I leant around the front of the buggy.

'Hi, Isabella,' I said. 'Are you ready for an adventure?' Isabella nodded. 'You need to make me a promise though. . .' The little girl looked confused. 'You're in charge. . . you are our navigator,' I said, knowing she would likely have no idea what that word meant, but enjoying the look of confusion on her face all the same. 'You need to tell us when to go left, right or straight on, okay?' That she understood.

She looked at her dad and flashed him a big grin, then pointed down the road ahead. And we were off! Headed for an afternoon of running down quiet back roads towards the city.

The group of Evanton runners had been such a wonderful

distraction that morning, I'd forgotten how tired I was. But with fewer people around and less-enthusiastic teenage whooping, my feet got increasingly sore as the day progressed, and I struggled to keep pace. I loved watching Steven with Isabella in the buggy though — the way he checked in on her, chatted to her about the scenery and made sure she was well plied with drinks and snacks. It was clear he was a 'fun dadda' and that they had a special bond. It made me think that if Jamie and I had a daughter one day (and I hoped we would) that he would have that kind of relationship with her. My own dad had always made me feel like I was the most special person on the planet, so I know how beautiful a dad–daughter bond can be. In between growing envious of Isabella's snack hoard and daydreaming about any future kids, I tried the failsafe trick of not thinking about how tired I was, but soon it was impossible to think about anything else. I had to admit it. I. Was. Pooped.

I was enjoying taking made-up instructions from Isabella, which sometimes included 'Left-Right!', 'That way!' or simply 'Rarrrr!' (which, of course, meant straight on), but soon the miles caught up with me. Three miles shy of the city, Steven, Isabella and I dropped down to follow a cycle trail alongside the River Ness, and it was there that I really started to struggle. The conversation between Steven and me had naturally lessened as we both grew tired, but the chatter in my mind was now louder than ever. It was like someone had tuned into a lunchtime TV debate show and dialled the volume up to LOUD.

One part of my brain was saying, 'For God's sake, Anna

— it's only three miles to go. Suck it up. You can run three miles!' And the other part of my brain was shouting, 'Oh my, you're tired. In fact, you're sleepy. How about stopping here?' That latter part of my brain wanted to duck into the nearest hedgerow, curl up into a tiny ball and slip into a deep sleep. When the Kessock Bridge came into view, I was relieved. I knew that meant there was only one and a half miles to run to the city centre. All I needed to do was make it up and over the hunk of iron and tarmac, and I could stop and have a day of rest at last.

The ramp up to the bridge was smooth under foot and so I was convinced it was going to be an easy cruise from then on. But all hopes were dashed when the smooth pavement of the ramp ended abruptly and I saw that the walkway on the bridge was covered in sharp, set stones with extra pieces of gravel here and there. I let out a deep sigh. I should have expected it. I knew from past cycling adventures, during the colder months, the sections of road and pavement on bridges tend to ice over before the land surrounding it. It's to do with the bridge being more exposed to the elements and losing heat from all sides. So it made sense that, in the Highlands of Scotland — a place where the winters are cold and long — the pavement should be so very spiky to offer pedestrians and cyclists more grip in icy conditions. In fact, the pavement on this bridge had likely been designed to be as spiky as it could possibly be. Spikier even than the naughty tarmac of Shetland. Great news for the everyday commuter, but terrible news for my soles.

'It's okay. It'll be okay, Anna. It'll be okay. . . .' I said quietly, doing my best to give myself a pep talk.

I took a deep breath and began dancing along the white line at the edge of the spiky pavement, clinging on to the crash barrier to try to help alleviate some pressure from my soles and propel me along, but still it felt like I was running on glass. Steven had gradually eased ahead — he was likely tired too and eager to get the day's run done.

I continued the self-talk, reminding myself that there was just over a mile to go now, and that it really wasn't far at all.

'Not far, not far, not far. . .' I repeated, but on the fifth mantra, without warning, I lost it. My lower lip wobbled, and tears collected in the corners of my eyes. Soon they were streaming down my face, carving a watery pathway through the layer of road grime on my cheeks, dropping off of my chin onto the floor and topping up the water level in the River Ness beneath me.

The floodgates had opened and there was no closing them. It all just felt so unfair — I'd done my best to push on that week and not let anyone down, so why was this last section so bloody spiky? Surely, all of that trying on my part should have earned me some smooth surface? I had run 194 miles over the past nine days without a rest and the result was pain and frustration. And when I get frustrated, I cry. So I cried. I kept running while I had a good old sob (because stopping would only make the journey across the bridge last longer) and the tears splashed onto my thighs. I knew better than to try to hold back tears. That only gets you clogged up. Those drops of frustration needed out and running across the Kessock Bridge was the time to set them free.

7

Biting Off More Than
You Can Chew

In 2018, Jenny Graham of Inverness became the fastest woman to cycle around the world. She circumnavigated the globe, covering 18,413 miles in just 124 days and 12 hours, covering an eye-watering average of 148 miles per day. She broke the previous world record by almost three weeks and, what's more, she did the whole thing completely on her tod — solo and unsupported, carrying everything she needed on her bike. Needless to say, Jenny is one heck of a woman. I'd first met her at Kendal Mountain Film Festival (an annual event held in a beautiful part of Britain) in November 2018, and eight months later she had extended an invite for me to stay with her as I ran through Inverness.

After wiping the tears from my cheeks at the end of the Kessock Bridge, I'd waved goodbye to Steven and Isabella the mini adventurer, and then indulged in a solitary dinner of a shandy and a curry in a local bar. A well-timed summer shandy always seemed to re-right the world and, as an added bonus, didn't make me fall over as much as beer did. Although, I'm pretty sure that necking two shandies in quick succession after a long hot run instead of having one pint of beer defeated the object of trying to consume 'less alcohol'. It's like breaking a chocolate bar in half and eating it one half at a time. Much healthier, isn't it?

Post-shandy inhalation, I called Jamie. I shared the day's events with him, felt a little better and then hobbled my tired behind over to Jenny Graham's place. On the slow walk there, I made the decision to take two days of rest in Inverness instead of one. It wasn't what was on the schedule, but after a week of ignoring its cries, I finally needed to listen to my body. And my body said one day of rest wasn't enough to prevent me crying on any future bridges that I would cross in Scotland.

'McNuff!' Jenny flung open the door to her home.

'Jennnnyyyyyyyyy!' I gave her a hug.

'Och — how are your poor feet?' she asked.

'Errr. . . They're alright.'

'You're a madwoman. Come in, come in.'

There are no airs and graces about Jenny and that was reflected in her cosy and comforting home. Boxes of books about cycling were piled up in one corner of the living room, a few items of kit were strewn here and there and there were two large oatmeal-coloured sofas, which looked like the kind of place you'd want to fall asleep on a Sunday afternoon. Photos of friends and family were plastered all over the walls — in the hallways, stuck on the fridge in the kitchen and in the bedroom too, where they were framed by a string of fairy lights. Jenny's place made me feel like I was already part of the furniture, and I could happily sink into it and relax.

On the first evening together, we chatted about anything and everything else except the run. I had the pleasure of meeting Jenny's 20-year-old son, who (I can't believe I'm at the age where I'm going to say this) is such a nice young man. Wonderful manners, polite and easy to talk to, he was as cool as his mum is kind. Over a dinner of spaghetti bolognese, we spoke about life, love and past adventures. And, for the first time since leaving Shetland, I forgot I was on a barefoot run. And I mean, I actually forgot. Jenny was talking about Ben Nevis and some other nearby peaks and how they were beautiful places to visit, and I caught myself thinking, What am I up to this week? Maybe I'll go on a trip there, before remembering that I was in the middle of a 100-marathon barefoot run and not on a jolly.

Over the next few days, Jenny plied me with coffee, freshly baked cranberry bread smothered with peanut butter and endless ginger oatcakes. She was obsessed with oatcakes, which was understandable, given that we were in Scotland — the birthplace of the oatcake. And it just so happened that I ruddy love an oatcake too.

'I like the ginger ones the best,' Jenny said, cracking open a box and laying them out on the table with some strawberries. 'Because they taste like ginger biscuits. . . but they're "healthy".' She caught an oat crumb as it dropped from the corner of her mouth.

I took a bite of my first ginger oatcake. She was right. 'Wowsers. That's lush,' I said.

'I know, aren't they just the best?!' She chuckled. 'Although. . .'

'Although what?'

'I went into one supermarket and these oatcakes were in the biscuit section,' she looked genuinely disgusted.

'Well, I hope you didn't go there again. They are most definitely NOT a biscuit.'

'I know. Trying to make us feel bad for eating them. I will not be going back.'

In between chatting with and being fed by Jenny, I spent the two days of rest pottering around Inverness. I liked Inverness. It was more compact than the Scottish cities I was familiar with — Edinburgh and Glasgow — but it has everything that all good cities should have: a river, some cracking architecture and an array of fine coffee shops. I sat in many of those coffee shops, catching up on admin and giving interviews to journalists — one of whom wanted to write an online article on 'the top 10 things I had learned from the barefoot run'. Which, given that I was only 277 miles into the 2,600+ mile journey, was a tad premature. I did at least convince the journalist to adjust the wording to 'so far' and said that I was learning to relax and go with the flow, rather than grapple with my prefabricated expectations of what each day would be like. I also said that I had learned to listen to my body. These were things that, in reality, I was still in the process of struggling to implement, but they say that you preach what you need to learn, so there I was — preachin'. After finishing the conversation, the journalist asked me to send her the most 'gruesome shots' I had of my feet. I obliged by sending her some snaps of my peat-bog cuts and big swollen toe. Yummy. That'd get some clicks.

In contrast to the teary, wobbly mess I'd been on the run into the city, I felt more like myself again while at Jenny's house and very much 'at home'. Even more so because she'd given up her bedroom and had insisted on sleeping on the sofa. I spent each night curled up next to a Guinness world record certificate, which was casually propped against the wall in the bedroom. In the morning, I'd wander, bleary eyed, into the living room. Jenny would be sitting on the floor, still in her sleeping bag, hair in a messy ponytail on her head, clutching a mug of coffee, back propped against the sofa mid-conversation with one of her cycling friends elsewhere in Scotland. She'd wave me into the room before putting the phone on speaker.

'Hey, hey, guess who's here! It's McNuff! She's on that mad barefoot run. I can't believe she's made it this far in her bare tootsies. . . I know! Mad!'

When I'd first arrived at Jenny's door, I wasn't sure how much of my messy mind to reveal. But on the final evening, over some coffee and yet more ginger oatcakes, I decided that it was time to open up about the mental roller coaster I'd been riding since Skaw Beach. Perhaps Jenny had some advice.

'Jenny. . .'

'Yes, chick.' She was bright and breezy as ever.

'When you were on your cycle around the world, did you ever have any moments where you felt like. . . you might not, I mean, you weren't sure that you'd be able to make it?' I exhaled as I said it and felt relieved to have let my struggle out for a run around. Jenny thought for a moment.

'Do you feel that way?' she asked.

'I have been. I mean, some days. . . yes, I do,' I said quietly.

'Let me think. . .' I braced myself for her input. For the sharing of that one moment during her own long journey when she'd felt so weighed down by the burden of having taken on something that was so difficult, it took every ounce of her grit and determination to carry on. I held my breath. Jenny smiled.

'No.'

'No?' I gawped.

'No, sorry chick. I don't think I did,' she said nonchalantly, before refilling my coffee cup.

'Oh. . . okay. . . thanks.' I now felt foolish for having even shared the thought and wondered if Jenny's response meant that I really had bitten off more than I could chew. Jenny smiled again, shrugged her shoulders and took a sip of her coffee. I smiled awkwardly and took a sip of mine.

'Oh, no! Wait! I've just remembered!' she shouted, almost spitting coffee from her mouth.

'You've remembered?'

'Yes! Yes, I did! What am I saying? I totally thought I was going to stop!' She put her palm to her forehead and chuckled.

'You did?'

'Oh yes. There was a bit when I was cycling across Russia, on the Trans-Siberian Highway, and the road got crazy-busy. Huge trucks were thundering down and running me off it. I knew I had hundreds more miles of that road to go, and I was petrified.'

'I'm not surprised.'

'I know, and I remember thinking, "I can't do this, I just can't." And that was only eight days into the record attempt. . . you know, this massive trip that I'd told everyone about. . .'

'So what did you do?'

'Och, I pulled off the road, sat on a doorstep and had a good wee cry!' she said.

'Oh my days. Thank you. I mean, I'm sorry that happened, but that makes me feel so much better.'

'Yep, and I remember thinking. . . I've got to change tack. But then I wondered if I was being weak for not just pushing on through it, you know?' I nodded. I knew that feeling well. 'So, in the end, I decided I needed to cycle at night. The road was much quieter and it was easier to see the trucks coming with their headlights behind me. . . so when one came along I'd just get out of the way and let them by, then hop back on the road and carry on.'

There was a pause, during which I thought about how tough that must have been. I knew from my own experience of cycling on busy roads in the USA how terrifying it was, let alone when there were massive trucks, you were in a country where you didn't speak the language and you were trying to break a world record.

'Ha! I cannie believe I completely forgot. Funny how you forget those parts, eh?' Jenny shook her head and reached for another oatcake.

That night, I lay in bed and looked up at the string of fairy lights on the wall in her bedroom. Taking an extra day off in Inverness was the best decision I'd made in a long time. I took solace in the fact that someone as hard as nails as Jenny Graham had experienced her fair share of self-doubt on her own adventures. And, in that moment, I realised there is a hidden power in wondering if you've bitten off more than you can chew. Because it means that, in order to carry on, you must swim down into the depths of yourself and look for a version of you that you've never met before. A you that deserves to make it. And, of course, it feels like you're swimming around in the pitch black, without even knowing what this thing you're searching for actually looks like. But you have to trust that it's there. And that if you want to find that part of yourself, you will.

East & South Scotland

CULLEN BAY

ABERDEEN

PERTH

Donald

GLASGOW

EDINBURGH

KELSO

8

Itty-Bitty Gritties

I had to blame the sausage roll. There was no other explanation for why I spent quite so long taking a mid-run break at the coffee shop in the tiny town of Carrbridge. Okay, I could blame the coffee (of which I had two cups) and the quaint emerald stream on the outskirts of town (which I marvelled at), but really, it was the sausage roll. It was piping hot, peppery and delicious, and so I had three. It was well past get-your-ass-moving-o'-clock by the time I ran out of town. I was approaching the end of the high street when a white car appeared beside me.

'Heeyyyy! Heyyyy! Are you Anna McNuff?' shouted a guy in the passenger seat through an open window. His arm was outstretched and pointing at me.

'Errrr. . . Yep, that's me!'

I was now running alongside the car while it continued at a slow creep. I peered in through the open window and the driver gave me a quick thumbs-up. The passenger leaned even further out of the car and extended his hand for a high-five. 'You're awesome! Keep it up!' he shouted. Our hands met in mid-air and, with that, they drove off.

Since leaving Inverness there'd been a rise in the number of people on the road recognising me as 'that barefoot runner'. Sometimes, it was because the passer-by had followed the journey on social media (like a woman who insisted on buying me a croissant from a nearby cafe as I ran out of Inverness). But often, I was being recognised because of the growing media attention. Although I'd arrived on the Scottish mainland wanting to hide from view as often as possible, I was now more comfortable with being noticed. . . especially by those who already knew what I was doing and why. The interview I'd given in Shetland, on one of the main Scottish TV channels, had now been re-run a few times, and some regional interviews I'd done in Inverness were beginning to roll out too.

At Nethy Bridge, a woman following the journey on the news caught sight of a shock of pink hair dashing across the road in front of a local primary school. She and the kids at the school were very excited to see me, which made me very excited to see them too. After a series of selfies and a brief chat with the kids about why I was barefoot and why I had pink hair (which is, of course, because my mum is a unicorn), I took off down the trail, bound for Aviemore.

Later that day, I was 5 miles from my destination and I was struggling along a particularly gravelly section of the Speyside Way. Despite my soles having built up a decent amount of hard skin in the past three weeks, I had somehow managed to get two tiny pieces of grit stuck in them. One piece was on the ball of my right foot, the other was on the ball of my left foot and both of them were precisely where I would naturally land with each stride. I was midway through making a mental note to get the tweezers out that evening to dig the bits of grit out when a runner appeared beside me.

'Lovely evening, isn't it?' she chirped.

She was clad in a peach rain jacket with lilac shorts and had the bounciest stride I'd seen in a long time. She ran like a cross between a deer and a kangaroo (if kangaroos could run). I had to look closely at her feet to double-check that they were actually touching the ground with each step, such was the height of her bounce. I assumed the bouncy lady was out for an evening jogette and was being polite in chatting to me as she passed, but after a few minutes she declared that she'd used my GPS tracker to hunt me down.

'I've been watching you for weeks! I saw you were coming through town as I went to get the kids from school, so I threw them in the house and told them, "Mummy's off for a run!"' she beamed.

The bouncy lady and I ran together for a further 20 minutes, nattering away, following a trail of light grey as it meandered between tall pines which stretched upwards towards the slowly setting summer sun. The woman's enthusiastic running style and fine chatter made me forget about the grit in my soles and the gravel beneath them, and I upped my pace (and added some bounce) to match my stride with hers. I was just beginning to wonder how much longer I could keep up running at such a lick when. . . 'Oh, gosh, better run. Teatime!' said the lady, tapping her watch.

We parted ways with a hug, and I watched her bounce off round a bend. I didn't even get her name.

Exchanges like those cheered me right on up. They validated the journey and reminded me that, even though it felt like it was just me slogging it out through the country, there was a whole army of people with me in spirit, following from afar. An elusive, invisible cheer squad who came into view every now and then. The more people who delivered drive-by high-fives, gave gifts of food or bounced a few miles by my side, the more I was doing it for them as much as I was doing it for me. I wanted to make good on the faith they had in me.

It wasn't just the people who were raising my spirits in the Highlands; the landscape was putting in a good shift too. As I entered Aviemore, I ran into the western edge of Great Britain's largest National Park, Cairngorms National Park, home to the Cairngorm Mountains. I'd spent many a winter's evening while training for the run curled up by the fire with Nan Shepherd's The Living Mountain, which describes her life in and around the Cairngorms. Her descriptions of the landscape are so rich and vivid that I felt like I already 'knew' the Cairngorms. But when I rounded a bend and they came into view for the first time, I felt a flutter my belly. They were majestic. Ghostly peaks, reaching for the clouds — a mix of grey tops and green lower slopes. They seemed so masterful, so stoic. As if they held some kind of wisdom. And, as is always the case when I look at a mountain, I felt overcome with calm.

I had expected the scenery around Aviemore to be beautiful, but when I ran out of town the following day, something entirely unexpected happened — Scotland had a heat wave. A heat wave?! In the Highlands?! I couldn't believe it. Speak to any Brit and they will talk of Scotland's fine scenery but, sooner or later, mention the dark days, cold weather and tendency for it to rain. . . a lot. And yet, the July of 2019 was a scorcher. In a bid to beat the heat, I was running in as few clothes as possible (short of being naked) — just light shorts and a vest — but by late morning my body was glistening with sweat and my clothes were drenched. There were salt stains on the front of my shorts, a dusting of it had collected on my neck and the skin on my sweat-encrusted arms prickled with heat. I'd prepared for many challenges over the course of the journey through Britain, but I wasn't prepared for Scotland to have a heat wave. I was running on a mix of trail and quiet back roads, but soon the tarmac on the roads became unbearable. If I set up my camera to take some video footage, I couldn't stand still in one spot. Instead, I had to hop from one foot to another, making sounds like a chimpanzee: 'Ooo. Ahhh. Ehhh. OhMyGoshThat'sHot. Ahh. Eeee!' I swear, if I'd stayed in one spot long enough my soles would have melted, and I'd have been welded to the road.

When I passed Loch Pityoulish 5 miles out of town, I knew what I had to do. Without a second thought, I ran off the road, through a small wooden gate and down a trail to the water's edge. I slung my backpack under a tree and waded into the loch, fully clothed. Oh the relief! It was instant. I swear steam rose from the surface as I plunged in — like a hot pan taken from the stove and placed directly into the sink. I paddled around for a few minutes in the loch, dunking my head several times and doing my best to scrub the salt from my neck and back. I took a photo while in the lake and discovered that I even had salt on my eyebrows — so much of it that I looked like Santa Claus. For fear I might be mistakenly called into duty on Christmas Eve, I gave my brows a good scrubbin' in the lake too. I then emerged from the depths, scampered back up the shore, grabbed my backpack and took off along the sun-scorched road. The loch dunk had a cooling effect on my whole body, and the tarmac now felt more bearable under foot. I enjoyed 30 minutes of comfortable running and discovered that my wet hair acted as a neat ice cap. By lunchtime it was over 30°C and the layer of tar beneath the rock chips on the road had begun to melt. Where heavy tractors had turned into farm gates off the side of the road, their wheels had churned up the top layer of molten tar, leaving a wave of congealed rock in their wake. 'Woah. That is so cool!' I said, getting my phone out to take a picture of the mini tarmac sculptures.

The churned-up road had confirmed what I already knew — it was SCORCHIO. And 10 miles into the day, my soles were on fire again. Inspired by the loch dunking, I came up with a solution to maintain some level of chill for my feet. I survived the rest of the day by stopping every 20 minutes to suck water from my bladder and spit it on to my soles. I should clarify that by bladder I mean my hydration bladder, not my actual bladder. That would be weird. The bladder suck 'n' spit technique kept my soles cool enough to make it a couple of miles, and then I would repeat the process.

Heat Wave: 0, Barefoot Britain: 1.

The heat was certainly uncomfortable, but in a sick kind of way, I liked it. Because for once I wasn't thinking about all of the miles I still had to run. I had a more immediate problem to solve, and there were practical (or rather unpractical) things I could do to stay cool and keep moving forwards. Those things kept my mind occupied and my wayward thoughts in check.

At the end of a hot 'n' sweaty 20 miles, my sticky soles and I were collected at Grantown-on-Spey by a mum and her six-year-old son, Jake, who were hosting me for a couple of nights. They lived a 10-minute drive from town, so Jake chatted away in the car on the journey home, while I rested my dirty soles on the car dashboard (with the permission of his mum). Jake was a ball of energy — inquisitive about me, the run and every other aspect of my life. We got on like a house on fire.

The following morning, as Jake, his mum and I clambered into the car to make the return journey to Grantown, Jake decided he wanted to wear his ski goggles for the drive. Of course, I didn't ask why. It was clearly a logical thing for a six-year-old to do. Despite having had an in-depth conversation with him over breakfast about the merits of dung beetles, Jake wanted to chat some more as we drove. So, he continued to ask me questions, pausing every now and then to readjust his goggles and stare out of the window to process each answer.

'Anna. . . Do you ever wear shoes?'

'Sometimes Jake, yes.'

'Anna. . . Have you ever been to Africa?'

'Only North Africa. Tunisia, Morocco and Egypt. But I'd love to see some other countries.'

'Anna?'

'Yes, Jake.'

'Do you have any tattoos?'

'I do.'

'How many?'

'Just two. Do you have any tattoos, Jake?'

'Naaah. Not yet,' he replied nonchalantly, and his mum smiled. 'Well, except I've got these pretend ones I got from Angus at school. I put them on sometimes.' He brandished a packet of transfer tattoos he was holding in his lap.

'They look pretty cool, and that's very kind of Angus to give them to you.'

'Do you want one? I mean when you've done your running. Later. I could put one on you?'

'I absolutely do want one. But only if you choose which one. Deal?'

'Deal. And. . . and. . . and then you can choose where to put it,' he said.

Jake looked out of the window and adjusted his ski goggles again, seemingly chuffed that he'd soon be adorning me with new ink.

The promise of a new tattoo got the day off to a great start as I re-joined the Speyside Way and ran out of town. It was still warm but, thankfully, nowhere near as hot as the day before. And as an added bonus, the ground wasn't melting beneath my feet.

I ran away from Grantown on a rocky track through a towering pine forest, choosing my path carefully, hopping onto large, smooth stones and over piles of spongy pine needles wherever I could. The trail ahead was a kaleidoscope of greens and browns — slim, dark-green trees with chocolate trunks were covered with bright green moss that spilled onto the path at the edges. Down the middle of the trail, a river of rusty-brown fallen pine needles carpeted the ground. Everything was quiet, and it smelled exactly how you might expect — like a pine forest. I wanted to bottle that smell and take it with me for a day when I needed transporting to the serenity of the woods.

After a few miles, the trail left the forest and led onto a section that was smooth and grassy underfoot, although there were several patches of spiky gorse lining the sides. It was far enough off the side of the trail not to bother my feet but the perfume from its flowers was all-encompassing — they smelled of sweet coconut and vanilla. With a great surface to run on and surrounded by nature's aroma, I was on cloud nine. I was feeling incredibly Zen, weaving my way through the country-side, communing with the wildflowers, the trees and the birds who hopped across my path. Then. . .

'Bugger!'

Pain jabbed at my sole. That was sharp, I thought. I stood on one leg and inspected the bottom of my foot. And then I remembered. The bits of grit in my feet. They were still stuck in there from before Aviemore and I'd just landed right on one of them. Things went from hero to zero after that. It wasn't long before the Zen feeling evaporated and the 'itty-bitty gritties' in my soles began to bother me. The unwelcome pain from the grit also coincided with the trail getting rougher underfoot. Gone were the soft pine needles and grass; instead, there were patches of grey rubble. The grey rubble then turned to larger stones before opening out onto a field where the mud had been churned up by cows and gone rock-hard in the heat. It was like trying to run across a rocky riverbed. I almost rolled my ankles a few times and struggled to stay upright as I leapt from one peak of mud to next.

By early afternoon I was starting to get frustrated with my sore feet and the slow progress and decided I needed a break. I slumped on a fallen tree trunk and inspected my soles. When I poked at the areas around each piece of grit, I found they were red and hot to the touch. Yikes. That wasn't good. After inhaling a couple of cereal bars and a few chunks of cheese for lunch, I got going again, but the running was so stop-start that it was driving me bananas. I could make it a few minutes in mild discomfort but then I would land on an uneven surface and a small rock would press precisely on the point where the grit was. Vooomf! A bolt of searing pain would shoot through the sole of my foot, making me feel like I wanted to vomit. Think of standing on an upturned plug in the living room, only sharper. I would stop for a moment, swear, take a deep breath, wait for the pain to subside and then take off down the track, hobbling slightly but telling myself I was sure it wouldn't happen again. But then I'd land directly on the piece of grit in my other foot. I'd hit the roof, and even more swear words would pour from my mouth. To place a cherry atop the pity cake, I then lost the trail. It had contoured around a hillside but now ended abruptly at a patch of thorny brambles and stinging nettles. There was no way I was wading through them, not today. I was over it.

I slumped in the shade of a tree and checked the map. It was 2 p.m. I'd made it a measly 9 miles since leaving Grantown at 10 a.m. that morning. At such a snail's pace, I hadn't a hope in hell of reaching the meeting point I'd arranged with Jake's mum near Aberlour at 5 p.m. I needed to change tack. Much as I liked the idea of staying on the Speyside Way for the rest of the day, it was time to choose the path of least resistance. The surface on the trail was just too unpredictable, and I needed to pick up some speed. I also needed a surface that wasn't going to disturb the itty-bitty gritties so much, and that meant a flatter, smoother option: tarmac.

As I trudged back towards the road, I was desperately trying to keep my brain in check. 'Positive thoughts only, Anna,'

I muttered. Any miles were good miles, after all. At the back of my mind I knew the Speyside Way would have been perfect for a regular run with trainers on, but I quickly pushed that thought out — it was dangerous to dabble with thoughts like that. When I reached the end of the field, I hopped over a gate and set off down the road.

Despite my niggles and the nagging feeling that I was 'copping out' by taking the tarmac route, the road running did the trick. Progress was much faster, and other than a short stint on a busier stretch, I could run on minor back roads with little to no traffic. I munched up the miles and it felt good to be moving steadily again, but the damage done to my feet on the rough trail couldn't be reversed. The grit gods were angry; I had awoken a fire in them, and they weren't letting up.

My running style had now moved from a slight hobble to a wide-legged wobble as I tried to avoid landing on the bits of grit in either foot. Ladies, you know when you go into some public toilets and you have a wee, and then you realise there's no toilet paper left? Then, you have to do the danger waddle to the next cubicle, in search of some paper, trying to avoid any drips and hoping no one comes into the loos at that very moment. That's how I would have looked running down the road — legs wide, knees bent, backside sticking out, proceeding with tentative haste.

I was just thinking about how I'd cope the following day with an off kilter running style and such sore feet when a navy-blue people carrier pulled up alongside me. There was a young boy in the back, and he was wearing ski goggles. I checked my phone. I'd done 17 miles. It was a few miles short of where I'd hoped to get to that day, so I clambered in the car and slumped into the passenger seat, feeling defeated.

'Anna?'

'Yes, Jake?'

'Did you do all of your running?'

'I did. . . most of it.'

'Was it hard?'

'It was.' I sighed and there was a pause.

'Anna?'

'Yes, Jake?'

'I brought you a banana.'

And with that, as if by magic, all seemed right in the world again.

9

Allan the Welder

I love the shape of Great Britain. Yes, there are other countries that are larger and have equally enviable atlas outlines, like the United States, India, Australia or Italy (definitely the best-shaped country in the world). But there is something wonderfully animal-like about the outline of Britain. It looks part-dog, part-human, facing eastward across the globe, with a round nose (Aberdeenshire) and a large Elvis-esque quiff on its head (the Highlands). The torso (the Midlands) gets wider around the middle (don't we all?) and Britain's knees (Norfolk) jut out to the east, with the added flair of a cheeky leg (Cornwall) trailing westward into the Irish Sea. Since arriving on the Scottish mainland, I had enjoyed looking at the map of Britain and reflecting on the miles I'd run so far — I was now up to 340. But I took even greater joy in letting people know precisely where I now was on the outline of Britain. I had done the Elvis quiff and I was heading for the nose.

Beyond Aberlour, I followed the course of the River Spey north-east, through open pastures and birchwood forests, towards the Moray Coast. After leaving Jake and his mum, I'd decided to reduce my daily mileage to around 15 miles, just until the bits of grit in my soles became less red and angry. I knew the grit couldn't stay in there forever, or at least I hoped it wouldn't. And I was buoyed by the fact that, each morning, my foot had formed an extra bit of hard skin around the affected grit area. Little by little, that barrier of hard skin made the ball of my foot less sensitive and when I caught the gritty area on roots and rocks while running, it resulted in far fewer swear words. Happy days.

I didn't have any hosts or talks lined up for the following week of running through Moray and Aberdeenshire, and my main kit bag had been shipped ahead to Aberdeen. That meant I could just wake up, run until the sun went down and find a place to rest my head. Much as I missed having my fave jogging bottoms to slink into in the evenings and was running with slightly more stuff on my back (laptop included), it felt liberating to have everything I needed to survive for a few days. The running felt freer, somehow. I was just a barefoot wanderer with my laptop, a toothbrush, a coat, a bobble hat and a pair of thick socks for the evenings. I didn't even have any knickers. I never really wore them anyway, so I was a barefoot, knickerless wonder, roaming wild and free through the Scottish countryside.

With a reduced daily mileage and nowhere particular to be each evening, I was able to take my sweet time getting out of the door in the mornings. That meant I racked up 11 or 12 hours in the Land of Nod most nights. With less time pressure, I was also less concerned about the kind of surfaces I might encounter over the course of the day and, all in all, I could relax and enjoy the wonder that is the Speyside Way.

In contrast to the section of trail north of Grantown-on-Spey — which had ended at a bush of brambles (although I am now convinced this was my lack of route-finding ability rather than the trail) — the Speyside Way beyond Aberlour was a treat. It largely follows the route of an old railway line and for the most part is flat as a pancake. As an added bonus, much of the trail had been left au naturel. Grass had grown over where the train tracks used to be and every now and then I had the luxury of a section of luminescent green moss. I later learned that this spongy wonder is sphagnum moss, which only made me love it even more, because sphagnum is a wonderful word.

Not only did the luminescent glow of the sphagnum cheer me up, it was also like running on a thousand mini, fur-covered trampolines. In fact, it was so soft and bouncy and inviting that I lay down on it for a few minutes, just to see what it felt like against my cheeks. Well, it felt like the kind of fleecy blanket that your nanna might wrap you up in at Christmas time (if a little cooler) and it smelled of seaweed and woodchips. I wondered what a passer-by would think had they caught me at that moment, face down in the sphagnum, soaking up its earthy goodness. Although, given its alluring luminescent glow, perhaps they would have laid down and joined me.

In between moss-hugging, I enjoyed running through old railway stations, some of which had been neatly restored, with bold black and white painted signs, concrete platforms (complete with the white safety line) and the once-crumbling station house now transformed into a tearoom or a modest cottage. The Old Station at Cromdale was my favourite. It had a cream picket fence and a converted old railway carriage, which people could book to spend the night in. Other stations weren't always as beautifully maintained as Cromdale but they had equally intriguing names: Tamdhu, Ballindalloch, Dailu-aine Halt. Blacksboat Station was another firm favourite that was just a weather-beaten, white-stone outhouse, sitting alone by the tracks, miles from anywhere.

Each time I passed through a ghostly station, I got excit-ed. Not only did they affirm that I was making progress along the line, but there was a whiff of the illegal about running through them, as if a runner shouldn't be allowed to go where the trains once went. Sometimes, if there was no one else around, I would make a loud 'WOOOO! WOOOO!' noise as my shoulders drew level with the station platform, imagining I was a steam train of my own design, fuelled by sausage rolls, milkshakes and cheese.

As I rumbled on down the track, I began to wonder what other routes there were across the country that used to be train lines and were now footpaths. I knew there were lots of these 'rail trails' in the USA — I'd cycled on a number of them — but I assumed that we Brits (who love our public transport) would still be using all of the railway lines for, you know, trains and things. But the more I read, the more I learned that there were rail trails all over Moray and Aberdeenshire.

These lines were part of a local network of tracks that were historically used to transport herring, seal oil, farming produce and livestock, but they ground to a halt as the demand for the line changed and they eventually closed in the late 1970s. In my railway read-a-thon, I also discovered there were rail trails further south too, in the Peak District, Bristol, Bath, Devon and Somerset. I made a note of where these old lines were and aimed to seek them out if at all possible. If the rail trails in the south of Britain were anything like the spongy Speyside Way, I could book myself a one-way ticket, hop aboard the heavenly foot-spa express and ride that first-class carriage all the way to London Town.

In a state of rail-trail reverie, I kept the barefoot wheels in motion along the Speyside Way. With a better surface and less of a need to concentrate on the ground beneath my feet, I was able to zone out for a few days and tune in to podcasts and audiobooks. I listened to Oprah Winfrey's memoir, What I Know for Sure, as well as a Viv Groskop podcast interview with world famous performer and clown Petra Massey. Petra spoke about how she copes with nerves while performing and overcoming a fear of being judged, while on stage and in life in general. 'The thing you need to accept is that we are all ridiculous. Some of us choose to embrace it and even celebrate it,' she said. Which led me to conclude that I was quite ridiculous and that this barefoot run was a celebration of that. Her words were timely as I began to pass more people on the trail. Most of them would notice I was barefoot, and so the comments came thick and fast. 'You're brave!', 'Isn't that sore?', and 'You've got no shoes on!'

Ordinarily, towards the end of the day, my response to these comments was just a nod or smile. But after listening to Petra's words, I did my best to use each remark as an opportunity to embrace and celebrate my own ridiculousness.

Other than the railway line and the River Spey itself, if the Speyside Way is famous for one other thing — its whisky. There are over 130 distilleries in Scotland and a disproportionate number of them are scattered along the shores of the River Spey. Despite never having liked whisky, I was determined I would leave Scotland with a greater appreciation for it. I had noted all of the distilleries that I'd passed since leaving Aviemore, like Balmenach, Tormore, Cragganmore, Aberlour and Craigellachie. Some of them were close enough to the trail for me to be able to smell the malty fumes escaping from the old stone buildings. Funnily enough, I never fancied a wee dram at any point during a long hot day of running, but I made a promise to all of the locals that I met (who were very passionate about the liquid gold) that I would keep an open mind about whisky. Until then, I'd stick to shandies.

As I neared the estuary of the River Spey, the trail opened out and I ran alongside fields of barley. The wind had now picked up and I watched as it moved, in waves, over the crops; the crests of the waves caught beams of sunlight as the wind danced across the surface of a honey-coloured ocean. It was mesmerising. I was now back up to running 17 miles a day and the pieces of grit in my feet weren't causing me too much pain, so I was already in a cracking mood that day, but the sight of the shimmering field raised it higher still.

In the last mile of the day, I deviated from the trail to head into Rothes to find a B & B, taking a route across a field to avoid a busy road. When I saw the town come into view from the middle of the field, I let out a whoop, excited at the prospect of a hot shower and a snuggly bed for the night. . . maybe I'd even get Love Island on the telly-box.

I was thinking so much about the comforts awaiting me that I got lazy with my foot placement. I didn't look before I leapt into a small gully, where there were the sharp roots of a recently cut-down tree. One of the roots went slicing into my foot.

'Crap!' I shouted, quickly followed by, 'You idiot, Anna!'

I limped onwards for a few steps, then sat down to assess the damage. Oh dear. Bright red blood was trickling out from a flap of loose skin on the pad of my foot. It wasn't too sore, but some mud had got stuck in the wound, and so, after calling in the first aider (who lives somewhere in the corner of my mind), I cleaned it with antiseptic wipes, patched it up as best as I could with some tape and hobbled on into town with my tail between my legs. That evening I made a new rule — no daydreaming about the day's end until the day is done.

Thankfully, the cut wasn't as bad as first feared, and by morning, the flap of skin (which I was convinced was making a bid for freedom) seemed to have reattached itself to my foot. So I whacked a couple of steri-strips over the cut, taking care to run the strips between my toes so they stayed put while I ran. Feeling like I had snatched victory from the jaws of defeat, I set off for the North Moray Coast.

Since leaving Aviemore, I'd loosely followed the Speyside Way and I was sad when it came to an end. I felt like the trail and I had history together. I had taken parts of it with me (quite literally) and left parts of me on it. We were forever bonded. I took the final few steps on the trail at the small town of Portgordon, where the North Sea lapped at the shore of a pebble beach and the air smelled of brine. Perhaps it was because thunderous, charcoal clouds loomed large on the horizon, but the sea looked more grey than blue at Portgordon. The grey sea was mirrored by concrete walls and heavy, cracked paving slabs which lined the seafront. The houses in town were mostly grey too, or brown, with the odd rogue white one thrown in here and there.

There was hardly anyone around as I ran through — just a man in a navy jacket walking a little white dog near the harbour. Except for the whoosh of the wind and the squawk of seagulls it was a quiet place which, combined with the greyness, gave the town a melancholic feel, but I liked that. It's nice to indulge in melancholy from time to time after all, and after a week of being inland, there was something soothing about being alongside the sea again.

Despite the cut I'd sustained at Rothes, my feet and body were feeling tip top as I headed east along the coast. I'd set myself the conservative target of running 17 miles to Buckie that day and by 4 p.m., I'd done just that. I should have been elated to make Buckie, but I'd made the 17 miles with relative ease and now I was having second thoughts. I still had some juice left in the tank and it felt strange to stop running when I had energy to spare. It was early July, so there were still six hours of daylight left to play with, which meant I could run further if I wanted to. Did I want to? The next major stopping point was Cullen Bay, 6 miles further along the coast. Was I an idiot to try to run extra miles with grit in my feet and a cut still healing up? I decided to take a break in a greasy spoon and mull things over.

Over a feast of jacket potato, beans, cheese, extra cheese and a strawberry milkshake, I worked out that if I did decide to run some extra miles it would mean I could get ahead of schedule. So long as I tacked some extra miles on to days of running later in the week, I could stay put for two nights and take a whole unplanned day of rest.

I checked out my options for nearby accommodation and found that there were some B & Bs in Buckie, but there were also a few hotels in Cullen Bay. 'Stuff it!' I said aloud. I scrolled to the Cullen Bay Hotel and clicked 'book' before my brain or body had a chance to change its mind. The room was non-refundable. I couldn't afford to waste that kind of money. I had no option now but to cover those extra 6 miles. It was game on.

I ran out of Buckie at a fast clip, charged with adrenaline, spurred on by the Cullen Bay challenge and the prospect of covering 23 miles, which would be the furthest I'd run in a day so far. More importantly, if I made Cullen, it would mean exceeding my expectation for the day's mileage rather than falling short of it — what a novelty.

I was tanking it down the road out of town, eyes firmly fixed ahead, sucking in large lungfuls of sea air when I heard a shout.

'Heyyy! Hey youuuu! Youuu!'

I looked to my left to see a man wearing black boots, a faded red boiler suit, safety glasses and a white hard hat. He was striding towards me across a car park.

'You're that one off the telly! With neeey shoes on. It's you, int it?'

I stopped running and walked a few paces back to where he was now standing, on a grass verge at the side of the pavement. His dirt-covered face was a picture of wonder and he seemed unable to contain his excitement.

'It is, that's me!' I said.

'I knew it! I juss knew it. Och, I cannie believe it! Bwilliant. I think it's bwilliant, what you're doing. Fur the young gurls 'n' all that. Bwilliant.'

'Ah, thank you,' I said, basking in his outpouring of energy. 'What's your name?'

'Oh! I'm Allan. Allan the welder,' he replied, and I thought it was quite lovely that he'd added his profession to the reply.

'You're a welder?'

'Aye, aye. . . I'm up here fer work. You know, on a contract, and I was just gettin' in ma van and I sin you there, with ney shoes on!'

I chatted with Allan the welder for a few minutes, during which his excitement didn't waver. As the conversation came to a natural close, I decided I'd better let Allan get back to his job of welding and me back to my job of barefoot running.

'Well, Allan the welder. It's been a pleasure meeting you. Thanks for stopping me.'

'Och, no. It's my pleasure,' he said, touching his hand to his chest before extending it for a handshake.

'I'm a hugger, you know, Allan. . .'

'Oh, I love a hug!' Allan squealed. So, we did a half hug, half handshake. His hands were rough. I could feel the calluses on them and he smelled of dust and tin, but Allan the welder was a softie in every other way.

Fuelled by Allan's good vibes, I forged on along the coast. The further east I ran, the more beautiful the coastline became and the more dramatic the cliffs grew, in size and shape. The wind continued to pick up as I followed a quiet, sandy trail that ran along the clifftop and through the small town of Portknockie. The sea had grown rougher since I'd joined the coast at Portgordon — patches of white were now visible on the expanse of grey as great foaming crests leapt from the water and collided with jagged cliffs.

From Portknockie, I picked up a cycle route where the surface was either smoothly laid tarmac or a mixture of grass and sand, all of which made for swift and easy progress, and the miles passed in a flash. Just as my legs began to tire and the energy gleaned from the encounter with Allan the welder wore thin, I spotted a blue sign at the side of the cycle trail which read 'Cullen Bay Hotel'. I let out a victory cheer as I bounded up some steps to the main road and looked longingly across it at my sanctuary for the next two nights. The hotel looked perfect: old-fashioned and welcoming. It was a long, white building surrounded by lush grass, with large windows framed in blue wood which looked out onto the sea. There was even a quirky turret at one end of the building which made it look like a mini castle. Having run 111 miles since my last day of rest in Inverness, this place would be my fortress — somewhere to retreat to and gather strength for the barefoot battle ahead. I skipped across the road, brushed the sand from my legs and shoved open the heavy blue door to the lobby.

10

The Return of the Mojo

Cullen Bay is a special place. A near perfect sweep of golden sand, it curves around the windswept North Sea. It's bookended by steep black cliffs with green tops at one end and a modest harbour with a collection of colourful, quaint houses at the other. At the eastern end, closest to the harbour and houses, there's an assortment of jagged, biscuit-coloured rocks, which form a series of shallow pools, most of which get covered at high tide. In between the pools are two larger spires of rock, rising some 30 metres into the air, each one shaped like a shark fin. One fin is smaller than the other and, when the tide is in and the base of the rocks are underwater, it appears as if you're witnessing a baby shark and its mother swimming back out to sea.

The night I arrived at Cullen Bay, I celebrated the 23-mile day by treating myself to dinner at the hotel. Well, I told myself I was celebrating. Truth be told, I couldn't be arsed to walk the 20 minutes into town to find another place to eat. So, I showered, put my sweaty running clothes back on and made my way down to the dining room. I chose a table directly in front of a wall of windows, overlooking the sea.

I know some people feel awkward eating in cafes and restaurants on their own, but I adore it. Or rather, I have grown to adore it. When I was younger it felt weird, pointless even, to be sitting alone. As if everyone was looking at me. But the more the years go by, the more I appreciate the chance to sit, be still, to read a book or just to stare into space and have a good old-fashioned think. And when all of that is accompanied by delicious food and drink, well, that's an added bonus. All in all, dining alone feels as if you're taking yourself on a date — it's a real expression of self-love. And, given that I'd showed up for my 'date' in sweat-soaked Lycra, I was probably the only person who was going to put up with my runner's musk anyway.

After explaining to the friendly waitress quite why I was eating dinner in my running kit, I dribbled over the menu for a good 10 minutes. It didn't take long to settle on ordering a giant plate of carbonara. I'd been told by countless locals that I should try Cullen skink while in town — a local haddock delicacy that was famous Scotland-wide — but I wasn't feeling the fishy vibes that night and, based on how much I was salivating over the menu, my body was clearly asking for creamy carbonara. So, (in the spirit of self-love) that's just what I got. Fresh tagliatelle with chunky bits of bacon and a rich creamy sauce was washed down with a large glass of red wine and some Eton Mess for afters. Bliss.

Full of carbs and recharged by a solid night of sleep, I spent my day of rest wandering around Cullen. I sat in a coffee shop, bought some Cullen fudge to post back to friends as gifts and spent a few hours catching up on admin in the bar of the swanky hotel in town (which I hadn't been able to afford to stay in). I also took the chance to perform a full assessment of the itty-bitty-gritty situation in my feet, although I chose to do this in my bedroom rather than in the bar of the swanky hotel.

It had now been 10 days since the bits of grit had first wedged themselves in my soles on the way into Aviemore and I was in awe of what my body had done to them since then. My body had identified the grit as a foreign object which had no business being in my foot. It had walled it off with hard skin and was shoving the bits of grit slowly outwards. Each morning, I noticed the grit was closer to the surface of my soles. So much so that, on the afternoon in Cullen, I was able to pick out one of the pieces of grit and the accompanying section of harder skin and place it on my bedside table. Yummy.

I had a feeling that these gritties wouldn't be the last ones I'd pick up on the way to London, but I was reassured that, after a few days of pain and discomfort, my feet would do their thing and expel the unwanted evil (albeit in slow motion) in due course. I had lived in my body for 34 years and I had no idea it could do that. Bloody amazing! I was in love with my feet and their hidden grit-ejecting superpowers all over again. After picking the piece of grit out of my foot, I decided I would keep each piece in an empty Vaseline lip balm tin, for posterity. Maybe I'd show them to my grandkids one day.

Sporting one grit-free foot, on the second evening at Cullen Bay, I took a stroll along the beach just as the sun was going down. Despite the swanky-ness of the hotel I'd hung out in earlier that day, I was grateful I'd chosen to stay outside of the main town. Not only because it was cheaper but because it was quieter too. It was now 2 July, and one full month since I'd started at Skaw Beach. A lot had happened in that month and processing the events of the days on the road seemed easier to do when in a quiet place. The days of rest were important for that. They didn't just offer a chance to reset physically; they had the same effect on my mind too. They allowed me to disconnect from the run so that I could reconnect with myself.

I'd use the time to reflect on the week that had passed and focus on the one to come. That usually entailed homing in on what was causing me to feel apprehensive. There was always something: a talk I was worried I wouldn't make it to, a stretch of the route I was unsure of or a host where the logistics hadn't quite yet fallen into place. . . I knew better than to ignore the nagging concerns. They only got bigger if neglected, after all. So, on a rest day, I would let my thoughts drift to each worry, like a butterfly resting briefly on the stem of a wildflower. Never staying long enough to get bogged down but taking time enough to acknowledge it and take flight again, feeling lighter.

It was a blustery evening at Cullen Bay and, despite it being the middle of summer, the wind whipping in from the North Sea was biting. I walked all the way to the end of the sand and sat on a rock beneath a wall of black cliffs. I watched the waves roll onto the shore along the soft curve as the sky transformed into a smudged patchwork of lilac and blue. Copper-tinged rays streamed through gaps in the clouds and landed on the watery sheen left by the receding tide. I had a feeling it would rain that night but, for now, the only moisture in the air was from the sea spray. I let out a deep sigh and shut my eyes, feeling the North Sea squall gather up grains of sand and scatter them across my face. I felt at peace. I felt free. And there was an overriding sense that I was in between places. Practically, I was in between hosts, in between talks and in between any public running stages. But I felt in between in every sense. As if the journey were resting at a crossroads and if I let out one more breath while on that rock, there would be a shift in its direction, in my mood, in my feelings about the road ahead. I held my breath for a moment. Then I let it go.

The following morning, I woke at 10 a.m. and realised I'd slept through breakfast. I managed to score a cup of coffee and some leftover pastries from the friendly waitress who'd served me at dinner on the first night, and I took off from the hotel at midday, heading east along the coast on a series of small back roads. My legs felt fresh, there was zero pain in my feet and, all in all, I felt. . . different. In fact, I felt. . . marvellous! What fresh madness was this? Best of all, I felt like me. Hallelujah! Where had I been hiding all this time? I wondered. I must have been hiding from myself. And then, I clocked it. I knew exactly what had happened. Somewhere in that rest day, in the truckload of sleep, in the healing of my feet and aided by the swell of the North Sea, I had rediscovered my mojo. Oh, how I had missed that mojo.

I was so excited by my new lease of life that I took a break after 10 miles to sit on a bench and share the good news with those following the run. Goodness knows they'd had enough doom and gloom updates over the past month, so I was eager to share that I was having a good day. I loaded up my phone and tapped out a breaking news report:

RECENTLY FOUND: Anna's Mojo.

LAST SEEN: The Shetland Islands.

Presumed to have been kidnapped by a rogue puffin, Miss McNuff's Mojo was reported missing early on in her attempt to run through Britain in bare feet.

Speaking to us yesterday from the shores of Cullen Bay, the Girlguiding ambassador reported that she was in high spirits, having recently been reunited with the beloved mojo, following the completion of a 23-mile day and the consumption of delicious Aberdeenshire ice cream.

'I finally feel like I've hit a rhythm,' said McNuff. 'The feet are sore, and the days are still tough, but something feels different. I'm excited again about what's to come.'

And it was all true. What a relief. I let a broad grin spread across my face and took off again along the road, waving at the cars who beeped as they passed and enjoying the sound of the wind rustling through the tall trees. It was as if they were saying, 'Welcome back, Anna, welcome back.'

After running through the town of Banff (which reminded

me how much I loved Canada), I ran across the bridge to spend the night with a local family in Macduff (which reminded me how much I loved my surname. . . and Shakespeare). I told adventure stories in my host's living room to a small group of teenage girls before sleeping in the spare bedroom. The 18-mile run from Cullen to Macduff had been tiring, but I was delighted that my mojo hadn't gone anywhere over the course of the day. In fact, I was now tucked up next to, nay spooning, my mojo. It was well and truly back, and I hoped it was here to stay.

After leaving Macduff, I continued to munch up the miles, heading south on an inland route towards Aberdeen. I cracked out a 24-mile day on peaceful back roads which cut between rolling green fields under cloud-streaked skies. At the town of Maud, I fired up my own personal steam engine again and began to follow a trail along the path of another old railway line: the Formartine and Buchan Way.

When I joined the rail trail, I spotted two men dressed in high-vis jackets working on restoring the old Maud railway station. I tried to creep, undetected, from the gravel car park and onto the line, hoping to get out of sight before they clocked me. They looked engrossed in the business of restoration and so I thought I'd got away with it. But then I heard a call.

'Hey! Hey! Lass!' I ignored the shout and ran a few more steps. 'S'cuse me? Heeeyy! Lassie!' Bugger. Short of pretending I was deaf, I needed to stop. It'd be rude not to. I spun around.

'Hello.'

'What are ye doin'?' the man panted, now having jogged down the line in his work boots to where I was.

'Oh, I'm running.'

'Aye, I can see that. Where are ye running to?'

I paused for a moment. 'To London' seemed too much to comprehend. It was still even too much for me, so I settled on a closer, more digestible, target.

'Aberdeen. This line goes all the way there, right?'

'Aberdeeeeeen?!' the man screeched.

'That's right.' I took a few steps and began to move off down the track.

'You can't.'

'I can't?'

'No. You can't. Not all the way to Aberdeen.'

'Oh. Is the trail blocked?' I asked, thinking that perhaps this high-vis man had some insight into construction on the line ahead.

'No, it's not blocked, but it's thirty sumthin' miles to Aberdeen. And there's all sorts of things on the trail — stones and twigs and leaves 'n'. . . all sorts.' He shook his head.

'Oh, I'm sure it'll be fine. I'll give it a go. I've run from Shetland. I think I'll be okay. Thank you though.'

The man opened up his mouth again to speak, but I was already three steps gone, running over the stones and twigs and the 'all sorts', down the trail, into the shadow of the trees and rapidly moving out of sight.

'You're mad, you are! Good luck! Take care!' he shouted after me, and I raised a hand into the air in acknowledgement.

I was all for polite conversation, but sometimes it's best to agree to disagree. I didn't need the warden of Maud (as I had now dubbed him) to think I couldn't run to Aberdeen; I just needed to maintain the fragile belief that I could. And if you ever see someone poised and ready to pump you full of worry that is not your own, it's always best to run away, at speed.

As I expected, the surface on the Formartine and Buchan Way wasn't as bad as the man had made it out to be. It was a mixture of mud and gravel with a grass verge and so, with some careful foot placement, it was manageable. Plus, no stretch of surface ever lasted too long. Sometimes it was a joy (on the mud) and then other times it was a pain (on the gravel), but when the gravel became too much I would pick my way along the grass verge at the edge. This meant that sometimes progress was slower than I wanted it to be, and sometimes slow progress frustrated me, but I was armed with a secret weapon: Tina Turner.

I've been a fan of Tina my whole life — well, ever since my parents had introduced me to her music as a kid. I'd been listening to Tina's autobiography on audiobook since leaving Cullen and decided that if she could survive the hardships of being a Black woman in America in the 60s and 70s, an abusive partner and cancer. . . I mean, if she could do all of that and still rock it out on stage in a sparkly dress and denim jacket (which I had witnessed first-hand at a concert when she was 74 years old), then I could do a little run to London.

Beyond the challenges she'd overcome, what I admired most of all about Tina is that she had always wanted to do things 'her way'. The songs she sang, the way she performed — just as the lyrics say in 'Proud Mary' — Tina wanted her music to be 'rough'! She liked her sound to be raw, edgy and honest and she was willing to fight to make it that way. I'd very much like to be more like Tina when I grow up.

Twelve miles further along the Formartine and Buchan line, I detoured into Ellon to get a coffee. While Tina was doing a cracking job of distracting me from the task at hand, the need to constantly think about my foot placement on the trail was frying my brain. I always liked to be able to break up the day of running with a stop if I could, and that day I needed it more than most.

Even though the return run to Ellon would add 3 miles, I decided it was worth it for an hour of being still and on my tod. While the need to be alone might sound strange because I was on my own for much of the day, there was something about sitting still on my own as opposed to running that served a different purpose. I think we all need that in life — a mix of being in motion and coming to a halt. Given the extra miles, there was a lot of pressure for the coffee stop in Ellon to be absolutely perfect. Thankfully, I am a well-trained coffee-shop seeker and inexplicably drawn to establishments where fine coffee is served.

I was soon sitting in Ellon, feeling smug, having sought out The Coffee Apothecary — a gem of a place with wooden cladding on the walls, funky old church chairs and glass-topped tables made from old pallets with vintage records slid under the glass. In the process of making the decision to run into town, I had struck a deal with the schedule demons and made a promise to them (and myself) that I was only to order coffee and decent, healthy food. But then, I saw the doughnut. It was sitting in a glass cabinet at the serving counter. It was double the height of a usual ring doughnut, all fluffy and white and coated in sugar which caught the light and made it sparkle. The doughnut spoke to me. I was powerless to its sugar-coated-batter-y whisper.

When the ring of my desire arrived at the table, I tried to take a bite but discovered it was so big that I couldn't fit my mouth around it, so I had to cut it with a knife. I declared from that moment on that all doughnuts should be large enough to warrant attack with tools. I would like to add that I did order a cauliflower salad too, which was nowhere near as big as the doughnut but almost half as delicious (so, still very delicious). That was my one rule with eating naughty food. So long as I ate the good stuff too, then all was right in the world.

With a sugar-coated face and a belly full of batter and cauliflower, I felt a veil of lethargy lift. I polished off the rest of the doughnut of dreams and licked my fingers, pressing them into the plate repeatedly to make sure no spare morsels of sugar were left behind. I threw my pack onto my back, thanked the cafe staff for their fine fare and took off down the road, back towards the rail trail.

On the outskirts of town, I stopped briefly to check the map. I was outside a house with a large front garden, and a woman was weeding the flower beds a few metres from me. She was in her mid-sixties, with short grey hair and wearing a set of slim, rectangular glasses. The woman stopped what she was doing and looked up. I smiled and went back to checking the map on my phone. A minute or so later she appeared at the end of the driveway, trowel in hand and gardening gloves tucked into the front pocket of her jeans.

'Hello?' she said.

'Oh, hello,' I smiled, looking up from my phone.

'Are you okay?' She furrowed her brow.

'Yes, I'm great, thank you.'

'Are you sure?' she asked again, this time pulling her glasses down her nose and peering at me over the top of them. I got the feeling she didn't trust my first reply.

'Yes, thank you. I'm great. I just had the most spectacular doughnut,' I said, smiling again.

'A doughnut?'

'Yes. It was gigantic. At that coffee place in town. It's very good, isn't it?'

'Do you need some more food or something?'

'Oh, no, I'm stuffed! I ate a cauliflower salad too.'

'How about some shoes? Do you want some shoes? Are you in trouble?' She pointed at my feet.

'Oh! No, I'm fine. I'm on a challenge. It's a barefoot run,' I replied. I hadn't even clocked that she might have been concerned about my lack of footwear. I had actually forgotten I was barefoot for once.

'Oh!' The woman heaved a huge sigh of relief and pushed her glasses back up her nose. 'I saw you there and I thought you looked like you'd been running, and I wondered if you were running from someone and that perhaps they'd taken your shoes, and that you were in some kind of trouble,' she said. 'I was going to offer you some of mine.'

'Ah, that's so lovely of you. I promise you I'm barefoot out of choice. . . Thank you, though, that's very kind.'

'Okay, deary. Well, you take care of yourself,' she said, looking down at my feet again, before turning and heading back to her garden.

How lovely was that? The woman was genuinely concerned that I might be in some kind of trouble and was willing to offer me her shoes to help me out of it. It wasn't the shirt off of her back, but it was close enough.

After recovering from the overwhelming quality of doughnuts

and kindness in Ellon, I followed the Formartine and Buchan Way for a couple more days. But as I neared Aberdeen, I was eager to get back to the coast, largely because I could see on the map that there was a long stretch of beach leading into the city and also because locals had told me that it was sandy and flat and wonderfully run-able. I wanted to get onto the beach as far north of Aberdeen as I could so that I could make the most of what I hoped would be care-free miles where I wouldn't have to think so much about what was beneath my feet.

It was difficult to see exactly where I should make the transition from the inland road to the shoreline because many of the tracks leading away from the road were covered in rubble, or they looked like they ended at farms or crossed private land. I settled on traversing the dunes at the small town of Balmedie. On paper, it was the right decision, but I made a poor judgement call in choosing exactly where to get across and ended up on the wrong side of a stream, surrounded by a patch of swamp, complete with chest-height stinging nettles.

Short of backtracking to find a bridge over the stream, I decided I'd just have to pick somewhere to wade through the swamp and that that somewhere might as well be where I was standing. Having learned from my nettle encounters on the John O'Groats trail, I prepared myself before wading in by pulling on a long-sleeve top, gloves and leggings — minimising the parts of me that could get stung. When I was finished with my nettle suit of armour, the only exposed parts of skin were my head and feet. I let out a war cry as I waded into the swamp, thinking that if I kept moving I could make like a pond skater and hop-skip across the wet earth, skimming over the nettles to the other side.

The stench of the swamp made me gag — it smelled like a mix of a ripe compost bin and a freshly opened can of tuna. Halfway into the battle with the nettle swamp, it became apparent that I was less of a pond skater and more of a pond sinker. With each stride, my foot disappeared up to my ankle and, at one point, I sank all the way up to my thigh in the sludge. There was a moment of panic as my foot got sucked deep into the earth and my imagination went wild, conjuring up all of the things that could be lying in wait in the watery mud. Rusty pieces of metal, discarded heroin syringes, dead bodies and even MUD MONSTERS. . . So, fuelled by the potential of a smack-addicted mud monster wielding a piece of rusty metal about to inflict damage on my foot, I threw my body forwards, letting out a feral cry as I faceplanted into the stinging nettles. My cheeks prickled with heat, but I stayed focused on the task at hand. I frantically waggled my sunken leg. . . and the mud monster released it with a loud sluurrrp.

By the time I made it over the final dune and onto the beach, I was sporting scratches on my neck, stings on my face and I now smelled of tuna and compost bin. But all of that was worth it for the sight in front of me. Five miles of uninterrupted golden sand stretched from beneath my feet towards the skyline of Aberdeen. Every city I ran through was a milestone, but I'd been especially excited about making it to Aberdeen because Aberdeen was the precious 500-mile marker that I had been working towards since Shetland.

I wasted no time in bounding down the dune and onto the beach, letting my toes sink into the cool, soft sand and raising my arms in the air, whooping and hollering as I went. There wasn't anyone else around to hear my shouts, but I wouldn't have cared if there was. Knowing there was now nothing between me and the city except miles and miles of soft sand was a relief. I immediately felt my body relax.

Once I made it onto the flat beach, I let my legs stretch out and, with each stride, I felt charged with electricity. Like a Duracell bunny, I was convinced I could run forever like this. I bounded on under blue skies and gently rolling clouds, splashing through small streams, enjoying the sensation of cool water running over hot, tired toes. It was a calm day, and the North Sea was like a mill pond. The glassy waters stretched out like a mirror beneath the sky. I could see red and blue oil tankers and the ghostly outline of wind turbines — dozens of them. I knew many people considered wind turbines to be ugly — a blot on the landscape — but I liked the ones in the sea. There was something otherworldly about them — like gentle giants standing ankle-deep in the glassy blue.

A mile into the run along the beach, I spotted a seal that was making its way back into the water. Perhaps he'd been hanging out on the sand all morning, catching some rays, or was returning from an inland visit to some friends for brunch in the dunes. The seal shuffled forwards and then stopped to look at me. I wondered whether it was as amazed by me as I was by it. The answer was a clear 'no', as it promptly resumed the belly shuffle towards the water and disappeared into the shallows.

Knowing that I needn't concentrate on the surface beneath my feet, I put in my headphones, loaded up Tina on audiobook and ran for an hour along the sand, carried onwards by the sheer joy of being able to run freely. I ran as far along the beach as I could until I reached the estuary of the River Don. It was too wide and deep to wade through it, so I knew I'd have to head inland to cross a bridge over it. And from that bridge, it was a straight shot into the city centre. I was almost there.

Just shy of the river, the beach narrowed and there were half a dozen small tidal pools. I skirted around many of them, opting to run above them on the soft sand of the dunes, but on the last few, I decided I should stop fannying around and just wade through. I was almost there, after all, and running on the dunes was using up extra energy. All I wanted was to take the most direct route possible into the city centre for a long-awaited rendezvous with a big plate of food, a shower and a warm bed.

I'd now switched from listening to Tina's audiobook and was working my way through Lizzo's latest album. I wanted to skip to 'Good as Hell' to celebrate my approach to the city, so I was busy fiddling with my phone as I crossed the final tidal pool, and I wasn't concentrating on my foot placement. I'd just hit play and was joining Lizzo in doing a hair toss and checking my nails when I stubbed my foot on a large, submerged boulder. With an earphone in one hand and my phone in the other, I didn't have any hands free to stop me falling, so I toppled sideways, dunking my whole body into the salty pool and scraping my leg on the rock on the way down.

'Waaaa!' I yelped, attracting the attention of some nearby dog walkers and raising a few eyebrows.

Embarrassed, but delighted that I'd managed to keep my phone and earphones dry, I laughed at my own stupidity. After stumbling out of the pool and resuming running, I noticed a stinging sensation in my right leg. I looked down to see blood seeping from patches of raw, exposed skin on my shin. There was grit and sand stuck to the graze and blood trickling down to my ankle. I thought that running into the city sopping wet and streaming with blood wasn't a good look, so I found a secluded bush on the shore of the river estuary, just shy of the bridge over the river, and ducked into it. I peeled off my sodden shorts, and there I stood, cowering, naked from the waist down in the bushes, listening to the rumble of the inner-city traffic, blood on my legs and doing my best to clean the sand and grit from the large graze on my shin. Sometimes life's challenges come in the form of oxygen-starved mountain tops, arid deserts and raging river crossings. And other times, they come as a result of selecting a bangin' Lizzo track while trying to cross a 3-metre-wide rock pool on a beach in Aberdeen.

ANNA MCNUFF

11

Adventure Pace

How do you fancy a trip to 'The Silver City with gold-
en sands?' Sounds glorious doesn't it? In a bid to encourage
post-wartime holidaymakers to take a trip to Aberdeen, that's
exactly how a 1950s marketing campaign described the city.
Since then, it's collected many other, less flattering, nicknames,
such as the Granite City, the Grey City and (my personal fave)
Furry Boots Toon — which has nothing to do with fuzzy footwear and everything to do with the way an Aberdonian will
ask you where you're from. Furry Boots Toon = Where abouts
are you from?

Dominated by granite buildings and grey paving slabs,
Aberdeen is certainly. . . grey, and depending on who you
speak to in Scotland, the city gets mixed reviews. But if there
was one thing I liked about Aberdeen, it's that it was different.
Plus, I actually found all that grey to be soothing. Especially the large smooth paving slabs, which were mighty kind to
my tired soles as I ran into the city. The architecture of Aberdeen is beautiful too. There are plenty of large colonial-style
buildings with extravagant pillars, broad stone steps and copper domed roofs, which add some green razzmatazz to an

otherwise greyscale vista.

Thanks to my fight with a rock pool on the outskirts, I was running late when I arrived in the city. I had time for a quick 30-minute turnaround at a budget hotel (which included a 10-minute shower, five minutes of getting dressed and a 15-minute cat nap) before being collected by a local Girlguiding leader. She drove me back north to Haddo House, where I was going to spend the evening sharing adventure tales with 50 youngsters.

By 6 p.m., I was standing in light rain in the middle of a large field, watching girls aged between seven and 15 dash between tents in their wellies. One group was playing on a large wooden climbing frame, another gaggle was sitting in the porch of a tent playing cards, and two eight-year-olds were top to toe in a large canvas hammock — apparently they needed to 'chill out' before dinner. Watching the girls hang out, I thought back to my camping experiences as a youngster, some of which had been as a Girl Guide. At least these girls were agreeing to show up for dinner; I remember climbing a tree and refusing to come down from it at all, no matter how much the leader tooted her whistle. But I also remember that all of the time spent outdoors, running, chatting, making plans, was priceless.

Dinner for the group was a vat of pasta with bolognaise sauce and lashings of cheese, and dessert was s'mores with a side helping of adventure tales. I blew up my inflatable globe and danced around the campfire, brimming with energy, all of the day's hard work and hard running forgotten in a flash.

The following day, I was feeling refuelled from the night at the campground and had racked up a juicy 12-hour sleep. I made my way towards the William Wallace statue on Union Terrace and was touched to find there were 10 runners waiting at William's feet. It was a fine place to choose as my departure point from the city, opposite what locals refer to as the iconic buildings of 'education, salvation and damnation': the Central Library, St Mark's Church and His Majesty's Theatre. I did a quick scan of the crowd. There was a mix of men and women, and I noticed that one of the men was barefoot. I went about the usual routine of hugging everyone hello and asking their names, and midway through the hug-a-thon I stopped at a familiar face.

'Chris!' I said and gave him a big hug.

Chris was a friend of my younger brother. They'd been at school together and, as my brother and I were only one school-year apart, I'd hung out with Chris a fair amount through my teenage years — at parties, rowing regattas and, more often than not, at the bus stop after school. Considering that I grew up in Kingston upon Thames in Surrey, 500 miles from Aberdeen, it was bizarre to see him there. Despite having not seen him in 15 years, I took comfort in having someone on the run who knew me of old. Your roots can be what hold you steady through turbulent times, after all. And it felt nice to be reminded of mine.

'Hello, McNuff Senior,' said Chris, referring to me as he

always did. 'Where's the junior McNuff? Didn't he fancy a jog too?'

'Ah, he's busy being grown-up and sensible,' I replied. Which, in part, was true. My younger brother was far more grown-up and sensible than I would ever be.

'That sounds about right. . . We heading to Betty's today, then?' Chris asked, referring to 'Aunty Betty's', an apparently legendary ice-cream shop which was at the end of that day's run.

'That we are. Is it good?'

'Oh, it's goooood. Just so you know. It's the only reason I'm here,' he grinned.

With an old friend in tow, the group and I set off through the city streets, winding down side roads and dodging pedestrians on the pavements. I felt immediately at ease. One of the bonuses of running through a city with other people was that passers-by took less notice of what I was wearing (or not wearing) on my feet. They were too distracted by the pack of brightly clad runners moving towards them at speed to look down. And even if they did notice I was barefoot, I was too engrossed in chatter, gathering up the whens, wheres and whats of each individual who'd come out to play, to notice them looking at me strangely. City running with a crowd was a win–win.

After a fill of nostalgia with Chris, I decided to make an effort to get to know people in the group whom I hadn't met before, notably the guy in bare feet. I looked over my shoulder and spotted him towards the back: a dark-haired man in a red T-shirt and black shorts.

'Hi. . . Giorgio, is it?' I asked, moving alongside him.

'Yes, that's me,' replied Giorgio, and I detected an Italian accent.

'So, how's it going?'

'Okay. . . good. Well, I am a bit tired actually,' he said. That was music to my ears. It was sometimes tough to keep up on the public running stages when locals turned up feeling fresh and sprightly.

'You know what, Giorgio. . . I'm bit tired too. But ssssh, don't tell anyone.'

'Okay. I will keep it a secret.' He shot me a sideways glance and grinned.

Giorgio went on to tell me that he'd been looking forwards to joining in the run for a while and had taken a day of holiday from work to come out to play. That really touched me. Annual leave is a precious thing, after all.

'So, how far have you run barefoot before?' I asked, wondering if he was planning to run all 21 miles to Aunty Betty's ice-cream parlour.

'Well, this says we have run three miles,' Giorgio said, tapping his watch. 'So that would mean that the furthest I have run barefoot is. . . three miles.'

'What? This is the furthest you've done?'

'Yes.'

'And how far have you run before in shoes?'

'Three miles.' He smiled.

I had to hand it to Giorgio. It turned out that he'd never run more than a mile, even in shoes. And there he was, taking a day off work to run as far as he could in no shoesies along the Aberdeenshire coast. Unfortunately, 20 minutes later, just as we hit the 5-mile marker, Giorgio's ambition caught up with him and he began to lag behind. He hadn't banked on running so far and had no food, water or any way of getting home from where we were standing, on a bridge over the coastal railway. We had a whip-round in the group and managed to pack him off with some snack bars, a packet of jellybeans and a fiver to get the bus back to the city. Go big or go home, they say, and Giorgio had done both.

After Giorgio left, other members of the group peeled off at intervals, either looping back to the city or ducking out at a train station we passed along the way. Before each of them went, they commented on how they'd been surprised that the pace of the group was so enjoyable they'd wanted to keep going.

'I thought you'd be so much faster!' one woman blurted out. 'I mean, not that you're not fast, it's just—'

'Well, I'm delighted to be a disappointment.' I smiled. And truly, I was. I'd have hated for people to come for a run and then be clinging on for dear life. As the public running stage sign-ups had grown, I'd noticed that there was a misconception that, because I was on a long journey, I would always be running at breakneck speed. Don't get me wrong, I love a good lung burning run as much as the next person. There's always a time and a place to smash it. But that's only once in a while. My style is more stop-and-smell-the-roses. Yes, I'm running, yes, I'm going from A to B, but the joy is in the movement itself for me. I'm sure the tortoise got a much better view of the landscape than the hare, after all. So, I run at Adventure Pace, which can be defined as follows:

Adventure Pace:

Thou shalt run and chat (and stop for coffee) and repeatedly congratulate oneself for being so adventurous.

By 12 miles through the day of Adventure Pacin', it was just me, Chris and a woman in her late forties called Jo. Jo was a talented runner and showed no signs of tiring as we padded on along small back roads under clear skies and sunshine. It was pushing 28°C, and by mid-afternoon, the tarmac was hot beneath my feet. After we passed 15 miles, the heat took its toll, and my pace began to slow. At that point, I knew I'd make it to Stonehaven sooner or later, but I wasn't keen on destroying myself to get there. I had to get up and do this all over again the following day, after all, so I took my foot off the pedal and set my feet to cruise control. Chris wasn't used to running more than a few miles, so he started to struggle too and was grateful for the steady pace, but Jo showed no signs of letting up. The distance between Chris and me and Jo kept stretching out as she powered on, so we nicknamed her 'the Husky'. I imagined Chris and I were on a cumbersome sled and that there was an invisible tow line stretched out in front of us as Jo the unstoppable Husky pulled us onwards along the coast, and towards ice-cream glory.

An hour later, when we arrived at the beachfront at Stonehaven, I was more done than a Sunday slab of roast beef. My soles were sore and, after a day of chatting with other runners, my cheeks were worn out from smiling. Strangely enough though, I didn't struggle to run the final 10 steps towards the sign that read: aunty bettys. The queue was out the door and stretching along the pavement, so Chris, Jo and I wasted no time in getting in line. When we reached the inside of the shop, I discovered it was like a treasure trove, partway between a room at Willy Wonka's chocolate factory and Honeydukes sweet shop in Harry Potter.

Trays of ice cream were lined up behind a large glass counter — raspberry, chocolate, mint choc-chip, butterscotch — and on a shelf on the back wall were glass jars of toppings and bottles of syrup. I could see chocolate sprinkles, rainbow sprinkles, raspberry sauce, fudge sauce, gummy bears, bon bons. . . I took a deep breath. There were many big decisions to be made inside Aunty Betty's. Not only did I have to choose between one scoop of ice cream or two, but I also had to make a call on which flavour to go for, which type of cone to have it in and then which sprinkles to add on top. I needed to get this right. The last thing I wanted was to fall short in my ice-cream selection and get ice-cream envy after a 21-mile run.

'Chris,' I whispered, trying not to draw attention to the fact that I was feeling overwhelmed.

'Yes, McNuff Senior?' he whispered back.

'What flavour's the best?' I asked.

'Hmm, that depends. They're all good. There are no bad choices at Aunty Betty's.'

'Right.'

'But. . . actually. . . Make sure you get a waffle cone. Its structural integrity is far superior to the wafer. You'll only regret choosing the wafer,' he added with a nod.

'Any flavour. Waffle cone. Got it. . . errr, Chris?' I whispered again.

'Yes?'

'How do I know which topping to go for?'

'That's easy,' he smiled. 'Just say "all of them".'

Standing outside Aunty Betty's, looking out onto Stonehaven Marina, I licked and slurped at a waffle cone filled with two scoops of lemon meringue ice cream and ALL the toppings. Sticky strawberry sauce was trickling down the cone onto my fingers and a gummy bear had just made a bid for freedom and landed face down on the pavement. I quickly rescued another bear from the same fate (with my tongue) and thought back over the day.

In contrast to the number of people who had run with me on Shetland and through the Highlands, today had been a big group. As I passed through more populated areas the run was gathering attention online and it was being reflected by the number of people joining me on the road. In the evenings, I would look up the next open running stages and check in on the number of sign-ups. Numbers were now creeping into the tens, twenties. . . and there were even a few stages down south where more than 50 people had signed up. For the first time since leaving Shetland, I felt like I was being carried along by an energy that wasn't my own. As if I had dived off a stage and into a crowd and was now surfing south — the hands, strength and chatter of strangers keeping me airborne.

South of Stonehaven, the sunshine disappeared and I ran through a few days of thunderstorms. On those days, I would wake up to pouring rain, run all day in it and finish up running in the rain. As I'd sent my main kit bag ahead to Aberdeen, I was only carrying a light rain jacket, so it was never long before the jacket had soaked through and was clinging to my skin. My leggings would follow suit, holding more and more water until it felt like I'd wet myself. When the weather was like that, I tried to pretend I was anywhere except on the road. I would retreat into the hood of my jacket, listen to an audio-book and do my best to be transported from the adventure to another time and place in my mind.

By the time I made it to the coastal town of St Cyrus, the

skies were blue again and the temperature gauge was back up to reading 'FIRE OF A THOUSAND SUNS'. I gave a talk to a group of girls at a local church hall and was collected by Guide leader Maureen, who was hosting me for a couple of nights. Maureen had short brown hair, wore glasses and was a softly spoken woman of a quiet nature. Well, that was how I found her in the time we spent together, but for all I know, she could well go out raving at weekends. I enjoyed a relaxed car ride back to her home in Montrose, nattering away. At one point, the conversation turned to the evening I'd just spent talking to the Rainbows, Brownies and Guides.

'It's lovely, you know. The energy you bring to the girls,' said Maureen.

'Ah, thanks, I try my best. And actually, I get a lot from their energy.'

'No, really, Anna — it's special. They don't often get a chance to hear from someone so. . . different.'

'Well, I'll take that,' I said. 'I like different.'

'So do we. I'm very grateful you were able to visit Angus and Aberdeenshire.'

'And I'm very grateful you're putting me up for the night. So that makes us even.'

'Well, my husband Stuart can't wait to meet you. I warn you. . . he's rather excited,' Maureen said as we pulled into her driveway. It was then I realised that I hadn't even asked if she lived alone, with kids, had a partner or anything. I really had just been nattering. 'He's a keen runner, you know. . . he'll talk your ear off about that,' she continued.

When we walked into the house, Stuart was standing in the hallway, ready to greet us. He was lean and athletic looking, had short white hair, a round face, bright blue eyes and (as of a few seconds ago) a broad grin across his face.

'Ooop, we've got a celebrity in the hoose!' he beamed, reaching out his hand to shake mine. I bypassed the hand and went in for the hug. 'I've been so excited to have you stay. I've been telling all of my run buddies about you and what you're doing. And your pink hair! Would you look at that pink hair! It's even pinker in real life!'

I was touched. The idea that someone had been looking forward to having me come to stay wasn't something I'd ever considered. I would have always thought I would be more of a lightly pencilled-in event on someone's calendar, perhaps something they had organised months ago without thinking too much about it, and now there I was in their home, eating their food, sleeping in their bed and running baths with their hot water. But Stuart's reaction, although on the more excitable end of the spectrum, was genuine.

After enjoying a sumptuous hot bath, Maureen whipped up a delicious dinner of lasagne and salad. And while we got down to the business of eating it, Stuart began telling stories — about running, about his childhood, about his work as a joiner. Every now and then Maureen would interrupt.

'Och. . . you'll get used to his stories. It's nice to have someone else here for him to share them with because I've heard them all . . .' she would say, and Stuart would grin.

'Well, I'm up for some stories. It makes a change from talking about me,' I said.

'Ah, in that case, don't you worry — I've got plenty of stories still left to tell you. In fact, I was thinking of coming running with you tomorrow. Although, I don't know if I'll be able to keep up. . . How far are you going?'

'Errr, I think tomorrow's around twenty-two miles. St Cyrus to Arbroath if I can make it.'

'Oooh! That'll be the longest I've run in a while. What speed do you run at? I don't want to hold you up.'

'I've got no idea — but it's steady. Very steady. I call it Adventure Pace.'

'Adventure Pace. Right. Are we talking nine-minute miles? Eight-minute miles?' Stuart pressed, and I laughed.

'Honestly. . . I have no idea. I don't run with a watch. But definitely slower than that. I can guarantee whatever speed you have in mind, it'll be slower. . . I think you'll need to be prepared to set yourself to cruise control. I mean, you can go faster if you like, but I won't running be with you.' I smiled.

'Okay. No problem. I always like to go by the watch. I've never done cruise speed but I'll try it out tomorrow,' Stuart said.

'Great. And just promise me one thing?'

'What's that?' Stuart asked.

'You'll come armed with those stories?'

'Now, that I can do!'

The following morning I was back in Maureen's car at 11 a.m., with Stuart in the back seat. I wasn't feeling the sprightliest version of myself. Despite the comfortable bed in the spare room, my feet had kept me awake, tingling until around 2 a.m., when I'd finally dropped off to sleep. It was now mid-July, and it was already a hot day. I knew the temperature was set to rise into the high 20s, so I had the car window open, enjoying the cool rush of air as we trundled towards St Cyrus Beach.

Maureen dropped us off on a gravel track at the end of a beach trail. It was a quarter of a mile walk back along it to where we intended to start the day's run, and Stuart and I used that quarter of a mile as a warm-up. My leg muscles creaked and groaned as we ambled slowly along an enclosed grassy trail, lined with patches of hemlock, a steep set of cliffs off to the left and a 7-foot-high stone wall to the right. We passed a walled graveyard and I stopped to take some pictures. There were the remains of a small, stone croft house at the end and an array of broken eighteenth-century gravestones scattered haphazardly among a carpet of dry grass. The gravestones looked like a set of chipped giant's teeth, and I wondered if anyone knew the people who were buried here. Or were they forgotten souls, just a pile of lost memories in the earth?

I could tell that Stuart was excited about the day ahead. Booking a day's holiday from work to join me was an event in itself, but he was like a kid who had given himself permission to be let out to play. On the warm-up walk, he asked me a few times again about the pace I was planning to run, and I could tell he was nervous about the distance we were set to cover. Which was great because I was nervous that he would shoot off like a greyhound out of a starting gate — we were a right pair, both of us warning the other one that we may not be able to make it that far (in Stuart's case) or move that fast (in my case). Thankfully, the scenery was a wonderful distraction from our collective nerves.

'So. . . this is it,' Stuart said, as we popped out from behind the long stone wall and onto a wide, open beach.

'Wow,' I said, spinning 180 degrees and taking in everything in front of me. It was stunning.

It was low tide, and the waters of the North Sea were a way off from where we were standing, with small crests of waves rolling onto the shore. The golden sand was 50 metres wide and went as far as I could see in both directions, dotted with the footprints of dogs and their humans. Away from the sea, the edge of the sand led into short, bright green grass, which grew taller and wilder as it stretched away from the beach and merged with ferns and bracken. Above the ferns, the cliffs were bare and grey, undulating against the blue sky, their contours mirroring the waves of the ocean to our right. Halfway along the clifftop, I could see two small, white houses, but other than that, there were no buildings in sight. The onshore breeze was welcome in the stifling heat, so I stood still for a moment, burrowing my feet deeper into the cool, wet sand beneath the top layer. The scenery had been nice enough since leaving Aberdeen, but St Cyrus was wilder. It felt untamed, a little pocket of paradise reserved only for those who knew to go there.

Stuart and I soon got the journey underway. I was feeling tired so was grateful for the company, even if I didn't have the energy to talk much. I had gathered that Stuart was a very matter-of-fact man, so I felt like I could lay it on the line with him.

'Right then, Stuart. . .'

'Yes, Anna?'

'It's story time.'

'Story time?'

'Yes, you said you had plenty more stories to share. I want to hear them.'

'You do?'

'All of them.'

'Well, okay then. . .' Stuart took a deep breath and began. For the following 10 miles Stuart talked and I listened, gratefully. I learned that he'd run 23 marathons, but preferred shorter distances, like half-marathons and 10 kms. He always has a Yorkie chocolate bar before races and whenever he manages to put in a turn of speed during a race, he thinks 'that'll be my Yorkie kicking in!'

He told a story about how he'd once helped the police arrest a burglar who had broken into his home during the wintertime. Stuart had closely inspected the burglar's footprints and could tell the police exactly what shoes the man was wearing when he committed the robbery. 'That's runners for ye!' he laughed. 'We love our trainers! The police didn't believe me at first, but then they caught him red-handed — breaking into another house in the trainers I'd said he'd be wearing!' He beamed, and I admired his skill.

Stuart was a big fan of meeting 'famooose people', as he called them, and had clocked up his fair share of them over the years. He was especially keen on meeting or running with famous athletes and would often seek them out at races. He'd met Sonia O'Sullivan in a hotel lift on the morning of the London Marathon and had once almost beaten Liz McColgan at an amateur 13-mile event. He went on to tell me a story about another famooose encounter he'd had at a local running race where he'd met Billy Connolly.

'You met Billy Connolly?'

'Yes!'

'At a running race?'

'I did. And do you know what?'

'What?'

'I was so excited about meeting him and I thought I'd never get another chance, so I wanted to make sure I got a photo of us together. . . but I had to wait for ages, and then, when I did get the photo, we spent some time chatting. I lost track of time and heard the starter horn for the race go off while I was still with him. So I told Billy I had to go!'

'You missed the start of the race?'

'Aye, but I dashed across the line and managed to catch up with the main pack. And. . . when I crossed the finish line at the end I heard someone shout out "G'waaaaaan, Baldy!" It was Billy!'

After 13 miles of storytelling, we reached Lunan Bay and I decided that it was high time for a lunch stop. It was gone 3 p.m. and the coffee shack on the beach had stopped serving food, but we managed to find a hotel just down the road. They weren't technically open, but the manager was a kind man who could tell a woman in need of food when he saw one, and he ushered us inside to the restaurant area. The middle of a 22-mile run might seem like a strange time to stop for lunch, but I had learned to get better at listening to my body. Some days, it barely wanted to eat anything at all. Other days, I got to the end of the run and was ravenous, and on the odd occasion, I needed a full-blown sit-down meal in the middle of the day. And that day was a sit-down-lunch kind of day.

'Yer not gunna eat all of that and be able to run after, are ye?' Stuart gawped, looking at my plate as the manager set my meal down on the table — a hamburger, chips, a salad, a large pile of coleslaw and a milkshake.

'Oh, yes I am. Just watch me,' I smiled.

'That's unbelievable. If I eat more than an energy bar while I'm running I cannae move!'

'Well, I suppose we all have our talents, Stuart, and this is clearly one of mine.'

After leaving the lunch stop, I had no trouble running on my burger-filled tummy. We ran some more; the temperature rose some more. We then got lost, and (once back on track) Stuart launched into another story.

'When our kids were little, I would often hear a voice when I was passing their bedroom. . .'

'Go on. . .'

'It was a raspy voice, it sounded like an older woman. For a few nights, I thought it was the kids just messing around, so I brushed it off. But one night, I popped my head around the door. It was pitch black in the room and they were fast asleep. And it didn't even look like they'd just ducked back under the covers, you know? Like, they were actually asleep.'

'So it wasn't them doing the voice?'

'Well, I thought, "Who else could it be?" So, the next morning over breakfast, I asked them, "Kids — what was going on last night? Were you messin' about?" And they said, "No, Dad. . . we weren't. That lady just came out of the cupboard again to read us a story".'

'What on earth?!'

'Yeap. It was a ghost. Maureen saw her once too. She

was sitting up in bed and a lady just walked by the end of it. Dressed in old clothes and everything.'

'Blimey — was Maureen scared? I'd have wet myself.'

'No. She says it wasn't scary.'

'Do you know who she was? I mean, aren't ghosts supposed to have unfinished business or something? Do you know what she wanted?'

'I'm not sure, but she started appearing after we did some work on the house. So maybe we disturbed her with all our bangin' about.'

'I bet you're glad you're no longer in that house!' I laughed and Stuart fell silent.

'Stuart. . . You have moved since then?'

'Ah. . . no.'

'Which room is the kids' room?'

'You're sleeping in it.'

'Stuart!'

'Sorry, I wasn't going to tell you until you left. . . but, well, there you have it.' He grinned.

I didn't even think it was possible but, as we entered the final few miles of the day, Stuart ran out of stories. Not only that, but his legs began to tire too. I figured Stuart really was like a greyhound — used to running at speed, over shorter distances. Moving at a steadier pace for five hours was unfamiliar to his body. I, on the other hand, was more of a St Bernard: slower, always overheating, constantly hungry and often needing to rescue myself. When we spotted Maureen waiting for us on the roadside outside Arbroath Smokies fishmongers, she was a welcome sight for us both. We piled our sweaty bodies into the car and headed back 'home' for a final evening, in what I now knew was a haunted hoooose. That night I slept with one eye open, straining my ears to listen for the lady with the raspy voice.

12

The Power of People
(and Vegetables)

I have often wondered what the appropriate term is for a group of runners. All gatherings of animals have names, after all. Are they a pod? A gaggle? A collection? A pride? Officially, and in races, runners are 'a field' but, thinking about the groups who had joined me since I'd left Shetland, I decided that none of these terms did the runners justice. They didn't adequately describe the ethereal magic created by many brightly clad bodies in motion, powered by lungs and legs alone and surrounded by plumes of chatter. And so, given a runner's ability to skip lightly across the floor, I decided that a group of them should henceforth be known as a. . . fandango. 'Oh, would you look at that fandago of runners go, isn't it just majestic?' crowds would coo. Because, yes, yes it is.

Stuart's company set in motion a string of others wanting to come out and be a part of their own fandango along the Aberdeenshire coast. At Arbroath, five women from the Arbroath Footers Running Club turned up in matching red T-shirts and accompanying bright leggings to form a small yet mighty group and continue to speed my journey south.

The Footers and I followed the Arbroath promenade for half a mile before weaving along quiet, sandy trails through the dunes next to East Haven Beach. After leaving the beach behind, we cut inland and tiptoed across the exclusive Carnoustie golf course. Golfers clad in smart trousers and buttoned-up polo shirts with crisp white visors looked up from where they were sitting, sipping on frothy-topped beers at tables outside the clubhouse as we ran by, and after asking for permission from the golfers on the tee, we did cartwheels and roly-polies across the fairway, hollering as we went.

Nine miles into the day, the fandango of Footers and I stopped briefly at a corner shop to gulp down icy milkshakes and slurp on orange-flavoured Calypso ice lollies. Most of them then headed to get the train back to Arbroath from there, leaving just one member of the group to push onwards towards Dundee by my side. As the cranes and ships of Dundee Harbour came into view, we began to tire and descended into delirium together. We sang The Lion King's 'Hakuna Matata' at the top of our lungs and I soothed my tired soles by tiptoeing along white lines painted on the pavement all the way into the city centre.

That night, as I clambered in the shower, I thought about how wonderful it had been to be part of a group like that. With the Footers showing up, en masse, to join in with my journey, they had granted me temporary membership to their community. And how nice it felt to be a part of something beyond my barefoot club-of-one for a while.

As the week wore on, the days remained hot, the tarmac was spiky in places and the number of people joining in to run miles by my side grew. I'd now covered a total of 582 miles and was pushing the mileage up to 20+ miles on most days.

My feet were on fire each evening. They still tingled until the early hours, but it wasn't just my feet that I couldn't switch off – my brain was in overdrive at nighttime too. Where I now had more people running with me, I was chatting a lot of the day rather than spending time alone, processing my thoughts. And that meant that when all was quiet and silent in the evening, my brain launched into action. I'd chill myself out, relaxing as best as I could after doing all the admin for the following few days. I'd nestle my head on the pillow, almost fall to sleep — and then WHOOOSH! A thought would pop into my mind — usually a disastrous one about some part of the run yet to come. What if that section of trail is full of gravel? What if I don't make it on time to that Girlguiding unit? What if that person I just messaged thinks I'm being rude in asking if I can stay an extra night? What if, what if, what if. . . It drove me crazy, and with each question my heart rate went up a notch, until it was beating clean out of my chest. And that was it, I was wide awake.

The combination of tingly feet and a buzzy brain meant that, in contrast to the glorious 12-hour sleeps I was racking up in the north of Scotland, I was now only getting six or seven hours a night. That might sound okay, but I'd learned that I needed at least 10+ hours for my body to fully recover. There was also a direct correlation between how much sleep I got and how well I was able to cope with the difficult surfaces during a day of running. The less sleep I had, the more clogged my brain was, and the more painful my feet were. With less sleep in my system, each morning I'd wake up and wonder how I was possibly going to complete that day's run.

In Dundee city centre I met another group of runners at the Desperate Dan statue. If, like me, you're wondering why there would be a giant statue of a comic book character on a Scottish high street, it's because the publisher of The Dandy comic book — D. C. Thomson — was based in Dundee. Every day's a school day. It was a warm July day and I was grateful that Desperate Dan's chin was so large that it cast a shadow over me as I stood beneath it and chatted with the group, which included some hardcore runners (they had hydration packs on and everything), plus a mum, her two kids and a lady with a black cocker spaniel called Milo. Together, we set off for a 23-mile saunter to Perth.

Clusters of supporters lined the route out of the city, holding out bowls of sweets, and open boxes of Maltesers, which had partially melted in the heat. The crowd rang cowbells and shouted 'Allez, Allez, Allez!' as we passed, which made me feel like I was an elite cyclist in the Tour de France. Milo went as far as she could on her little paws (an impressive 4 miles), and the kids got in and out of their support car (driven by their dad) at intervals and sprinted past me, barefoot 'n' all.

The Dundee runners continued to be a fan-dango-tastic source of distraction, but I'd chosen a hot and hilly route towards

Perth. There was a lot of naughty tarmac — miles and miles of it — and, as the day wore on, my soles became sore, my legs ached, and my eyelids began to droop. I was running on empty and could feel the demons of doubt begin to whisper. . . There's a long way to go today, Anna, and then more after that. You're very tired. . . do you really think you're going to make it all that way? I shook my head and ignored the whispers, but they grew louder still. You're tired. So very tired. Don't your legs hurt? they hissed. I needed something else, anything else to focus on. Something to help me drown those voices out. And then, there it was, lying on its side in the middle of the road. . .

A turnip.

The turnip spoke to me, and, in my delirious and desperate state, I felt compelled to carry it to the finish line in Perth. And so, 16 miles through the day, I scooped that turnip up from the ground, placed it in the chest pocket of my backpack and informed the group that it would be joining us for the journey to Perth. For the following few miles, we passed the turnip back and forth like an earthy baton, stopping briefly to hold it aloft as we reached the crest of a hill and looked down over a patchwork of green fields, broccoli-topped trees and the River Tay, which flowed midnight-blue under late afternoon clouds. The turnip did a wonderful job of keeping the demons of doubt at bay — their voices in my mind were drowned out by laughter among the group. After 23 hard-won miles, I thanked the (now slightly warm and battered) turnip for the part it had played in getting me through the day and laid it at the foot of the Sir Walter Scott statue in the centre of Perth.

Despite the great company from fellow runners and the timely intervention of a root vegetable, I really began to struggle with fatigue over the following few days. The lack of sleep, the sore feet, the ongoing heat — it all started to catch up with me. Even though I was racking up the miles, I couldn't outrun my exhaustion. I began to feel detached, as if I wasn't running at all — instead, I was somewhere else, floating above my body and watching it all unfold.

There would be times when I was running with a group, and I would all of a sudden feel completely drained. Like I wanted to stop where I was, curl up in a ball at the side of the road and sleep for a thousand years. The group would be having such a nice time, and many members of it were going through their own personal battle — running further than they ever had done, coming back from an injury or doing their first run since becoming a mum — that I didn't want to share my pain. And besides, I told myself that the listener wouldn't know what to do with it.

I'd look around and note how everyone else was in trainers (because they were sensible) and know that they couldn't be feeling what I was feeling. They also hadn't run the day before and they wouldn't be running the day after and, in those moments of realisation, even though I was surrounded by dozens of kind, lovely people, I felt lonely. Sometimes the feeling was brief and other days it would come in waves — deep, rolling waves that would last for an hour or so. It would even happen while I was talking to someone, which, of course, made it worse because I wanted that person to be having a nice time and I didn't feel I could help them do that.

The reality was, I could have chosen to let someone know every time I was struggling, but what I needed was a hug from someone who really knew me. A hug from my parents, a close friend or Jamie. But I couldn't magic any of those people to the side of the road in Perthshire. So, I thought about something I'd come up with a few years back when I was asking my mum for advice to help me cope when I was feeling vulnerable and exposed.

I was right at the beginning of my relationship with Jamie and, as I fell in love, I became worried about getting my heart broken again. Mum is a qualified life coach, specialising in neuro-linguistic programming (NLP), so I've grown familiar with her techniques over the years. She asked me to use one of these to talk about the two versions of myself in my mind. I imagined one of the two versions of myself to be Strong Anna — she was brave and resilient and tall and knew that nothing could harm her. And then there was the other version of myself — a frightened little girl who'd loved so openly and so blindly that she'd had her heart smashed into tiny pieces as a result. Little Anna comes out when I am angry, tired, frustrated and in pain. The strong, brave version of myself protects and reassures the other one.

And so, in those moments when I was on the road, in pain and exhausted, I imagined that big, strong Anna giving the little girl Anna a hug. She knelt down, wrapped her arms around her, wiped away her tears, pulled her in close to her chest and whispered into her ear that it was all going to be okay. The feeling of being hugged by a stronger, protective version of myself stopped me from feeling like I wanted to melt into tears during the middle of the run. Instead of denying the way I was feeling, I had learned to acknowledge it and to comfort myself. That would get me just a little bit further along, and suddenly, I would feel a rush of relief. It was all going to be okay. Because big, strong Anna who lived in my head had said so.

***

A few days after the run with the turnip, I was curled up on the sofa in a house northeast of Glasgow, poring over a map of the area on my laptop. A woman called Claire had collected me after a day of running and was downstairs whipping up dinner, while I snuggled under a tartan blanket and tried to work out the best route to take from Stirling to the city of Glasgow.

Running into cities was always a tricky business. The outskirts were a minefield of hectic A-roads, and I didn't want to end up on one of those. When planning my route from Stirling to Glasgow, the issue wasn't too much choice, it was a lack of it. Usually there was a network of back roads I could pick my way along to avoid the A-roads. I'd make a vague plan and then wing it on the day, choosing whichever road looked best according to the three basic Ts of a barefoot adventure:

tarmac, trails and traffic. But between Stirling and Glasgow, there were big patches of land with no roads on them at all. I mean, I was pleased for that area of Scotland — how nice that it hadn't been bulldozed through and tarmacked over — but it was unusual.

The following morning, I told Claire I was nervous that I'd chosen a duff route to Glasgow and that it would be fraught with naughty tarmac, so she offered to drive me over the planned course on her way to dropping me at the start of the day's run in Stirling. It had taken me a while to pull my face out of my cereal that morning, and I'd had to have two coffees before I felt human. I was particularly tired, and my muscles felt like guitar strings pulled so tight that they could snap at any moment. I was looking out of the car window, scanning the tarmac and surface I'd be running on and summoning up the energy for a 21-mile day of running, when I heard the sound of the car indicator.

'So, this is the start of the climb,' said Claire, taking a left turn onto a narrow, winding road.

'The climb?' I asked.

'Up the mountain.'

'The mountain?'

'Yes, the mountain,' she laughed. 'You do know that the route you've picked means you're running over the Campsie Fells today?'

'The Campsie Fells. . .' I let the name roll around in my

brain. I'd heard it before; it sounded vaguely familiar, but I'd been route planning on a simple street map with no elevation profile, so. . . no, I'd had no idea I'd be running over them.

'Yep. . . These mountains are really popular with cyclists. This road is one of the top climbs in Britain,' Claire smiled.

It now made sense why there were so few roads between Stirling and Glasgow. There were mountains in the way. The moment I realised I would be heading into the mountains, I caught sight of something in the corner of my mind. It dashed out of sight before I could get a good look at it, but I could swear it was excitement. Despite my tired feet and my delirious brain, the Campsies had just served up a giant wodge of challenge cake with a side helping of lung-busting scenery sauce and, when placed alongside the prospect of a day of same-same drudgery, running up a mountain sounded wildly appealing. I grabbed the tail end of that excitement and held on tight as the car swerved around bends and we wound our way up, up, up into the clouds.

Running over the Campsies turned out to be just what the doctor ordered. The big, strong Anna in my mind was out in full force and, once out of Stirling, I followed a country road which ran alongside a stream and passed through clusters of shady woodland before opening out onto a wild and wind-swept plain. Patches of brown-topped long grass and white wildflowers lined the road as it rose and fell over small undulations, steadily climbing all the while. It was a cool day, I was running in light drizzle, and the road reminded me a lot of places I'd visited in Wales. All open and exposed, with only nature for company and not another soul in sight.

I was accompanied by a couple of runners (and a dog and a lady on a scooter) for the first few miles out of Stirling but, after that, I ran alone for the bulk of the day, which seemed to suit the solitary mood of the Campsies perfectly. I settled into my own personal rhythm, enjoying the dull throb in my quad muscles as I sucked in lungfuls of mountain air which smelled of pine and vanilla. It started to rain heavily around lunchtime, but I didn't mind. It was warm enough, and the water beneath my feet made the road surface softer. Soon, my hair became sodden. Water dripped from the front of my visor and splashed onto my legs as I passed a large reservoir, joined the main road through the fells and started the final big climb of the day.

There were now 7 miles to go and I could feel my engine start to falter, but I refused to let it. I was enjoying myself too much — so I focused on watching the white lines at the edge of the road move beneath me and let my feet carry me onwards. Softly splashing through puddles on the now sodden road, chug, chug, chugging towards the summit of the pass at Campsie Glen. There was a new burning sensation in my lungs and I relished it. It was refreshing to have pain in an area of my body that wasn't my feet, and I felt fit. I felt strong. I now felt like I could keep going forever, munching up the mountain miles. I settled into a groove and stayed in that glorious zone for an hour, until the top arrived.

At the summit of the climb, a local runner called Vincent was waiting at the side of the road. He was wearing a fluorescent orange top and his personality matched the brightness of his attire. The effort I'd put into the climb was starting to catch up with me, but Vincent's delight at managing to use my GPS tracker to find me was enough to fuel the final few miles. Together, we floated down the other side and into Lennoxtown.

The following day, Vincent's family came to wave me off from the start line, and I was joined by a large group for the journey from Lennoxtown into the centre of Glasgow. The group and I followed the Forth and Clyde Canal and turned the run stage into an unofficial litter pick, stopping to gather rubbish en route, collecting it in plastic bags and depositing it in nearby bins as we ran. On account of all of the smashed glass bottles I dodged on the way in, I believe that the city should officially be renamed Glassgow, but my feet and I survived and we ended the run at St George's Square in the centre of the city.

That evening, I checked in on the Barefoot Britain Facebook group and saw there was a post from Vincent.

Loved running with Anna yesterday! A real honour. The whole family came along to see her off this morning as she headed for Glasgow and my sister even joined in for a few miles. My youngest kid, Lewis (aged 3), kept asking throughout the day whether the 'Pink Lady' had finished her run yet. We kept him updated until she reached Glasgow and asked him whether he'd like to go running with Anna in bare feet. He looked very worried and said, 'Me no have the bear feet.' As it turned out, he was concerned that the 'Pink Lady' had stolen the bear's feet, and wanted to know when she planned on returning them to the bear.

Despite being a wanted woman for having stolen a local bear's feet, it was lovely to be back in Glasgow, a place I was fond of and had visited many times before. But this time around, I'd just be passing through. I was eager to keep pushing east as fast as I could because I was running towards a precious few days of rest — and a long-awaited reunion with someone very special.

ANNA MCNUFF

13

Loved up and Piped Out

Edinburgh is one of the best cities in Britain. There is a long list of things I love about the place and most of them are subtleties. I love how, on cold mornings, the cobbles glisten with frost, appearing like a sea of precious gems, set into stone walkways. And when the rain blows in (as it often does), I love how it pours through the streets, weaving between those cobbles like glistening tributaries of a river delta.

I love the ornate neoclassical buildings — how they turn honey-coloured in the dawn light and glow amber at dusk. I love that you can escape city life at Holyrood Park. And how wild or calm it can be up on Arthur's Seat at the highest point, depending on the weather. I love how, from up on a hill, the city looks like a giant chessboard, each landmark an ornately carved piece, moved into position and frozen by time. The imposing spire of the Scott monument on Queen Street (which I've always thought looks like a rocket ship, ready for take-off), the tall, round tower and Grecian-style pillars of the National Monument up on Calton Hill, the spire of St Giles' Cathedral — which resembles a crown fit for a king. But most of all, I love the city at night, when the maze of secret stairwells and hidden alleyways are flooded with moonbeams. When all is quiet and the skies are awash with sparkle, the city feels the most alive.

Needless to say, Edinburgh holds a special place in my heart. Cities like Edinburgh were part of the reason why my route through Britain was so very wiggly — I wanted to really soak up everything the country had to offer. The bits I'd yet to fall in love with and those I was already head over heels for. Considering my love for Edinburgh, it seemed like the perfect place to meet up with Jamie for the first time since starting the run. It'd been six weeks and 700 miles of barefootin' since I'd last seen him.

Although we'd spoken most nights over the phone, and six weeks was a short time apart compared to what we'd done in the past, I missed him. So, when there was a knock on the door of my hotel room in Edinburgh's Haymarket district, I felt a tingle of excitement in my belly. I swung open the door to see a handsome devil of a man standing opposite me. Strong jaw, dark eyebrows, green eyes, five o'clock shadow and a cheeky smile. I noticed he had more grey hairs around his temples than when I'd seen him last, but I took that as an indication that he was well on his way to joining the George Clooney salt 'n' pepper hair club, and dang, that was sexy. There was a familiar yellow and black backpack slung over his shoulders, and he was wearing shorts and flip flops.

'Heeyyyyy,' he said, opening his arms wide for a hug. I rested my head on his shoulder and wrapped my arms around him, letting my body collapse into his. If there was one thing Jamie excelled at, it was looking after me. Knowing he could do that for the next few days was a welcome relief.

After my repeated struggles with sleep down the east coast, I'd decided that Edinburgh called for an extended break. Since leaving Shetland, I'd only taken one or two days of rest in a row, but the reality was that a rest day was filled with so much admin that I couldn't properly relax or recover. I was putting Polyfilla over the cracks rather than fixing the issue. And that left me permanently running on fumes. So, in Edinburgh, I planned to take four whole days off from running. Glorious.

It also didn't take me long to decide that Jamie and I were long overdue a date. I'd let him know to pack his skinny jeans (which always made me fancy him) and a clean T-shirt (a rarity), and that we would be having a date night while in the city. I'd even gone to the effort of splashing out £10 on buying a long black dress from a charity shop in Glasgow, so that I matched his skinny-jeans effort. On our first night together, I threw on the dress and we looked like an ordinary couple as we stepped out onto the town. Only the dirty, hardened soles hiding beneath my flip-flops and the sharp tan lines on my arms gave the game away.

As we left the hotel, hand in hand, darkness was beginning to fall, and my fondness for the city came flooding back. I thought briefly back to the first trip I'd made to the city five years earlier, just before we'd got together, and how life — and the city — now seemed richer with his hand in mine. I loved

Edinburgh, but I loved Jamie more. It was a double love-in and that made me all kinds of happy. So much so that I really did forget, if only for a few hours, that I was 700 miles into a 2,600-mile run. I'd sneaked through a portal into another time and place where, for that night, I was just an anonymous body in the city on a date with the man I loved.

I spent the following few days catching up on admin (sometimes in the bath and sometimes out of it), eating, drinking and sleeping. And, thanks to a new addition to my sole care kit, I was sleeping better than ever. A woman called Anna Hill in Glasgow had given me St John's Wort Oil to rub on my soles.

'It helps with nerve damage,' she said, and help it did.

I'd slather it on them before bed and it would keep the tingling at bay. That tiny bottle of oil really was a game changer. Where my nights were once full of tingling feet, they were now full of sleep and a renewed confidence that my feet were finally adapting.

One afternoon, I did a photoshoot for the cover of Women's Running magazine in Holyrood Park and, that evening, I visited the Scottish Girlguiding HQ to give a talk to the girls and leaders who'd gathered there. I also had a visit from the Body Goddess, Sylvia, who happened to be visiting the UK from America. I had convinced her to come up to Edinburgh so that she could treat me with her trigger-point therapy in person. Sylvia poked and prodded me for two hours on the hotel-room floor and fine-tuned my bod like it was an F1 racing car. Okay, it was more like a Hot Rod, but the engine was soon well-greased again and purring like a pussycat. Edinburgh was the reset I so desperately needed and, come the evening of the fourth day, I was ready for the road again. It felt like I'd ticked another giant milestone off and I also knew that, in a few days' time, I'd be running into England and leaving the Scottish portion of the journey behind.

***

Despite all of the R & R, when I opened my eyes on the morning I was due to leave the city, my heart was pounding and my chest felt tight. I lay still for a moment, staring at the ceiling, trying to pin down exactly what it was that was making me anxious. I recalled a dream I'd been having about putting on a rock concert in a large theatre, which looked like the Royal Albert Hall. I couldn't remember who was in the line-up for the concert and people kept coming up to me and asking who was playing. It was then that I remembered I hadn't actually booked anyone to play. Worst of all, I hadn't bought the bread for the lunch. Can you imagine. No bread for lunch?! Everyone had bought tickets and they were going to watch an empty stage and have no food for the interval. I had this overwhelming feeling I was going to let everyone down.

I let out a breath and threw back the covers. Whatever that was about, there wasn't time to dwell on it. I gave Jamie a long hug and an even longer goodbye smooch and felt sad knowing that it would be at least a month before I saw him again. But he had work to get back to in Gloucester, and I had an adventure to be getting on with too. I packed up my stuff, then headed out the door to meet a group of runners outside Girlguiding HQ to begin the journey towards the Scottish Borders.

I was running 15 minutes late (as was tradition), so I put a little skip in my step as I rounded the bend at midday, to see a group of 30 people gathered outside Scottish Girlguiding HQ. There was a loud cheer from the crowd and I noticed that the majority of them were women. Many of them were in running gear, but there were a few who looked like they'd just come down to wave me off in their lunch hour. It was by far the largest crowd I'd had run with me on a public stage so far, and any nerves I'd had that morning disappeared in puff of excitement.

'Right. . . Does anyone know the way to England?' I asked the group and they laughed. 'I'm serious,' I said, and they soon realised I was only half-joking. I'd chosen a vague route out of the city, but locals always knew best, so I was up for following someone else's lead, at least to get me out of the city.

'What route are you taking?' asked a woman in a visor.

'I was thinking of going via. . . err, hang on. . .' I said, pulling out my phone to check the map. 'The Grange, then Gracemount and then Bonnyrigg?'

'I can get you as far as Gracemount,' said a young woman at the back of the group.

'Marvellous. What's your name?'

'Katie.'

'Okay, everyone. Katie's in charge. She knows what she's doing. Everyone follow Katie.' The group laughed again.

After a few hugs and many smiles, we were ready for the off. I gathered everyone into a group behind my camera to film the start of the run stage.

'Ready, Team Edinburgh?'

'Yeaaaahhhh!' came the chorus.

'Okay, let's start a countdown together. . . ten. . . nine. . . eight . . . bugger!' I said, looking down at my backpack. It was missing one of the straps which went across my chest to help support the pack. It must have fallen off over past few days and I hadn't noticed. It'd be a nightmare to run with it like that — the pack would bounce all over the place. 'Does anyone have a piece of rope, or a string or something to tie this up with?' I tugged at the two sides at the front of the pack. A woman's hand shot out from the crowd with two small hairbands in her palm.

'Brilliant! Thank you. They'll do. I probably need a few more though. . . anyone else got a spare hairband?'

Another three hands shot forward. I linked four hairbands together, then fastened them to the backpack. I jumped up and down on the spot to check that the bands would withstand the weight of the pack across my chest, and they seemed to do the trick. Crisis averted. Marvellous. If ever I was in doubt as to who might be able to fix a backpack malfunction, it was a group of hairband-wielding women outside a Girlguiding HQ.

Following Katie's lead, we bobbed and weaved through the city streets, taking lefts and rights, parting and coming back together around pedestrians on the pavement. We passed the imposing stone building of the Usher Hall, a Nando's, and a couple of kebab shops and then skirted the edge of the Meadows — a beautiful carpet of green amid a city of stone where students and tourists lazed on blankets in the afternoon sun. Just as had been the case in Aberdeen, I was lost in chat, distracted from feeling self-conscious about running through the city with no shoes on. After 30 minutes, those who had nipped out to join me on their lunch break peeled off to head back to work, and 15 of us forged on.

Over the next hour, we followed cycleways and pavements through suburbia. We waited patiently to cross at large ugly A-road roundabouts, and runners left us at intervals. Each of them left with thanks and a hug, and Katie the navigator got an extra big thanks when she bowed out at Gracemount. Gradually, the houses and cars lessened, there were more and more green fields and fewer pavements to run on alongside the roads. At 13 miles, we made it to a pub in Bonnyrigg. I'm not sure what the regulars thought of a 10-strong group of brightly dressed, sweaty women tumbling through the door of their local at 3 p.m. but they treated us kindly, parting to let us go to the front of the bar and order up some drinks and grub. It was another hot day again, and I decided that there was just as much salt on my forearms as there was on my salted peanuts.

The majority of the remaining run gang left to get the train back from Bonnyrigg, leaving just three of us to complete the full 22-mile stage to Heriot in the Scottish Borders. As we left the pub, I was struck by how quiet it was, now that there were only three of us padding down country lanes. Much of the day had been noisy — cars, fumes, people, chatter, the thud of trainers on pavements — and I'd been surrounded by the cacophony of a city and its urban sprawl. And in the wake of all of that, the calm of the afternoon felt heightened. I liked it. I liked both things, in fact: a morning of madness and an afternoon of peace.

I think that any day should unfold like a good piece of classical music. There are always those parts in the music where things go bananas (this is a technical term) and everything is loud and intense. Someone's crashing cymbals and going at it with a tuba like there's no tomorrow. But then comes the calm. A flute, a soft violin, a sultry clarinet. And suddenly, the spaces in between the notes feel almost as important as the notes themselves. Energy and calm were my running yin and yang and I let that sense of completeness power me on through the afternoon.

By early evening, our fandango of three was still going strong and I felt wonderful. I had forgotten what it was like to come towards the end of day of running and still have energy left. We started up a long hill and had a cracking 180-degree view of the surrounding countryside. Meadows of long grass and clusters of trees stretched beneath a cloud-filled sky and led to the hazy outline of the Pentland Hills in the distance.

As the incline kicked up, the chatter between the three of us died away and we chugged upwards in virtual silence — the only sound was our breathing and the wind moving through the grass beside us. I looked out over the fields and exhaled. My mind was clear, and my body felt fantastic. I stretched my arms out to the side of me as I ran and let the warm air move over my palms. I watched the sun dip between a gap in the clouds and hover above the peaks of the Pentlands — a ball of burning golden light which set the fields ablaze. I was barefoot, running up a mountain in Scotland, in the warm summer air. And, in that moment, heaven was a place on Earth.

Over the following few days, I tracked east across the Scottish Borders. It rained on and off, but it wasn't long before the heat of the summer returned with full force. Sweat poured down my back and chest once again and my teeth were coated in a claggy dust, which got stuck on my tongue when I ran it across them. On one day, I celebrated reaching the 18-mile marker by sitting in the shade of a local cafe for an hour. They were serving ice-cold, frothy-topped chocolate milkshakes in mason jars and that seemed like the perfect thing to wash away the road grime in my mouth. I was partway through slurping down the remains of a second milky marvel when a blue car pulled into the gravel car park at the front of the cafe. It stopped right by where I was sitting and a woman in the passenger seat wound down the window.

'You must be Anna?' she said, smiling.

'That's me!' I replied as the woman stepped out of the car.

I did a double take. There was something so familiar about her. She had high cheekbones, a pale complexion, piercing blue eyes and a welcoming smile. Her hair was curly, dark-blonde and cut short, just above her shoulders. They were the kind of curls that if you gave them a gentle downward tug would spring right back up onto her head. I didn't think I'd ever met this woman before, but I felt a rush of emotion when I looked at her. There was a warmth, a memory from some-where. I looked again. She was the spitting image of my nan.

'Aww, how are you doing?' I said, opening my arms for a hug. Regardless of whether or not I'd met her before, I felt compelled to hug her.

'You don't know who I am, do you?' the woman said. I released her from the squeeze and eyed her closely. 'We're re-lated, aren't we?'

'We certainly are. I'm your dad's cousin, Lee.'

'Ah, that makes sense! You look like the spit of my nan, you know. . .' I said.

'Ah, that'll be my Auntie Helen.'

Lee's Auntie Helen was my 'Nanny Nuff'. Her full name was Helen MacGregor MacPherson McNuff. I wasn't sure if you could get a name more Celtic than that if you tried. Even Jamie's dad — Donald McDonald — didn't come close. My nan was a tour de force — ice-blue eyes, bold energy and lots of theatrics. She had 13 brothers and sisters, and a lot of nieces and nephews, so getting everyone in the same place at the same time was a challenge and I'd still yet to meet many of my Scottish rellies. Sadly, Nanny Nuff passed away when I was in my early teens, but I had many fond memories of her, and it was lovely to be reminded of those in meeting Lee.

Lee and her husband had been keeping tabs on my progress for a few weeks. That day, they'd been hiking nearby and seen that my tracker had stopped at the cafe, so they seized the chance to say hello. Lee spoke softly and had a calming energy about her, so I was enjoying her company. I chatted with her for 15 minutes and then the conversation started to come to a natural close.

'Now, before I go, here's an important question,' Lee said.

'Go on.'

'Is your dad as handsome as always?'

'He is,' I replied. If that wasn't too weird a thing to say about my dad.

'Och, he was always such a wee darlin'!' She beamed and I nearly melted at the expression. Her accent was something I loved so much about the Scottish side of my family.

I ran away from Lee brimming with energy. Not the kind of short sharp fix that might only last a few hours, but something more nourishing, like I'd just been reminded of the deeper connection I had with the country I'd been travelling through for six weeks. It was the weirdest thing. It had taken me running through most of Scotland in my bare feet to meet one of my Scottish relatives for the first time. Wasn't life a wonder?

***

A day later, the chat around the dinner table turned to bagpipes. Anna Hill — giver of St John's Wort Oil in Glasgow and saviour of my soles — had sorted for me to stay with her mother and father-in-law on my last night in Scotland. I'd just discovered that Donald, her father-in-law, could play the bagpipes. I'd always found bagpipes to be a fascinating instrument. The sound is synonymous with Scotland, and I could never quite work out how so much noise could come from inside one small animal-skin bag and a load of wooden pipes.

'When you leave Kelso in the morning, I'll pipe you out,' Donald smiled.

I laughed and carried on eating because surely, he was joking. But come the following morning, Donald appeared in the breakfast room wearing long white socks, a white shirt, a kilt and a sporran.

'Oooh, you look lovely. Are you off somewhere nice today?' I asked.

'I am. We are. To Kelso. This is for you.'

'What?'

'He's piping you out,' Anna said, taking a sip of tea.

'You're what? But I. . . I thought you were joking?!'

'Not at all. It's a fitting way for you to leave, and it'll make sure they look after you over the border,' Donald said, matter-of-factly.

I couldn't believe it. It seemed like an awful lot of effort to get dressed up in full Scotty attire, and to get the bagpipes out, just for me.

It's difficult to describe the feeling I had, standing outside Kelso Abbey, with Donald — the one-man bagpipe band — piping for me. Well, really he was piping for us — me and the group of runners who had turned up to join in. I decided he was playing those pipes for everyone who had helped me in Scotland. For Jane on Unst for getting me started. For the girls who made me a bracelet on Yell. For Shona and the Manson Massive. For Gill and Jim (and Biscuit the cat) and lovely Jenny Graham too. For all of the other hosts who had given me a bed for the night and fed me. For every runner who had laced up their shoes and come out to play, for those who had ferried my kit bag along and anyone else who had kept me on the road and kept me moving.

I felt a swell in my chest and a wave of sadness. I had loved immersing myself in everything Scotland had to offer — its pristine beaches, rugged coastline, windswept moors, boggy bogs, towering mountains and meandering rivers. I had failed to learn to like whisky, but I had loved getting to know Scotland better. In fact, I had adored it. And I knew that there would now forever be a piece of my heart painted white and blue.

'The North'

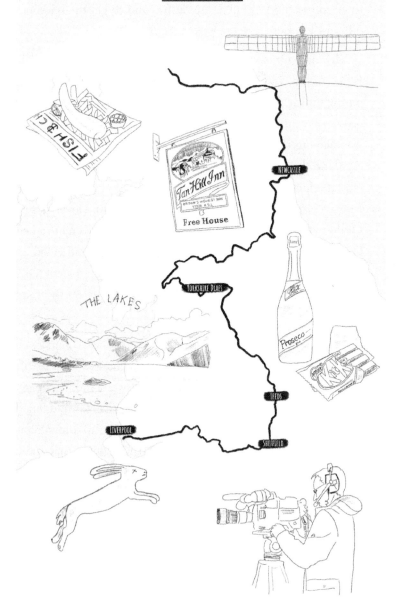

14.

Operation: Sandy Soles

There is a deep-rooted part of me which believes that you shouldn't be allowed to even think about reaping a reward until you have worked really, really hard. There is, however, a radical, alternative school of thought, which is that not everything in life has to be quite so difficult. If there is an easy — or easier — option available, we can take that and it's not a crime to do so. It doesn't cast a shadow on our character. It doesn't say we are lazy. It is, in fact, a neat way to make things effortless whenever you can.

Since leaving Skaw Beach at Shetland, I had learned many things about my self-imposed hardship. Mostly, I had learned that I sometimes make things more difficult for myself than is absolutely necessary. I hop eagerly aboard the struggle bus so that I might feel worthy to claim any rewards that come my way. Even if that reward is something as simple as taking a day off from running. But after having experienced the effortless joy of running barefoot for 7 miles along Balmedie Beach into Aberdeen, I decided that there was the option to get off the struggle bus at any time. If I could find some more sandy beaches and make things easier on my body, then that's just what I would do.

So, before leaving Scotland, I'd put a post out online, asking the general public if they knew of any long stretches of sand. There was a flurry of responses. Some of them recommended places which were too far off-route like the Outer Hebrides, West Wales, Cornwall and Norfolk — but there was one set of replies which caught my eye.

Northumberland! The beaches there are amazing and if you timed it right with the tides you could run on sand for miles and miles — @VickyandRuby

Druridge bay in Northumberland is a lovely bit of beach — @Joannae29

Totally agree with Northumberland for the best long sandy beaches! — @Sarahlredman

Northumberland? Did they have beaches there? All I knew about Northumberland was that it was home to Newcastle upon Tyne, a city famed for its wild nightlife, a deep love of football and for being the birthplace of Byker Grove-boys-turned-TV-presenter-superstars Ant and Dec. I'd never heard about any beaches there, but after the case put forward by Team Northumberland, I was ready to launch a full investigation.

Originally, I'd intended to take an inland route from Kelso to Newcastle. Heading onto the coast would mean adding an extra 40 miles to the route, cancelling two public running stages and working out how I could still make it inland to a Girlguiding talk that was booked for the end of the week. But when placed next to the prospect of some carefree jogging on glorious golden sand, these seemed like minor issues. The Northumberland coast was calling me. Operation: Sandy Soles was a GO.

I spent my first night across the border in England in a room above a pub in the small town of Wooler. It was a cosy place. Large rough blocks of grey stone on the outside, a wooden bar, regal red carpets and an ornate seventeenth-century fireplace on the inside. The smell of ale and pork scratchings filled my bedroom and the sound of punters clinking glasses in the bar went on late into the night, but when I ran out of town the following morning, I felt bright and breezy, ready to greet my first full day of running through England's green and pleasant land with open arms. And it really was green and pleasant. A checkerboard of grassy fields rolled off towards the horizon, broken only by the faint grey line of a road or gravel track. Frilly hedgerows ran between the fields and clusters of trees were dotted here and there — the kind that looked like florets of broccoli: thick trunks and big bushy green tops. There'd been a thunderstorm overnight and the roads were still wet, so there was a strong smell of hot summer rain as I padded over the cool pavement and out of town.

Heading east, I followed a mixture of trail and road, hopping on and off an ancient pathway called St Cuthbert's

Way. I didn't know much about St Cuthbert, but I'd googled him while in Wooler and discovered that he is (or was) rather famous. Born in 634 AD, St Cuthbert is the patron saint of northern England and is widely described as a preacher, a monk and a hermit. I'm sure he'd have had exactly those three words on his business card back in the day. St Cuthbert was responsible for leading the charge in northern England for conversion to Roman Christianity and, in his later years, he retired to Inner Farne Island, off the Northumberland coast, not far from the Holy Island of Lindisfarne. He even built himself a wall so that he couldn't see the mainland from his little patch of island paradise.

After the excitement of being piped out of Scotland, I too was in search of some solitude. . . and the quiet back roads of Northumberland delivered it. I was enjoying the peace and quiet so much that I ran without listening to any music or podcasts. There was only the sound of my feet padding beneath me, the rhythm of my breath and the 'sssh' noise as one of my arms repeatedly caught the side of my backpack midway through its swing. On days like those, nothing felt complicated. I was at one with the landscape and the task at hand, and that led me to wonder whether I was overdramatising the whole adventure. It was just a run, after all. All I had to do each day was get up, move my legs and keep making forward progress, however easy or difficult that may be.

Of course, I made things more difficult for myself by running a mile in the wrong direction on the trail. But aside from that navigational faux pas, my first day in England was a belter. I continued on St Cuthbert's Way for as long as I could, enjoying its soft squishy grass underfoot. I followed it over stiles, through hip-height ferns and up short, sharp hills with panoramic views of the surrounding landscape. In the early afternoon, I left the trail behind and kept heading east along quiet back roads towards the coast. I could smell the sea air and glimpsed blue-grey waters in the distance between hedgerows. When the silhouette of Bamburgh Castle appeared, I let out a squeal. It looked picture-perfect — a square, central tower, surrounded by turrets, perched on a grassy mound above the dunes of Bamburgh Beach. The brown-grey stones had taken on a rusty glow in the afternoon sun, and it seemed like something out of a child's toy set. I wanted to reach out, pluck it from the landscape and put it in my pocket, saving it for a day when I needed to remember just how fabulous Britain was. Beyond the castle, the Farne Islands were just about visible through the offshore mist. I could make out the tall tower of Farne Lighthouse and, not for the first time in the journey, I wished I had more time to explore.

As late afternoon turned to evening, I headed south, weaving slowly towards the sandy beaches, taking lefts and rights along backcountry lanes just inland from the coast. I hadn't spoken to anyone all day, so I began to enjoy the odd interruption from passers-by and local wildlife. A man on a white horse clip-clopped past, nodding as he went. A pigeon cooed from the bough of a nearby tree. A black hen bobbed across the road in front of me, her steps as jerky as mine had become in the last hour, and I wondered if she'd had a long day on her bare feet too. I passed a woman and her dog who were leaving the road to head off through a gate and onto a footpath in an adjacent field. The woman stopped and did a double take.

'You've got no shoes on!' she said.

'You're right,' I smiled.

'Are you sure that's a good idea?' she pressed.

'It's absolutely a good idea!' I shouted over my shoulder, almost out of earshot. And I actually meant it.

Eventually, I transitioned from the road to the beach and ran on soft sand beside the dunes, as seaweed pawed at the shoreline. I passed through sleepy seaside towns and smiled at the procession of early evening dog walkers — poo bags in one hand and balls to throw in the other. Wafts of sickly-sweet cigar smoke escaped from dimly lit pubs and fused with the warm summer air, reminding me of when my uncle used to visit and smoke Hamlets in the garden when I was a kid. Hungry holidaymakers dressed in beach shorts and scrappy vests emerged from glass-fronted fish and chip shops, clutching precious newspaper parcels dotted with patches of fat. Smells of malt vinegar and freshly cooked chips filled the air, and my stomach began to rumble. I pressed on, on the lookout for a place to lay my head for the night after covering 23 miles, so that I could do it all over again tomorrow.

On the second day of running down the coast, I'd just left the beach at High Newton-by-the-Sea and was passing a row of small, terraced houses with long, narrow front gardens, when I heard a shout.

'Nooooo!'

I stopped and looked back down the road behind me. There was no one in sight, so I assumed I'd imagined the call and set off again. Perhaps auditory hallucinations were all part of the underlying fatigue.

'Noooo! No, No, No,' came the voice again, and this time I identified it as having a thick Geordie accent. Unless I really was hallucinating, the voice had to belong to someone.

To my right, a grey-haired man appeared from behind a bush in his front garden. In one hand, he was clutching a walking stick and waving it in the air. He stopped when he reached his waist-high white front gate.

'Hello?' I said.

'No,' he replied.

'No?'

'No.'

'Yes?'

'Nooo. You cannie be runnin' with no shoes on.'

'Oh, really?'

'No. You'll get plantar fasciitis.' His eyes were wide with a look of deep concern. I smiled. For him to be worrying on my behalf about an injury to the arch of my foot was very specific and quite touching.

ANNA MCNUFF

'Oh, I'll be okay, thank you. I've run from Shetland and no sign of plantar ye—'

'Nooo!' he interrupted. 'I've had it. I tell ya! And it's agony!'

'Ah, I'm sure it is b—'

'Oooh, you'll get it if you carry on like that,' he interrupted, pointing at my feet. 'You. Will. Get. It,' he said again, this time with extra staccato to make sure that I had fully grasped the gravity of the situation.

It was at that point I realised it didn't really matter what I said in reply. I could have told this man I was a tap-dancing unicorn from outer space, and he would have ploughed on with his deep concern for my feet and the impending plantar-fasciitis doom, regardless. His mind was made up.

'Well, I better get going,' I smiled, starting up into a run and moving away. The man opened his front gate and shuffled out onto the street after me, shouting again. 'Noooo! Plantar Fasciiitisssss!' he called as I ran around the bend and out of sight.

I couldn't help but laugh as I made my way to the other end of town. On some days, I would have found the man's insistence irritating, but I found it more funny than annoying. I thought the concern was sweet. And, in reality, what I'd just witnessed was a classic fear vomit. He literally couldn't hold in his fears about plantar fasciitis. Convinced I would get the injury because that's what had happened to him, he had scattergun vomited his fear all over my running gear. I was used to it by now. I had been dodging my own fears about the journey, as well as the fears of others, since even before the run began. Sometimes, those fears came in the form of a comment online, sometimes they were delivered by well-meaning friends (who you'd really rather hadn't said anything at all). And, sometimes, a fear vomit would appear out of nowhere, charging at you from down the garden with grey hair on its head, waving a stick from beyond a white picket fence and shouting at you about plantar fasciitis. When that happens, it's best to smile, brush the fear vomit from your shoulders and carry on as you were.

Beyond High Newton-by-the-Sea, the days of running along the coast all began to merge into one. I'd put in an order with the Ministry of Marvellous Surfaces for some miles of smooth and easy coastal running and my request had been granted. The overwhelming memory I have of that week is one of real beauty — pockets of seaside activity with vast stretches of golden sand in between, often with nothing but the clouds and the wind for company.

After Bamburgh, the castles came thick and fast. Dunstanburgh Castle, near Craster, was a firm favourite — a spectacular jumble of crumbling grey, perched on a section of grassy land cut off from the road and only accessible by foot. As I followed a trail around the base of the castle, I was suddenly engulfed by a swarm of orange and black.

'Butterflies!' I shouted as they fluttered around my head.

I stopped running and stood stock-still — there were dozens

of them and even more resting on top of the long grass next to me. I'd never seen quite so many butterflies in one place. Well, perhaps on a David Attenborough documentary, but never in real life. I imagined that the butterflies knew about the run, somehow. They were beating their tiny wings as hard as they could to cheer me on and propel me onwards down the coast.

The further south in Northumberland I got, the more the word spread about my change in route. There were no officially organised public running stages on the coast, but people still found me from time to time by using my GPS tracker, and those who thought I would be running inland discovered that I was now barefootin' right by their front door.

One afternoon, near Amble, a red car beeped at me then pulled into a lay-by up ahead. The supporter was a man with round glasses, a ginger beard with flecks of white in it and a smile that took over his whole face. He'd just finished his last day working for English Heritage at the nearby Warkworth Castle and said that he knew I was in the area so he had left work early to see if he could find me. He proclaimed himself a 'master stalker' and asked if he could poke the soles of my feet. Of course, I agreed. After he'd marvelled at just how hard my soles were, I dished out a hug and waved him on his way.

Ten minutes later, another man pulled his white van over at the side of the road. He was wearing a race finisher's T-shirt and looked as fit as a fiddle as he hopped out and bounded alongside me, insisting that I carried on running while we chatted so that I could keep my momentum.

'Anna, so glad I've found you! I knew you were in the area, and I was driving by, and there you were! I just love what you're doing,' he said.

'Ah, thank you. And thanks for tracking me down,' I said.

'Total pleasure. And your message that girls are hard. . . or something. It's really inspiring.'

'That's exactly the message,' I laughed. We chatted for a while longer, and he asked if his wife and daughter could join me for a run out of town in the morning. I told him it was the more the merrier.

'Well, I'd better go. Keep it up, Anna!' the man shouted, peeling off and pumping his fist into the air. And with that, he was gone.

Each brief exchange with a supportive stranger like these two made it feel like what I was doing actually mattered — that the run affected someone other than just me. It was easy to forget that during the miles spent alone in my head.

The scenery and unexpected visits from cheery supporters through Northumberland really helped to distract me from the long days, but by the time I made the outskirts of Blyth, the extra miles I'd run along the coast had caught up with me. I'd covered 100 miles over the past week and the wheels on my one-woman wagon were threatening to fall off. I first noticed it when I was running with two other women on a national cycle route alongside the River Blyth. I was enjoying the smell of fresh rain on the ground and the sound of it dripping through the leaves of the trees. But when the cranes and boats at the Port of Blyth came into view, something changed. My legs felt weird. Hollow. As if there was nothing in them but air. My pace slowed dramatically and all of my muscles ached. It happened so suddenly, like someone had flipped a switch. I only had 2 miles left to run for the day, but it might as well have been a marathon. I did my best to keep a smile on my face and keep chatting, but my mind was whirring. I was used to having tired legs, but this was different. And what was really worrying me was that the lack of spring in my step was accompanied by a new, tugging sensation in my right calf.

Despite the calf niggle and hollow legs, I pushed on for a further 23 miles to Newcastle the following day. Arriving in the city put me back on track with the original running route, which meant that I now had big groups of runners joining in — I had places to be and people expecting me to be there. There was no time to be injured. And besides, when faced with the prospect of thinking about a potential problem or sweeping it under the rug, I am often one to reach for the broom. So, even though I was concerned about the pain in my calf, I decided not to think about it (it's really a very good tactic, you know). Business as usual, I told myself. I got my oversized barefoot broom out and I swept away. Sweep, sweep. I ran some more. Sweep. I gave some talks. Sweep. I told myself the calf would miraculously heal overnight. Sweep, sweep.. until, my calf went POP!

Thirteen miles into what was supposed to be a 25-mile run to Newton Aycliffe, and a bolt of pain shot up the back of my leg. It felt like an electric shock—which I translated as the muscles shouting, 'FOR GOODNESS SAKES, ANNA, WILL YOU LISTEN TO US?!' Immediately afterwards, I was reduced to limping and I knew I had to stop. I told the kind and patient group of runners I was with that I wouldn't be going any further that day and felt terrible about it. A few of them said that they were relieved that they'd only need to run 13 miles and not 25, which somewhat eased the blow, even if they were making it up.

I was ferried home by a local family — the Barnetts — and that evening, I called Sylvia (the body goddess) to get her advice. She was now back in California and, as usual, she sent the most calming video message. She instructed me to use my fists at the point where the curve of the calf muscle dips up behind the knee and said to 'squeeze my calf like a juice box' from both sides. It sounded bizarre, but I knew to trust Sylvia. So, I followed the instructions, and I squeezed that lower leg as if it were a carton of Um Bongo.

She also gave me instructions to release a second set of trigger points at the bottom of the calf and signed off her video message by saying: 'Now, Anna, it's gonna hurt like hell, but you need to go hard. Don't back off until that muscle releases. Don't do it more than once, just do it, do it right. And hard.' I poked around on my lower leg until I found a tender spot, just where Sylvia said it would be. I took a deep breath and jammed my thumb into the muscle and began to count backwards from ten, breathing deeply through a wave of nausea until the pain subsided.

After a chat with Jamie, who reminded me (as always) that I still had plenty of time to make it to London, I took an unplanned day of rest in Newton Aycliffe to allow the calf to calm down. I tried to stay positive over those 24 hours. To be honest, I was amazed that in the 830 miles I had run so far, I'd only had to deal with one major muscle complaint.

Much to my surprise, on the second morning in Newton Aycliffe, my calf had gone from zero to hero. There was a red patch on it and a dull ache but no pain at all. I tentatively walked from the bedroom, down the stairs and into the kitchen and still. . . no pain. It seemed too good to be true — had Sylvia's juice-box therapy done the trick?!

Over the following few days, I tried my best to be sensible (well, more sensible than usual). I dropped the mileage back down and built it up again slowly, from 16 miles, then 18. . . nudging up towards 20+ mile days, which was the distance I was covering before my calf had thrown its toys out of the pram. The major bonus of having kind hosts in the area was that I didn't always have to run to a set destination. Logistics Queen Abby had made sure they were kept up to date on where I was and how I was getting along, and I knew it would only take them an extra five minutes to whizz down the road to collect me, if I ran more or less on any given day. So, not only were these kind strangers giving me bed and board, but they were now acting as my rehab crew.

One afternoon, I was thinking a lot about the calf injury and realised that, in attempting to ignore my body's cries for help, I'd narrowly avoided a disaster. I wasn't entirely sure how — it had to be luck of some form — but my body was quick to pick up an injury and quick to heal. I was grateful to my bod for putting up with me as I continued to put it through the wringer. It felt like I'd been on the edge of a precipice, about to tumble into it, and at the last moment, a safety rope had pulled me back from the drop. And yet, in a strange way, I drew strength from it. Much as I hated all of the unknowing when there was an interruption to the flow of the journey, each time I came out the other side, I felt stronger. Wiser. Braver. Like I'd unlocked a little room in my castle of confidence I didn't even know was there. There was no doubt I'd gone boom and bust on the Northumberland coast but, with the support of Sylvia, cheery roadside supporters and those kind hosts, I'd managed to scramble my way back on track.

ANNA MCNUFF

15

The Mighty Power
of Hugs

If ever there was an antidote for a weary body, it is the Yorkshire Dales National Park. It's a place where the earth rises and falls like waves on a green ocean. Drystone walls and rivers run through the landscape like arteries, leading to tiny towns nestled in quiet valleys filled with moors, waterfalls and many, many sheep. I'd only visited the Dales a handful of times, but I'd always found it to be welcoming. It was a place where everything felt. . . friendly. When I think of the Dales, I think of softness. Of spongy grass and soft rolling hills. Of forest trails and moss-covered pathways. All things that were wildly appealing to my bare feet. I was so eager to spend time in the Dales that I planned to run across them twice — once from east to west and then, a few days later, in the opposite direction.

After leaving Newton Aycliffe, I made a beeline south-east, following back roads to Barnard Castle, and then on to Bowes. I scampered across a main road and was just beginning to wonder when the infamous hills of the Dales were going to start when voooof! The road kicked up towards the sky in front

222

of me. It wound around a bend alongside a drystone wall, and up, up, up I went, huffing and puffing in the late-morning sunshine, blowing the cobwebs from my lungs after what had been an unsettled week.

It was a long, hot upwards slog for the following hour. The road turned to gravel at Sleightholme Moor, so I opted to run on the grass instead — dancing around thistles and sheep poo all the way to the top of the climb. I then enjoyed a plate of warm chips and a cold shandy at the highest pub in Britain, the Tan Hill Inn. I'd heard a rumour that they let sheep hang out in the inn, so I was very disappointed to find that there were none propped up at the bar. When I asked the manager about it, he muttered something about health and safety and said that they weren't allowed to have animals in the pub anymore. Which was a shame. Because I'd have quite liked to have shared a plate of chips with a sheep.

By 4 p.m. I was back on my way, and the road that led away from the pub was a dream. There wasn't a whiff of gravel in sight and I was now running across an open moor on some of the smoothest tarmac I'd encountered on the journey so far. A slick black road ran out from beneath my feet, rising and falling towards the horizon under a cold blue sky. The air was warm but not suffocating and the road ahead was deserted, but for a few sheep. I always loved coming across sheep on runs. Especially in the Dales, where they hadn't had their tails trimmed. As the sheep trotted down the road, their fluffy white tails waggled around like a wayward arm and it looked like they were waving at me. From their bum. There is surely nothing more joyful than having a sheep wave at you from their bum. Better still when you are barefoot on a warm summer's evening, running across wild moorland in the beautiful British countryside.

So, I ran, and I ran, and I ran. I ran so much that I thundered past where I was supposed to meet my host for the night. I messaged to let her know that I was moving ahead of schedule and was just going to keep on running until she had finished work and wanted to pick me up. By the time she collected me from the roadside, I'd made it 21 miles and felt like a new woman.

***

When I lived in London, the Lake District was a mythical, far-off land — a place that took almost a whole day to travel to. But I have fond memories of visiting there as a kid. When my mum was training for something called the Saunders Lakeland Mountain Marathon with a good friend, we used to go to the Lakes so that they could practise their navigation, and Dad could practise his parenting skills by juggling three unruly children. I think the latter was actually a greater feat of endurance because Dad always finished the weekend looking more wrecked than Mum. Those trips as a family laid a foundation for a love of the area, but it wasn't until I moved to Gloucestershire that I began to visit more often. In just three short hours, I could be transported from the soft folds of the Cotswolds to the rugged, towering fells of the Lakes.

Of all the towns in the Lake District, I like Kendal the best because it's not as busy as other areas, but there's still plenty going on. There's old-world charm to it — a dinky clock tower, cobbled streets and some hipster coffee places to sit in and watch the rain trickle down windowpanes. Kendal is like the last bed in the Goldilocks fairy tale. . . it's just right.

The town is also the location for an annual adventure film festival and, over the years, I'd grown fond of the team who run the festival. So, when planning the route for Barefoot Britain, I'd made sure Kendal was included. In truth, it made no sense to go there at all. But the route was far from logical in every other way, so I decided to go all-in and make it as illogical as possible. I was always on the lookout for arbitrary reasons to go somewhere and there were two reasons to go to Kendal: a) I liked the place, and b) I knew some people there.

Despite these two compelling reasons, I'd left it to the last minute to tell those I knew in town that I was running through. I told myself that this was because I was 'busy' on the run with all of the admin that needed doing, but I'll fess up. I hadn't contacted the Kendal gang because they were an adventurous bunch, and I admired them, and the last thing I wanted was to tell them that I would be dropping in for a shandy or a rosé in the sunshine in early August, only to have something go tits up and me not make it to town at all. Letting down strangers was bad enough, but letting down friends felt even worse. It was only after leaving Newcastle that I finally wrote an email out to the Kendal Mountain team and hit send.

McNuff to Kendal family, McNuff to Kendal fam. . . come in. . . crch. . . over.

I should have emailed waaay sooner, but my brain wasn't allowing me to believe I would actually make it this far. . . But now Kendal is just 10 days a-wa-hey!

I'm running into town on Friday Aug 9th, taking a day off on the Saturday then running out on Sunday 11th.

I wondered if any of you have a spare bed and would be willing to have me darken your door for a couple of nights?

No worries at all if not! I can sort some other accommo, but I'd rather stay with one of you lot. Because then I can make inappropriate jokes.

Yours in barefootedness,

McNuff xx

Over the next few hours, the replies from the festival team came in one by one. Two of them were on holiday in Barcelona. One was down south to visit family. Another was in France. And two others lived out of town, so it wasn't going to work staying with them without a car. Brilliant. Top marks for organisation. Thankfully, there is no shortage of nice people in Kendal and a young local couple swooped to the rescue and offered to host me at their cute terraced cottage, just out of the town centre.

Taking a day of rest in Kendal was neat timing because it tipped it with rain. And I don't mean gentle pitter-patter, I mean biblical bucketing. It rained, and it rained, and it rained some more. Gone was the gorgeous weather I'd had, chasing sheep tails across the north of the Dales, and down came the rains, washing out every spider in the vicinity. In a rare break in the downpour, I took a stroll through town and gawped at the River Kent, all brown and violent, smashing its way through the landscape, dragging driftwood and clumps of branches as it went. Still, I didn't mind the rain. It was a wonderful excuse to dash between the local coffee shops, sample a flat white in each and take shelter from the storm.

The following day, I was expecting a small turnout at an open running stage from Kendal to Sedbergh. It was a Sunday and the weather forecast said it was due to rain again — both things which led me to think that only a few people would turn up. And besides, the runners of Kendal are hardy fell-running types. These were people who ate 800-metre peaks for breakfast and nibbled on 300-metre knolls for snacks. I was sure they all had serious running business to attend to in their fell shoes and short shorts, swinging hiking poles as they went. Joining me for a 17-mile run at Adventure Pace was surely too sedate, even for a Sunday. So, when I arrived to find a group of 25 runners gathered under the stone archway of Kendal Town Hall, I was gobsmacked.

'Ahhh! Hello everyone! Look how many of you there are!' I shouted across the street.

'We thought we'd give you a proper Kendal welcome,' said a lady in an orange running jacket.

'Well, I've got that alright!' I beamed, and my fondness for Kendal and the people there grew even deeper.

After the usual round of selfies, cheers and a countdown, the Kendalettes (as I shall now call them) and I set off at a clip away from the town hall, making our way over cobbles, along small back roads, up modest hills and out into the countryside. In a departure from the norm, the group included a mix of men and women — in fact, there were more men than I'd had on most of the running stages so far combined. I didn't think that Kendal had more male than female runners, but perhaps all that rain had dampened the oestrogen 'bat signal' I was unknowingly projecting into atmosphere. That, or my lady musk had been carried on the wind and was beginning to attract the males to the area. Whatever the reason, it was a nice surprise to have a mix of runners along for the ride, including a family, with two young boys and a black and white collie, a couple called Dave and Laura (who were recent converts to minimalist running) and one bright-faced mum-of-three whom I recognised from having posted several times about her runs on the Barefoot Britain Facebook group.

I was particularly impressed, though, by Martin, a man in his mid-sixties who turned up in bare feet and said he intended to run the whole stage that way. Shortly before leaving, Martin the barefooter opted to take things to the next level by getting bare-chested too. Which led me to wonder whether he would get gradually more scantily clad as the day wore on and end up butt naked by Sedbergh. Only time would tell.

With the Kendalettes by my side, the miles out of town passed easily. I moved steadily up and down the group, chatting to each runner for five minutes at a time.

On the smaller roads we ran in single file and I would slip to the back of the group (my favourite place to be). There, I could marvel all over again at just how many people had come out to play, and in the rain no less. I have a picture from that day which sticks in my mind. The line of runners is stretched out in front of me, streaking away from the camera like the brightly clad carriage of a Lake District locomotive, engines fully stoked by chatter, billowing steam up the climbs and free-wheeling the descents.

Five miles into the day, one member of the group announced that his parents lived just up the road. After a mid-run group vote, it was unanimously decided that we should all go and visit his parents' house. For a wee. And what a treat it was for those parents to have a trail of sopping, sweaty runners tiptoeing across their cream carpet and tag-teaming the downstairs toilet. While some used the bathroom, others chatted in the front garden and ate sandwiches. And when everyone had done their business and eaten their snacks, we set off again.

After the group pee stop, I began chatting to a runner in the group who looked particularly hardy. Angela, aka 'the running granny', was 60 years young and midway through training to be the oldest person to run from John O'Groats to Land's End.

She is a former surgeon and was doing the challenge to show women that age is no barrier to setting goals, and that getting outdoors is the best thing they can do for their health. She was also raising money to develop a health and well-being website and to make sure that older women had a means to stay connected to their local community, which she said was the key to good mental health and a long and happy life. I couldn't agree more. If the sense of community I'd experienced on the run so far was anything to go by, she was spot on.

'So, today's just a training run then?' I asked her, as we started up a climb.

'Yep, that's right,' Angela replied.

'Ah, well, in that case, I'm honoured. This must be a walk in the park compared to your usual distances.'

'Oh, no. It's a fantastic excuse. And the miles are fine. I'm running back again.'

'You're what?'

'Running back,' she repeated.

'To Kendal?' I shouldn't have been surprised, but I was impressed. That would mean at least a 34-mile run.

'Yes. Well, when we finish, I am. What time do you think that'll be?' Angela asked.

I thought for a moment. It was always hard to predict finishing times on the public running stages, especially with a large group, because there were often stops for wees and snacks. We'd once even had to stop for a male in the group to buy some Vaseline because his nipples were chafing. I took a wild guess.

'Oh, blimey, no idea. Five p.m.-ish?'

'Great. I've brought my lights. That'll be a nice run home for dinner,' Angela smiled. What a legend.

It rained on and off for the rest of the morning and every few miles someone would drop out from the group, needing to make a loop back to town. The Kendalettes gradually thinned out to a solid bunch of 10 — all of whom were in it to win it for the full 17-mile stage to Sedbergh. In the afternoon, the climbs came thick and fast, and my energy levels began to dip. I was busy thinking about which snack I should pull from my pack to get me out of the slump when I heard the sound of a motorbike approaching behind the group. I spun around to see a man whizz by. He raised one arm in salute as he went, a large wax overcoat flapping in the breeze behind him.

'It's Stace!' I shouted.

'Who?' came a chorused reply.

'Staccceee!'

I knew Stace's motorbike well. It was a real tank of a thing — a chunky silver frame with thick, knobbly tyres, wide handlebars, a furry cream seat cover and stickers from all over the world plastered on luggage boxes hanging off each side. It was a bike made for adventure.

Stace was a friend of mine from London. I didn't see him

very often, but he was always around when I needed him. An architect by trade, with the brain of an engineer, he'd helped me construct a groundsheet out of Tyvek for my first running adventure in New Zealand — which turned out to be the most durable, lightweight groundsheet known to humankind. He'd also once driven my bike a few hundred miles across southern England when a walking adventure turned disastrous, and I needed to switch to two wheels. Everyone needed a Stace in their life. He was a solid guy in every sense. Despite his brown-red beard, shaven head and bright blue eyes, he looked like Hagrid from Harry Potter when he wore his big wax motor-bike jacket. He happened to be travelling from Scotland to London that day, and so had looked up where I was and let me know he would appear at some point, for a 'drive-by hug', he said. A few minutes further on down the road, we found Stace standing next to his bike at a gravel lay-by, arms wide, open for the hug.

'I thought you were going to try to hug me while riding by?' I shouted as I ran toward him.

'Yeah, well, I didn't want to drive over your tootsies,' he said, engulfing me in one of his trademark bear hugs.

'Ah. Thanks so much for coming out to find me,' I said, folding into his arms but trying to keep my face out of his beard so that I could breathe. He smelled of sweat and engine oil, but I knew that he smelled better than I did, so I hugged him tighter still — even though I could barely get my arms around him in his thick overcoat.

'You're a nutter, do you know that?' Stace released me from his chest.

'I know,' I replied, before turning to the rest of the group.

'Hey, everyone — this is Stace. A friend of mine from London. . . he gives the best hugs. . . Anyone want one?' The runners looked confused.

'I don't bite, you know.' Stace opened his arms out wide.

'Go on, get in there, get yourself a hug each and then we'll get going again!' I coaxed, and soon a line of runners had formed by Stace's bike.

A few of the group hung back initially — they didn't know this large, bearded man on a bike from Adam, after all — but once they saw the post-hug glow emanating from those who had been embraced, they were in the queue as quick as a flash.

'Oh, wow. Now that's a hug,' said one runner, walking away with a breezy look on his face.

'Oh, my, I liked it!' said another, seemingly confused.

'Stace, they should prescribe your hugs,' said a third, and I couldn't agree more.

Once Stace had squeezed as many people as possible, he got back on his bike, waved us all goodbye and carried on with his own journey to London. I couldn't quite get my head around the fact that he'd be there in a few hours, while it was going to take me another couple of months and 1,700 miles to make it. But if the company I'd picked up in Kendal was anything to go by, there were plenty more good vibes to be scooped up along the way. And so, with my energy levels now restored by Stace, onwards on my wiggly route we ran. Through the Yorkshire countryside and east towards Sedbergh — just a group of brightly clad (and partially clothed), slightly soggy runners, fuelled by the mighty power of hugs.

16

Kit Kats and Prosecco

Hi Anna, there's a woman in Cumbria who owns a group of holiday cabins, apparently there's a hot tub. She says she wants to have a party in the hot tub and invite some of her runner friends over for dinner. Is that cool?

Way back when, before the run even began, this was the email that popped into my inbox from Abby. It arrived just a few days after I'd put a call out, asking for members of the British public to volunteer to host me, and it led me to wonder whether all offers of accommodation en route would be quite so luxurious. Of course, my answer was a swift **YES PER-LEASE**. The months since then had flown by and I had forgotten all about the offer of some hang-time in dreamy Cumbrian cabins in a place called Artlegarth. That was until Jennie and her kids turned up to join in for the final quarter of a mile into Sedbergh.

Artlegarth is a dinky place. I'm not sure it counts as a town; it's more a collection of houses, on a single-track lane, off an already minor road which cuts across Cumbria between Kirkby Stephen and Sedbergh. It's 10 miles east of the Lake

District, on the northern fringes of the Dales, and is one of those places you wouldn't arrive at unless you had a reason to be going there. But I find that those are the best kinds of places of all. That said, many people do seek out Jennie's lodges and, according to the website, I was heading to: 'Exclusive luxury log cabins with hot tubs and stunning fell views, located on a private seven-acre site, offering peace and tranquillity.' Bloomin' marvellous.

Jennie is a curly haired whirlwind of a Liverpudlian and a mum to three young girls — Ruby, Harrie and Annie. When she moved from Liverpool and took over the holiday-let business, she refurbished all of the original lodges on the site but also built three new ones, avec hot tubs. Jennie and her girls live in a farmhouse not far from the lodges, so I assumed that I would be staying with them. Best keep the smelly barefoot runner out of the way of any paying guests, I thought. But as we rumbled down the long driveway towards the farm, Jennie let me know that she had other plans.

'So, I've put you in one of the new lodges. . .' she said, in a Scouser accent that I was already loving so much.

'The new ones?'

'Yeah, you've got a kitchen and a couple of bedrooms to take your pick from. . .'

'What if I want to sleep in all of the beds?' I asked.

'Then, you can do just that,' she smiled.

'Oh, Jennie, you're making me feel like a princess.'

'You just wait, Princess. You've got a hot tub on the decking outside too, so you can have yourself a good long soak in that as well. . . Well, after my running friends have left. I've invited a few of the gals over for a BBQ. . . that okay?'

'Fine by me.'

'Grand. You'll love 'em.'

I asked Jennie about her own love of running and she said that she didn't really see herself as a runner, but she did love to run, whenever she got the time. She then nonchalantly gave me a tour of 'my' lodge: a peek in each of the bedrooms, a glimpse at the fridge stocked full of food she'd bought for me, and, of course, the all-important instructions for how to work the hot tub. . . you know, all of the usual things someone does for you when you've only just met. The decor inside the lodge was next-level swanky: funky lighting, accented wallpaper, bold patterns and a ruddy good spattering of cushions. I always admired a good bit of interior design, especially when people were liberal with the cushions.

'Who did you get to do all this?' I asked.

'Do what?'

'The rooms. Who did the design? They've done a cracking job.'

'Oh, nah, I did 'em myself.'

'Really?'

'Yeah. Piece of cake,' she said. I had a sneaky suspicion

that there was more to Jennie than met the eye.

The lodge had a large open-plan kitchen and living room, with ceiling-height glass doors that led out onto wood decking and the hot tub. Jennie nipped off to make a phone call and I stepped outside onto the decking. I sat down on some wooden steps, facing out towards the hills and stayed there for 10 minutes, taking it all in. It was approaching dusk and pastel colours dominated the sky — pinks blended with corals and merged into peach and lavender. Evening clouds gently fused and dispersed in the breeze and, except for the soft rustle of wind moving through the grass, all was quiet.

'Anna?'

'Mmm hmmm.' I spun around to see that Jennie had joined me.

'It's beautiful, isn't it?' she said, sitting down next to me on the step.

'It is. So serene,' I sighed.

'Now. I've got a very important question for you.' Jennie furrowed her brow.

'Is it which one of your luxurious beds I'd like to sleep in?'

'Well, that is important information, but you can tell me later. What I want to know right now is. . . would you like a Kit Kat and a glass of Prosecco to take into the bath with you?'

It wasn't a question I needed to ponder for long. I had a truckload of admin to do in the bath, which, of course, would be eased by the flow of Prosecco and a chocco fix. And so, while Jennie's runner pals turned up and the party got started out on the decking, I slunk into a bubble bath, sipped on a chilled glass of Prosecco and enjoyed that satisfying crack that comes from snapping a finger of a Kit Kat clean in two.

Later that night, when the running gals had left and the BBQ coals had gone cold, Jennie and I slipped into the hot tub to polish off the bottle of Prosecco together. Jennie emptied the bottle into tumblers before turning off all the lights on the deck except for the blues and reds beneath the water of the hot tub. The sun had long since disappeared and the inky black sky was speckled with gold. With moonlight falling onto the deck, we sat and watched the stars sparkle from the comfort of the tub, as wafts of steam rose from the water, and set about putting the world to rights.

I'd been intrigued by Jennie from the moment I met her, but in the whirlwind of my arrival and with the BBQ with friends, I hadn't had much of a chance to really get to know her.

'So, is this how you spend all of your evenings then?'

'Oh, me? Yeah. I just leave the kids to it, you know. They can whip up a plate of fish fingers and fend for themselves. . .' She smiled, and there was a pause. 'No, you know what, Mc-Nuff — I thought I'd make an exception for you. The girls are with my mum.'

'Aw, well, thank you. This place is pretty special, you know.'

'I think so.'

'It's so. . . peaceful,' I said, taking a sip of Prosecco.

'If you'd have met me ten years ago, you'd not have had me pegged for the peaceful life,' Jennie said.

'Really?'

'Oh, yeah. I was the one with the penthouse flat in Liverpool, driving around in a bright yellow Hummer.'

'A yellow Hummer? Nice.'

'Aye. I was proper flashy, me.'

'And you're not flashy anymore?'

'Ha! What do you reckon?' Jennie said, gesturing to her wayward curly hair and a face reddened by the hot tub. 'Nahhh. I'm more about the wellie boots than the high-heeled boots these days.'

'Well, I'm sure you rock the wellies. Did something change, then? I mean, to make you move out here?' I asked, and Jennie thought for a moment. She leant back against the side of the hot tub and sank a little bit lower into the water.

'Good question. . . I just didn't feel like it was for me anymore. That life, I mean. Good job. Good car. Or bad car, depending how you look at it,' she smiled. 'Good money. I should have been living the dream, but I wasn't. It wasn't filling me up, you know?'

'I get it,' I said, thinking back to my own experience of feeling unfulfilled in years gone by — a feeling that led me to buy a giant pink bicycle, leave my office job and head off to pedal through the USA.

'And then, well, also — something my boss said hit a nerve. . .' Jennie continued. 'I'd been working for this waste management company for ages, doing super-well, worked my way up to Operations Director, blah blah blah. The company got bought out, and I wanted to leave to do some travelling and then set up my own thing. So, I told my boss about my plans, and d' you know what he said?'

'What?'

'That I'd make a really good go of having "a little shoe shop or a flower shop" or something like that. Not that there's anything wrong with those businesses,' Jennie added quickly. 'They're ace, but it was like he assumed that the only kind of business I could run on my own was something "little", you know?'

'I bet that went down like a lead balloon.'

'Oh, it got right on my tits! So now, I'm in the shit business.'

'Oh, come on, Jennie. This isn't a shit business,' I said, gesturing to the lodges.

'No, literally. My other business. I run a waste disposal company.'

As it turned out, when Jennie's boss had dampened her spirits, she'd taken off on some travels and then gone ahead and set up a multimillion-pound environmental waste management company. The lodges came after that. How in the world she had the time to raise three kids and run two companies was beyond me. Jennie explained that it hadn't all been plain sailing, either. After giving birth to her third daughter, she and her partner had parted ways, leaving her flying solo with the kids. It wasn't where she'd hoped to end up, and she was still working through the aftermath of the break-up, but she seemed philosophical about it all.

'Well, I don't know, you've just gotta keep seeking it out I guess — the shiny bits in life, I mean. You've got to find those in all of the mess and surround yourself with the bubbly people,' she said, raising her tumbler of Prosecco towards me.

'Well, I know one thing for sure. Those girls are bloomin' lucky to have you,' I said. 'And I've got a feeling that it's all going to be alright for you. No, actually, I know for a fact that it's going to be alright. You seem like the kind of person who always works it out.'

'Well, I'm not sure I believe you yet, McNuff, but you make a good case. Let's drink to that.'

Jennie hadn't had it easy. She'd really been through the wringer over the past few years and to have made the time and put aside the energy to take me in for a few days — I was blown away. What I was doing paled in comparison to running multiple businesses with three young kids. In place of being able to run with a whole bottle of Prosecco in my backpack, I thought that I would take Jennie's gritty determination and bottle that instead. I'd then crack it open on a day when I needed to remember what hard graft really looked like.

The following day, Jennie took a break from being a mum and a business owner — or rather, she put it on pause — and joined me for a 22-mile run from Sedbergh to Hawes. She said it was further than her usual 10-km jaunts but, in true Jennie style, she was up for giving it a bash.

When I met a small group of runners outside St Andrew's Church, the skies were blue and filled with candyfloss clouds. Many of the group were Jennie's friends, who she'd managed to strong-arm over a burger bap the night before into joining me for a run. But also in the group were Dave and Laura, a couple who had been part of the Kendalettes and returned for round two. Clearly, the sight of my weather-beaten feet was enough to lure them back — that or it could have been the glorious scenery and the prospect of running on quiet roads through the Cumbrian countryside.

Much as I'd loved having a big group join me out of Kendal, what I loved more than anything on the journey through Britain was the variety. A change in pace, a change in group numbers, a shift in energy. The mixture of running in a big group, a small group, with just one other or running alone — I liked it all in balance.

The smaller group of runners meant that I could take my time to chat to each and every person, and I was especially keen to speak to Kendalettes Laura and Dave. Dave had a white cap on, turned backwards, which matched the laid-back vibe he was giving off, and Laura had bright blonde hair cut in a neat bob and was wearing black Capris and a purple T-shirt. Dave told me that he'd done long distances before, but for Laura distance-running was a new thing. She'd only ever run 5 miles until she joined me for a 7-mile run out of Kendal. And now, she was back for a second day on the trot.

'I'm not sure how far I'll go today. Probably just a few miles,' she said as we set off from town, and I was cool with that — any miles were winner's miles in my eyes.

After the first hour of excited chatter, we settled into Adventure Pace as a group, following quiet roads through the hamlets of Millthrop and Gawthrop — both of which I thought had ideal names for the setting of a murder mystery. A blackish-grey river of mottled tarmac flowed out from beneath my feet and passed between dry stone walls which looked like they'd been there for hundreds of years and were partly obscured by bushes and bramble. Closer to the frayed edges of the road, bursts of wildflowers were dotted here and there — little purple renegades in a landscape of green and grey.

I often ran at the back of the group, and from there I had a good view of Jennie in her green T-shirt and black leggings, her bright-orange backpack bobbing up and down, matching the rise and fall of the tight brown curls on her head, as if both things were linked by some kind of invisible string. I smiled and thought about how people's running styles tended to match their personalities. If you'd never met Jennie, you could guess that she was the optimistic and determined sort, always 'on the bounce' from one thing to the next — just by the way she ran.

After admiring Jennie's bouncy style, I spent some more time chatting to Laura. She told me how she'd recently set up a new business for 'movement photography', where she was commissioned to create beautiful artistic images of people running. An alternative, she said, to what's usually sold after running events — which, in my case, would be an image of me with eight chins and a look of pain etched across my face. I didn't do many official running events, but I always preferred the image in my mind (in which I am a galloping goddess) and to remember that from the day, rather than the reality of a 5 foot 10, lolloping, multi-chinned, sweat monster. So, I have never bought a running event photo. But what Laura described sounded like something I would actually like to hang above the mantlepiece.

'It's so graceful, you know — running,' she said. 'Or any movement at all, actually. There's a real beauty in it. No matter how you run.'

I thought that was quite lovely. To want to search for grace in even our most exhausted, graceless moments.

As the group and I ploughed on through the countryside, there were very few cars on the road and that made it feel like we were on our own private running track. We loosely followed the path of the River Dee, mirroring its meanders, and by the 6-mile marker, the bulk of the ladies had turned around to run home again. We were now down to a hardcore fandango of four: me, Laura, Dave and Jennie.

'Feeling alright, Laura?' I asked. I didn't want to draw attention to the fact that she'd already run further than she said she would, but I was keen to check in with her.

'Yeap. I feel good.'

'Happy to crack on?'

'Very happy.' She smiled.

And so on we went.

It was soon after leaving the village of Cowgill that the run gods served up a new challenge. The route got more undulating, and the hills came thick and fast. And yet, despite the exhaustion of the previous week, I felt strong. The surface was manageable, I had fine company and I enjoyed the novelty of hills being thrown into the mix.

We were halfway through trucking it up yet another long hill when I stopped to look back. The scene behind me was majestic: folds of straw-coloured hillsides tucked neatly into the valley, which made the earth appear like half-kneaded dough. A solid line of grey-white clouds hung low in the sky, hovering just above the tops of the hills, with just a thin strip of blue visible between the two. Faint wisps of white spread out from the bulk of cloud, as if someone had hooked the edge of a ball of cotton wool and dragged it upwards into the sky. A line of trees ran across the horizon, tracking the path of the railway, which led to the most spectacular viaduct. From where I was standing, I could count six arches, although I knew there would be more obscured by the trees at the edges. It was a picture-perfect postcard if ever I saw one, made even more perfect by the smiling faces of Jennie, Laura and Dave, trucking up the hill behind me. When they saw me looking back, they each gave an almighty thumbs-up or a wave. I waved back and turned to run on.

When I made the top of the hill, I stopped for a regroup and to check the map. We'd covered 13 miles. Blimey. That was Laura's longest ever run, and she was still going strong. Jennie looked sprightly too. There were now just 9 miles left to run and I was sure it all had to be downhill from there — we'd be in Hawes in 90 minutes, tops. Just then, a man on a blue bike, laden with panniers, appeared over the crest of the hill. I smiled as a flop of his strawberry-blonde hair escaped from beneath the bike helmet. I knew exactly who it was.

'Alright, Al. Fancy seeing you here!'

'Hello, Anna. I was worried I wouldn't find you! But then I remembered that I'm on a bike and you're on two feet — you're very easy to catch.' He smiled.

Alastair Humphreys is no stranger to adventure. Among other things, he's cycled around the world, rowed across the Atlantic and walked the perimeter of the M25 motorway. He's also slept out in a bivvy bag in more places around the UK and beyond, than I could even count. Al was now midway through another adventure — cycling around Yorkshire, where he grew up, and stopping to interview interesting people along the way. So far, he'd spoken to small business owners, Michelin-starred chefs, creative entrepreneurs, CEOs, bikepackers, a poet, a life coach, a climber and an urban wildlife professor. But that day, he had come to interview me. Once I'd stopped running, of course.

When the rest of the group joined me at the top of the hill, I made some introductions to our newest group member on his bike, and we all set off together —with Al now in the role of chief cheerleader. Of course, my belief that it was all going to be downhill was misguided and, as the hills continued to roll, the group spread out again. On one long downhill, Jennie was tanking it ahead — she had a real turn of speed on the down-hills and I struggled to keep up with the Scouser steam train. Laura and Dave had slipped further back and Al was using his pedal power to zoom back and forth between all members of the group — keeping our weary minds entertained and dis-tracted from the hills and the summer heat with his chit-chat. I'd just about managed to catch Jennie on an uphill section when Al appeared beside us.

'Laura looks like she's suffering,' he said.

'Oh dear. Poor love. She's doing amazing. You know this is the furthest she's run?' I replied.

'Ah, that explains it.' There was a brief silence before Al added, absent-mindedly, 'Running is so slow.' And in that mo-ment, I could have punched him.

He was right, of course. And if there was one thing you could always count on Al for, it was telling it like it is. Truth be told, Laura wasn't the only one suffering. The ground had become increasingly hot over the course of the day and the tarmac had grown spikier. The soles of my feet were beginning to burn, and I had just about used up the last of my energy catching Jennie up. I wasn't in the best mood for acknowledging that I was a slow-moving creature, but instead of opting to reach out and lamp Al one, I decided to laugh.

'Will Laura be okay?' Al asked.

'Yeah. I'll drop back and see how she's doing,' I said.

'Okay then, and in that case. . . if I was a nicer person, I'd stay with you all until the end. But if I whizz ahead down the hill now, I can get in a whole extra beer before you finish. . .'

'Al, I would be a terrible person if I didn't want you to have an extra beer. Go!'

'Great! I'll find us a pub and I'll sit outside. See you in a bit.' And with that, he took a few hard pedal strokes and disappeared around a bend.

With Al now gone and the thought of a cold beer planted in my mind, I dropped back to check that Laura was okay. I could see that the grin which she'd had on her face near the viaduct had now changed to a grimace. She was clearly slipping into the depths of her own personal pain cave, but I had a feeling she wanted to push on and make it to Hawes. I slotted in next to her and matched my stride with hers.

'Hey Laura, how you doing?'

'Oh, hiya Anna. Okay. I'm fine. I mean, I might cry soon. But I'm fine,' she puffed.

'Oh, you go right ahead and cry. Crying is great.'

'Okay, I will.' She mustered a half-smile and then fixed her gaze on the road ahead.

'Do you want me to just leave you to it?' I asked. Because I knew that when you are as tired as Laura was, the last thing you wanted was to have to make conversation, or worry that you're slowing others down. But equally, I wanted to check that she didn't feel like she was being left behind.

'Yeap, you carry on. Dave's here.' She gestured to Dave, who was running just behind her, and he waved. 'I'll be good. You carry on and I'll see you in town.'

'For a beer?'

'For a beer!'

'Gwaaaan, Laura! See you at the end!' I shouted as I ran off to catch back up with Jennie.

I was already impressed that Laura was pushing past the furthest she'd ever run before, but her honesty was even more impressive. She hadn't even tried to hide her pain; she'd put it out there, in the open, with a relative stranger — and she had then added that she fully intended to move right on through it. What a woman.

It took us over two hours to cover those final 9 miles to Hawes, during which I repeatedly promised Jennie that there couldn't possibly be any more hills, only to round the bend and see another one loom large on the horizon. The Scouser steam train drove the pace in the final few miles and, at last, we made it into Hawes. With sweat-encrusted faces and weary legs, we found Al on a picnic bench outside The Crown pub, already one beer deep. He went off to get a round in and returned with a side helping of salt and vinegar crisps, as well as some Nobby's Nuts (everyone loves Nobby's at the end of a run). We were halfway through supping our long-awaited beers and shandies when Laura and Dave came into sight. Laura was tanking it down the hill: arms pumping, head down, that same look of determination still on her face.

The group broke into cheers and started shouting.

'Gwaaannn, Lauraaaa!' I hollered, much to the bemusement of others at the pub, but I didn't care.

Jennie started going for it on the cheering now too. 'Yeaaahhhh, Lady!'

Laura upped her pace even more and raised an arm in the air in acknowledgement of the cheers. I stood up on the wooden picnic bench and almost toppled off it, but once I'd righted myself, I put my fingers in my mouth and whistled loudly, as the rest of the group continued to cheer Laura all the way to the pub: her own personal finish line.

Al already had two cold pints waiting for Laura and Dave by the time they'd arrived and, once they'd caught their breath, they each took that first satisfying sip. After getting stuck into what was left of the salt and vinegar crisps (the Nobby's were long gone), Laura sat back from the table and let out a sigh.

'So. . . how was that?' I asked.

'Tough,' she smiled.

'I'll say,' Jennie chipped in.

'Is that the furthest you've run?' asked Al.

'Yeah. . . well, yesterday was the furthest before now. What was that, Dave — seven miles?' And Dave nodded. 'But that's just beaten it, a bit. . .'

'A bit?! That's more than a bit, Laura — you smashed it!' I said.

'That's some training plan. Five miles one day, seven miles the next and then twenty-two. That's not mucking around, is it?' Al laughed and there was a silence. 'You do know what you've got to do now though?' he asked as he took another sip of beer.

'What's that?'

'A marathon.'

'Oh no! I have to, don't I?' Laura put her head in her hands.

'Well, you don't have to,' I chipped in, 'but just so you know — if you flattened today's course and ran for the same amount of time as you did. . . you'd have made a marathon. No problem.'

There was another brief silence as Laura took a few more sips of beer.

'It's funny, isn't it,' she said, fiddling with a crisp packet on the bench in front of her.

'What's that?' I asked.

'I'd always told myself that I'd never be able to run even a half-marathon.'

'Did you?'

'Yeah.'

'Why?'

'Well, I thought half-marathons and longer stuff were for. . . you know, super humans.'

'And yet you've just run twenty-two miles.'

'I did,' Laura smiled.

17

Uh. Oh.

I love maps. Really, I do. If there was an inanimate object that I could marry and have babies with (aside from a block of mature cheddar), it would be a map. In days of old, before we got good at cartography and were able to accurately depict the landscape, maps were mostly created from stories — fables passed from village to village, the stuff of myths and legends. They were brimming with mystery and intrigue and possibility. As kids, we learn that maps are a gateway to the unknown, an invitation to adventure. X marks the spot. And if you turn modern grid lines at a 45-degree angle, they look very much like Xs if you ask me. There is always hidden treasure waiting to be discovered within any map. Especially a British one.

According to the map of the Yorkshire Dales, there were a few different routes I could take for the onward journey from Hawes. I decided to continue to search for buried treasure in the landscape by heading east, then turning south to pick up the path of the River Wharfe, where I'd follow the Wharfedale Valley all the way across the National Park to Otley.

When planning the route for the day, I noticed that there weren't many turnings to take, so I opted to scribble down town names on a scrap of paper and just use that to navigate. Not having to get my phone out to check the map repeatedly meant that I could run more freely, with fewer interruptions. Because if there was anything likely to interrupt my appreciation of running through the splendour of the Dales, it was my mobile phone and the oversized, never-ending to-do list attached to it.

I did a brief scan of the villages I'd be passing through and noted that there were some cracking names. Some of them sounded distinctly Yorkshire-esque, like Thoralby, Bishopdale, Buckden and Grassington, but others seemed fresh out of a fantasy novel: Askrigg, Aysgarth, Cray and Starbotton. Were there elves living in Aysgarth? Dwarves at Cray and wizards in Starbotton? I had high hopes that I'd meet hobbits with big dirty feet like mine in Appletreewick too, but only time and some barefooted exploration would tell.

Fuelled by a few solid nights of sleep at Jennie's lodges, I was in high spirits. I was running alone for the first time since leaving Kendal and I felt as strong as an ox. Well, a running ox. Do oxen run? Anyhoo, I felt fabulous. It didn't take me long to find my personal groove. With my legs swinging back and forth like a metronome, I settled into the kind of rhythm where you can run all day. I was drunk on the good vibes from the excellent company of the past few days and at one with the rolling green hills around me. And so, I got lost in the wonder of it all. Despite my foolproof plan to 'remember where to turn off on the road', I ran into a town that I didn't recognise the name of: Carperby. I stopped to check my scrap of paper. Carperby. . .

I didn't think I was supposed to be running through Carperby, but it was so small that perhaps I hadn't noted it down. I ran on for a while longer, resisting the urge to get my phone out and check, before realising that I had definitely taken a wrong turn. Bugger. I let out a sigh, pulled my phone out of my rucksack and fired up the GPS app to see where I'd gone wrong.

'Oh, you muppet, Anna,' I said aloud. I'd run a mile past the turn-off junction. That meant I'd just added an extra two miles to what was already a 22-mile day.

Just then, it crossed my mind that I wasn't standing off to the side of the road enough. Traffic had been light, but it was a good idea to make sure I was tucked out of the way should any cars come a-rumblin' down the valley. I took a backwards step with my left foot and it landed in something cold and wet. I assumed it was grass or mud — it had rained a lot recently and all sorts had been washed from the fields onto the road. I was too engrossed in the map to bother to look down at my feet, so I stood in the cold, wet, sloppy stuff for a minute or so longer. Once I'd worked out precisely where I needed to run from that point on, I glanced nonchalantly down at my foot.

'Oh, my god. Oh, my god!' I leapt from the ground like a cat on a hot tin roof. My stomach lurched and a wave of nausea rose in my throat.

I'd stood in a dead rabbit.

I jumped around for a minute, not knowing what to do with myself, before going back to inspect the scene of the crime (no, I'm not sure why either, I just couldn't help it). I stood over the poor, deceased, grey-brown bunny and felt a twinge of sadness. I realised that my heel must have been in its stomach, which is why it had felt so cold and slimy. I never liked to see a dead animal, least of all one I've stood on. (Although I do promise the rabbit was dead before I stood on it.)

I sat at the side of the road for a few minutes, away from the scene of the crime, using up all of the antiseptic wipes in my first-aid kit to give my soles a good scrubbin'. When my feet were fully de-bunnified, I ran on, trying as best as I could to shake the thought of the event for the rest of the afternoon, but every now and then the image of the rabbit's black beady eyes and the sensation of a slimy organ on the sole of my bare foot would crash into my mind like a wrecking ball and make me shudder all over again.

I managed to avoid foot baths in any other roadkill as I continued my trundle down the Wharfedale Valley and, once again, the landscape was beautiful. I'd been impressed with the dreamy scenery of the Dales from the off, but Upper Wharfedale really tipped things up a notch. Originally carved out by a glacier millions of years ago, it's now a dramatic mix of grassy fields and limestone scars (which is a fancy word for an exposed limestone cliff). There are vast stretches of nothing but sheep-filled, rolling green, with stone barns dotted here and there on the lower slopes, and I could often hear the trickle of hidden becks, which ran alongside or under the road.

When the water of the Yorkshire Dales revealed itself, however, it was in spectacular fashion — like at Aysgarth Falls, where the River Ure drops dramatically down the valley over a beautiful set of staged cascades. I stopped on a stone bridge at the end of the falls to take in the view, watching the inky-green of the river part around moss-covered boulders and thunder past forest-lined banks. Where the water thundered over each ledge, it turned white and was streaked with brown. It looked mighty, and powerful. Feeling energised by that power, I fired up my soles and took off again.

It was late evening when I made it to the bottom of Kid-stones Pass. Given that I was navigating by town names written on a scrap of paper that day, I had no idea I'd be running up a mountain towards the end of it. I checked my watch. It was 7.30 p.m., sunset was in 90 minutes, and I still had 9 miles left to run before making it to Kettlewell for the night. I felt a pang of nerves. I couldn't afford to go much slower, or I'd wind up running in the dark. And I really didn't like running in the dark. The navigational blunder at Carperby and my run-in with the ghost of Bugs Bunny had lost me some time. Well, if I was being completely honest, I'd also lost some time because I decided to stop for a milkshake and buttered crumpets at the Aysgarth Falls visitor centre. But that's beside the point. One should never blame crumpets for anything in life, so let's blame the rabbit.

I had no idea how big this pass was other than it looked bloody enormous from where I was standing, craning my neck up a road which charged towards the clouds. I bit my lip — it was going to be touch and go, but the challenge was set. I sucked in a lungful of Dales air, turned the fizz of nerves into a wave of LET'S BE 'AVIN' IT and blew out my cheeks.

'Game on,' I muttered under my breath, and off I went, legs set to Wharfedale Warp Speed as I streaked up the road.

Despite my underlying nerves, I soon started to enjoy the climb. It was just steep enough to set my lungs on fire, but not so steep that I had to reduce my run to a walk. I kept my cadence high, taking small steps and relishing the sick burning sensation in my legs as my quads tugged at my kneecaps. I liked it when my muscles hurt like that; it made me feel alive — as if I was using my body in a way it was supposed to be used: for forward motion.

It was a lush evening to be out and about. Traffic on the road was light and the air was warm and still. I was running sandwiched between two scars, which rose steeply from the roadside and flattened out to long plateaus at the top. I looked up at them and wondered what it might be like to run across those tops — to dance along that line between the green of the dales and the sapphire of the sky. At the top of the pass, the road flattened out and I was able to pick up the pace for a few hundred metres until the descent began. From that point on, I freewheeled down the other side, letting my legs go just as fast as they wanted to and asking the rest of my body to do its best to keep up. The sun had now almost set and the last of its rays were scattered across the top of Kidstones scar. Sheep were grazing in the field below the cliffs and the setting sun had given each of them a fluffy golden halo, so they looked like a flock of woolly angels against a backdrop of green.

The valley sides got steeper still as I joined the River Wharfe at Cray and followed the road along its banks through the quaint villages of Buckden and Starbotton. My shadow grew longer and my legs grew tired, but in the lilac of dusk, I felt invincible. At 9 p.m., I chased the sunset all the way into Kettlewell and padded straight to the King's Head pub. I made a beeline for a tartan-covered stool next to an open fireplace in the corner and slouched down onto it, propping my back against the cool white brick wall behind. I let out a long sigh. It'd been one heck of a day, featuring a dead rabbit, stunning cascades, a lung-busting mountain pass and crumpets (let's not forget the crumpets). I'd made it another hot and hilly 24 miles and could only hope that, minus the dead animal, there would be more days like that to come.

After leaving Kettlewell, I hopped onto the Dales Way footpath and followed its grassy trail along the banks of the River Wharfe, over stone ladders and wooden stiles. I ran beneath ragged crags, across the cobbles of Grassington and past the imposing ruins of Bolton Priory until I reached Otley. At Otley, I was joined by a group of local runners, as well as an excited gaggle of Brownies. After a very loud and enthusiastic countdown to the start of the running stage, the Brownies sprinted with me, away from Otley town centre and up the hill to Ilkley Moor. They repeatedly asked their adult chaperones if they could take their shoes off and be barefoot too, and one especially energetic girl ran the whole way up the hill by my side, explaining just how much she really LOVED to run.

'And where do you like to run the most?' I asked.

'Outside!'

'Outside? Does that mean you run inside too?'

'Oh, yes. Mummy has a treadmill in her bedroom and sometimes I go on it. And I put it up to FAST!'

'Do you?'

'Yes, I loooooove it! I could run on it alllll day. Well. Not at FAST. Maybe at medium. But Mummy says she'll get a jelly belly if I don't let her go on the treadmill, so then I have to get off and let her have a go.'

The training this little girl was putting in (both indoors and outdoors) was clearly paying off because I could barely keep up with her on the hill towards the moor. Given how much she 'loooooooved' running, I assumed she'd be wearing some kind of fancy trainers. I looked down to see that she had Ugg boots on. Enthusiasm is always more important than footwear, clearly.

After the day spent running over Ilkley Moor, I slingshotted in and out of Leeds and by mid-August, I was headed for Sheffield. I'd been looking forward to making it to Sheffield for a while now because it was the next big milestone, at 1,000 miles into the run. But I was apprehensive about the miles into the city itself because, having been through plenty of cities by this point on the journey, I knew how ugly it could be. There were a few different routes I could have chosen to run to Sheffield, but I opted to follow an A-road into the city centre. Looking back, I know why I chose the A-road. I was tired, it was the most direct route and I wanted to make sure I made it on time to a talk at Sheffield Girlguiding HQ that evening. In short, I was keen to get there in a way that involved the least amount of brain power possible, and the A-road, with its big straight line on the map, was the winner. What I hadn't thought about is that the sides of A-roads are not only noisy, but they're often covered in grit, glass and all of the other gubbins that gets thrown out of car windows — nappies, McDonald's cups, glass bottles, cans of energy drinks (why is it always the people who drink energy drinks that seem to litter?) — all of it. Anyway, I chose the A-road route.

I was joined by a small group of runners for that day's 18-mile stage to Sheffield. When we hit sections of the pavement with grit or glass, I'd taken to dropping off to the back of the group and allowing a few metres of gap to build up between me and them so that I had a clear view of the ground in front of me. There, I would do my best to keep one half of my brain on the surface beneath my feet and one half of it on listening in to the conversation of the group. Just as we passed Sheffield Wednesday Stadium, I felt something sharp in the ball of my right foot. I called the group to a halt and shuffled to the side of the pavement to sit on a wall and inspect my sole. I could see a tiny cut, two millimetres across, but there was nothing in it. I had no idea what had gone into my foot, but it had gone in and out (perhaps it had even shaken it all about) and left behind only a small puncture wound in the hard skin. It made me feel uneasy, knowing that something had pierced the surface of my sole — it was like having a chink in my armour.

I also didn't like the fact that I couldn't see what I'd stepped on, but there wasn't any blood, so I didn't think too long on it. Picking up small cuts and scrapes had become part and parcel of the run, after all. I made a note to give it a good clean that evening, to be sure to keep the nasties out, and I was sure it'd heal in a few days.

At 5 p.m., the running group and I crossed over a couple of busy junctions. We ran up one last very steep hill and arrived at the Broad Lane roundabout. Just opposite it, a line of 40 girls and leaders had gathered on the pavement outside Girlguiding Sheffield HQ. They were waving homemade pom-poms and cheering and clapping as I padded the final few metres to the entrance of a red brick building. One of the leaders was standing out the front and waved me over.

'Anna! You're here! So glad you could make it. The girls have spent the afternoon learning about all the countries you've been adventuring in and making barefoot biscuits.'

How cute was that? I was super grateful for the effort the girls had gone to in order to give me a superstar welcome, but I was even more grateful that the leaders had managed to time a delivery of takeaway pizza with my arrival. Salty, cheesy goodness after an 18-mile run? Yes per-lease. So, while the girls finished up their various projects, I sat at the side of the hall and inhaled a few (read: many) slices of pizza. I then downed a cup of tea and munched on some very special foot-shaped cookies with Smarties in them, which had been lovingly baked for me by a Brownie called Rebecca. I used any puff I had left in my lungs to blow up my inflatable globe, then I took a deep breath and got up in front of the girls to start some storytelling.

The following morning, I woke up at a budget hotel in Sheffield city centre. I wiped sleep from my eyes and rolled over to check the time on my phone. It was 10 a.m.. I flopped back onto my pillow and stared at the ceiling. God, how my legs ached. Thankfully, it was a rest day. The only taxing thing I had to do that day was to catch up on some admin and mooch half a mile to a nearby coffee shop to meet a friend. I reckoned I could manage that.

Quite often, in normal, non-adventuring life, I will do my best to keep my phone on airplane mode for a few hours in the morning, especially if I'm trying to get anything done that demands some deep concentration. Sadly, much as I wanted to do that, I knew it wasn't realistic on this adventure. Days off were only days off from running — there was still a swirling tornado of questions from Abby to answer, talks to arrange and route-planning to think about. It was exhausting, but I figured that I was only doing this run once, so I was going to do it right.

I idly flicked my phone off airplane mode and threw it back onto the bed beside me. Bing. . . bing. . . bing. . . Bing! Bing! Bing! Bing! My phone lit up like a notification-powered Christmas tree. What the heck was going on?

I opened the first email. 'Hi Anna, Carys from ITV news here. We saw your piece about the barefoot run in The Times this morning. . . We'd like to send a crew out to do a piece on you, say, tomorrow?'

I opened the next email. 'Dear Anna, it's Jez from Channel 5 News. We've heard about your run and think it's fantastic. Can we arrange an interview?'

The next notification was a WhatsApp message from Alice, the PR manager at Girlguiding: 'Paul Ross at TalkRadio wants a chat. Can you do tonight at 11.30pm?'

Jeremy Vine was doing a segment on his Radio 2 show about barefoot running and they needed an expert for it. And so it went on. BBC Five Live, Daily Mail, The Sunday Times — everyone wanted a chat with the woman running through Great Britain in bare feet. There was a real sense of urgency to all of these messages — they had to speak to me NOW. Which did make me laugh, seeing as I had been running for over 1,000 miles and six weeks already, and I still had some 1,600 miles left to go. I wasn't exactly a fast-moving object. I was very easy to 'catch', so to speak. I wanted to tell all the journalists to chill their boots, that I wasn't going anywhere and that I had plenty of time to talk to them over the coming weeks. Did it have to be today when I just wanted to be still and drink coffee? But I had learned over the years that this is how the media works. Rarely are you flavour of the month, or even flavour of the day. If you are the flavour of the hour, you've got to roll with it. Any coverage was nice for me but, more importantly, the more people who knew about the run, the more it would help raise Girlguiding's profile. And perhaps that meant more people would get involved with the organisation and support young women across the country. That's what mattered the most. So, I started replying to emails from bed. I took phone calls in between brushing my teeth and getting in the shower, and I did what I would never advise anyone to do — I said yes to everything.

As it turned out, I could line up a lot of the interviews for the coming days, but I did have to apologise to my friend when I paused our catch-up coffee to take a call with a local radio station. She understood and had even ordered me a fresh, warm coffee when I made it back to the table. That's true friendship right there.

That night, I took a much-needed cat nap to recharge my battery for a late-night chat with Paul Ross at 11.30 p.m. Staying up late was worth it, if only for the intro he gave me: 'She's rough, she's tough. . . She's Anna McNuff!' he bellowed over the airwaves. I then took some calls with local regional stations — BBC Radio Gloucestershire and BBC Radio Wiltshire in the West, and Radio Jackie in south-west London — which were great for spreading the word among the local supporters en route.

The following day, I was bleary-eyed when I met a fandango of 15 runners and an ITV evening news crew outside Sheffield Cathedral. The day off hadn't been as restful as I'd hoped, but the wheel of adventure kept on turning and I needed to move with it. The runners kindly waited for me to give the interview with a reporter from ITV. He was a friendly man and inquisitive about the run and its aims. We talked about

Girlguiding and how adventure is for everyone, and that the outdoors is a place to go and just be your most marvellous self. Of course, I then went on to tell him about all the different kinds of poo I'd stepped in, and when I mentioned that I'd stood in a dead rabbit his face was a picture. But I didn't want to leave those parts of the run out. I was always hellbent on sharing the full truth about the journey, not just the perfect, sparkly bits. There is too much sharing of only the sparkly bits in the world already and it's unrealistic for young girls, or in fact anyone, to aspire to. The interview went out on ITV national news (minus the poo chat) and, in the video, there's a close-up shot of my feet. In that shot, you can see the small cut that I'd picked up on the way into Sheffield.

Interview done and dusted, the runners and I got underway on what was to be a 19-mile jaunt out of the city, into the Peak District National Park. The news crew filmed the start of the stage and then stayed with us for a while on the road — a camerawoman hanging out of the back of a car boot and filming as we chugged, en masse, up steep hills and along small country roads lined with hedgerows. The film crew then left, and from that point on, it was a very ordinary day. Well, except for the fact that I was given a piggy-back over an especially tough section of gravel over the Derwent Dam. Who refuses a piggy-back when they're offered one? Not me. Life is too short to refuse a piggy-back. But other than getting to ride on the back of another human for a short while, it was a very ordinary day. We ran. We chatted. We laughed, and we ran some more.

At the end of the day, I headed off to give a talk to some girls in the evening at an outdoors centre in Bamford. Towards the end of the talk, while fielding questions from the girls, I became aware of a dull ache in my right foot. I was sure it was just some nerve tingling. But there was also a nagging voice in the back of my mind which said that something about this sensation was different.

I was collected by a local host and ferried to her home, and I tried to ignore the ache for the rest of the evening. I was distracted through dinner, and when I crawled into bed that night, I did my best to rationalise the situation. It was two days since I'd cut my foot. If that tiny nick was going to flare up, surely it would have done it right away? I mean, I wasn't sure what the rules of foot wounds were but 'it' — and I was now viewing the cut as a thing I could bargain with — 'it' had let me run 19 miles. Surely, if it was a bad cut that wouldn't have been possible? I was certain a good night's sleep would encourage the cut to pipe down and, in the morning, all order would be restored.

18

The Ultrarunning Doctor

'Anna! Anna! Anna! Can me and my friend have a race with you on the field outside before you go?'

It was 9 a.m., and I was standing outside my host's house, chatting to her excitable daughter, Nyah. Overnight, the dull ache in my foot had progressed to a burning sensation, and then into full-blown throbbing. And man-oh-man, how it throbbed. By 3 a.m. I could think of nothing but the pain in the sole of my foot, and no matter what I tried to do, nothing eased it. What the hell was going on down there?! When morning rolled around, I'd managed to sit on the floor in the living room to get packed up, pull on some clothes and put a sock on over my foot — which really seemed to help, if only mentally. Because, if I couldn't see the cut, then surely the pain didn't exist. I then hobbled to the front door.

'Umm. You know what, Nyah?' I crouched down so that I was at eye-level with her.

'What?' Nyah pushed back a flop of chocolate-brown curls which had dropped across her eyes.

'I've got an even better idea. In fact, it's the best idea I've had in ages. How about I watch you run?' I said, trying to

269

sound as excited as possible.

'Me run? But I want you to run with me?' She wrinkled her nose and looked confused.

'But if I run with you then there's no one to judge who wins the race.'

Nyah thought for a moment before deciding I'd made a good point.

'Okay! But make sure you're watching!' she said, sprinting off with her friend to the field across the street.

After Nyah and her friend had raced up and down a few times (it was 'best of three'), her mum gave me a ride to Chapel-en-le-Frith in the middle of the Peak District to begin another day of running. My mind was in a million different places as we made the journey. I'd confessed to Nyah's mum that I had a sore foot, but I didn't want to share the extent of the pain I'd been in overnight. In truth, I felt stupid. Embarrassed, even. My brain was buzzing with a dozen what ifs. What if I'd run a different route into Sheffield and avoided the thing that cut my foot? What if I'd cleaned the cut better? What if I'd not had so much on, with the talks and all the interviews, and I'd been able to pay more attention to that tiny little wound?

Off the back of all the recent media attention, I'd agreed to give an interview to The Sunday Times, so Nyah's mum dropped me off outside a pub where I could find a quiet corner. I got out of the car and then smiled and waved, making sure that the car had rolled out of sight before I limped across the street. I know it might seem silly that I was trying to hide the injury, but when I've got a problem to solve, I need time to get my own head around it first — to process what's going on and work out how I feel about it before sharing it. I need to retreat into a dark, quiet corner to lick my wounds.

My dark, quiet corner came in the form of the pub. At 10 a.m., I sat down at a table opposite the bar and called the journalist from The Sunday Times. It was the weirdest thing, talking to a journalist about a long run when all the while I was wondering whether I'd be able to run at all. Doing the interview was like trying to pat my head and rub my tummy. I was desperately trying to listen to the questions, but I couldn't concentrate. I was away with the fairies. The sensible fairy in my brain was screaming at me that my foot was infected, but the optimistic fairy was still hopeful that I could 'run it off'. I'd had small cuts before that hurt when I walked, but after a mile or two of running. . . the pain went away. Perhaps this is one of those, I thought. I wrestled my way through the journalist's remaining questions and was relieved when the interview was over.

Slumping back in my chair, I stared into space for a few minutes. But sitting there was no good; I was only delaying the inevitable. I decided I had better at least protect the wound so that I didn't make it worse with my running attempt. I pulled some stretchy physio tape out of my bag and stuck it over the cut, winding it between my big and second toe to keep it in place. Then I packed up my bits and bobs and headed outside.

I began a speed-hobble down the street and passed a few people who recognised me as 'the barefoot runner' from the evening news.

'Great job!' shouted a passer-by.

'Well done!' said another.

I forced a smile through my grimace, but I had never wanted to be in possession of an invisibility cloak so badly as I did that morning. After a few hundred metres of hobbling, I was still in agony and the reality of the situation dawned on me. I felt a lump rise in my throat. I ducked down an alleyway on the edge of the town, away from the street, and melted into tears. I was so very tired of my thoughts going round and round like a merry-go-round, so I got my phone out and called Jamie. He answered right away.

'Hello, my dear.'

'Hello, J — can I just have a cry on you?' I sniffed.

'You go right ahead.'

So, I did. I blurted out about how much my foot hurt and how it was the worst day to not be able to run. Over the next 48 hours, I had three talks to give and members of the public waiting to join me in Stockport, then Manchester. I had also arranged to visit a Girlguiding festival to speak to 1,700 young girls. This was not a time to be injured. I sobbed a bit, sniffed a bit, then sobbed some more. I got angry, then sad, and then angry again. I felt such a weight on my shoulders and the feeling of it was almost physical. And the worst thing was that I knew it was from all the pressure I'd piled onto myself. . . all of the promises I'd made and the fact that I'd crammed so much into the journey on top of all the running. In that moment, I was tired of having to make all of the decisions, and I was clean out of energy to pep myself up. I felt trapped. I poured all of this out while Jamie listened, and then there was a silence.

'And you're sure you can't run on it?' he asked.

'J, it's agony!' I snapped, wondering if he'd heard anything I'd just said.

'I know, I know. It's just sometimes, when things hurt, you get running and they stop hurting. Did you give it a good crack, like half a mile?'

'Well, no. I only did a few hundred metres, but I can barely walk.'

'And you're sure you don't want to try again?' he asked softly.

I hung up the phone, having agreed to give it another go. It was tough love, but maybe Jamie was right. If this was going to stop me from running for a while, I didn't want to have any regrets. I needed to be absolutely certain that there was no way I could carry on. I took off, away from the alleyway, and ran for a quarter of a mile. It was like running with a drawing pin jammed into my foot. An old, rusty, thick drawing pin. I pushed on for a minute longer before hobbling to stop. This was ridiculous. There was no way I could walk the distance I had to cover that day, let alone run it. I collapsed onto a nearby bench and pulled out my phone. I'd got all of my emotions out while speaking to Jamie — they were busy soaking into my tear-stained top — and now I was on to the practicalities. I needed to find someone to take a look at my foot so I could work out exactly what I was dealing with. I'd accepted that I was injured and that this would take some time to heal, but I at least wanted to know I was doing everything I could to get back on the road as fast as possible. The clock was ticking. There were still 1,570 miles to go until London, and I desperately wanted to run them. I racked my brains for ideas of what to do in a place where I knew no one. I could easily get a bus to the city of Stockport from where I was, but then I needed to find a doctor I could explain things to who would really get it. I bit my lip. I hated asking for help at the best of times, least of all when I was down and out. But by not asking for help, I was only getting in my own way. I sucked in a deep breath and posted on Twitter:

HELP NEEDED. Does anyone know a doctor in the Stockport area? I'll fill you all in later.

I set the phone down on the table. I doubted it would work, but it was worth a shot. A minute later a notification had popped up; someone called Caitlin had replied.

There's an Ultrarunner called Adam in Stockport. Not sure which surgery he's at. — @Adfirth

274

Thanks Caitlin! @Adfirth I'm sure you're super busy! But if you see this and you're able to help or happy for me to give you a call then that would be wonderful.

Later that morning, I managed to get Doctor Adam on the phone.

'So, Dr Adam, I'm on this run.'

'Uh huh.'

'It's a long run.'

'That's great.'

'I'm doing it for Girlguiding.'

'Brilliant.'

'And, well, I'm running with no shoes on.'

'Okay. . .'

I sped up my words, hoping that if I could get them all out before Dr Adam drew breath, then he would think me less unhinged.

'And I've got a cut in my foot which I'm pretty sure is infected. And, well. . . I wondered if you might have time to take a proper look at it? I wouldn't ask, except. . . I'd love to get back on the road as soon as I can. I know that sounds mad. I know this is all a bit strange. But I—'

'No problem, Anna.'

'No problem?'

'No problem. Where are you now?'

'I'm right by Stockport train station, but I can come to you. I can get on a bus or in a taxi or something — whatever's easiest?'

'No, no, you stay put. I'll come to you, but it won't be for a couple of hours.'

'That's fine, brilliant, in fact. Totally brilliant. Thank you. What sort of time do you think?'

'Well, I just need to go and run a marathon on a running track first. . . as soon as that's done, I'll head over — let's say three p.m.-ish?'

I hung up the phone and I was buzzing. What were the chances?! Not only had I found a local doctor who was willing to help, but an ultrarunning doctor no less! He would surely understand the need to get myself fixed up and back on the road, pronto. Dear Universe, thank you.

As promised, Dr Adam came to see me after he'd run his track marathon. It felt strange to be meeting him for the first time and showing him my gammy foot within minutes, but I figured he must have seen worse. He took one look at my foot and said it was infected.

'How long do you think it'll take to heal?' I asked.

'It's tough to say; all bodies are different. It could be ten days, it could be a month, or longer. You'll just have to sit tight and let it do its thing. Sorry, Anna.'

I was gutted. The idea of being off my feet for 10 days was a blow, but what if it was months before I could run again? What with all of the intricate logistics of the Girlguiding talks and the running stages, surely that would mean cancelling everything and the end of the run entirely.

Dr Adam wrote out a prescription for some antibiotics. He then even drove me to a pharmacy to collect them and took me for a cup of coffee. Over the coffee, Adam shared stories from his own running adventures — the previous year, he'd run over 50 miles around Manchester, darting between all of the uniquely decorated bee sculptures that'd been put up around the city in 2018, raising money for a mental health charity. Just as I'd hoped, Dr Adam really got it.

I'm not sure if it was the antibiotics, Adam's calming vibes or the power of a good cup of joe, but when I hugged him goodbye, I felt so much calmer about the whole situation. I still didn't have a firm answer on how long my foot would take to heal, but I was back in the driving seat. I had a way forward, something to pin my hopes on. Everything would get easier from there on in.

After seeing Adam, I caught a train from Stockport to Manchester and holed up in a hotel at Piccadilly Gardens. I'd already planned for Jamie to visit me while I was in Manchester; the only difference was that I hadn't managed to run there and I had a ballooning, infected foot. I'd hoped that the antibiotics would at least help to lessen the pain but, 24 hours after seeing Adam, I was still in agony. Pus had now pooled under the many layers of hard skin, resulting in a yellow bulge on the bottom of my foot. I'd had my fair share of injuries over the years — broken bones, torn muscles, a slash on my arm (from rollerblading into a wall — that one left a big scar), so I couldn't understand why this tiny cut was so painful. That was until I remembered that there are 7,000 nerve endings in one foot. Goodness knows how many of them I'd upset. I also wondered whether all of the hard work I'd put in to building up the hard skin on my feet was now my undoing. Rather than escaping naturally through the skin, the infection was trapped under those many hardened layers.

Jamie was as laid-back as ever when he arrived.

'Hello, my love,' he said as I opened the hotel room door. I gave him a kiss and then a giant hug — one of those hugs where you let yourself flop for a little while in the other person's arms and wonder if they would notice if you just stayed there until the sun went down.

'How you doing?' he asked.

'Not great, J, not great. . .'

'Well, that makes sense. I didn't expect you to be bouncing off the walls.'

'I'm pretty frustrated. I might not be the best company,' I warned.

'You're always the best company, my dear,' he said nonchalantly, walking past me and into the bedroom before sitting on the edge of the bed. 'Come on then. . .'

'Come on what?'

'Let's see it! I want to see this foot. Is there pus? Oww, I do hope there's pus!'

For the first two days in Manchester with Jamie, I barely left the room. Even getting off the bed to go for a wee was a no-no. The second I moved my leg from its propped-up position on a pillow and onto the floor, a searing pain pulsed through my foot. There was a delayed reaction on it, perhaps half a second, while the blood took its time to reach the infected area, and that always made it worse, because I knew it was coming, and I had to wait that half a second each time before I could deal with it. It felt like someone had let a thousand tiny sharks with razor blade fins loose into my blood stream. As they swam through the infected area, their fins made a thousand tiny paper cuts. I'm not someone who likes to take painkillers — I'd rather feel what's going on (and I've seen one too many videos about what ibuprofen does to the lining of your stomach) — but that week, I was living on them.

As the week wore on, I progressed from being able to make it to the toilet, to being able to get to the restaurant on the floor below for meals. On the fourth day of being in the hotel, I managed to go outside and hobble across the road to a coffee shop. That was bliss! Oh, the freedom, the wind in my hair, the glory of being on the move at approximately half a mile an hour.

In all of that being still, I had a lot of time to think about the journey ahead. I was doing my best to keep everyone updated

— Girlguiding, the runners who'd signed up to the open stages, hosts and those following online too. I was feeling the weight of everyone having invested time and energy into the run, and I wanted to be able to let them all know what the plan was. Abby and I had a mega spreadsheet on the go and that spreadsheet had been keeping me on track — making sure the Girlguide members got their visits and that runners who'd signed up got enough notice of where and when to join in. But I needed to make a decision about what to do about the miles I'd missed.

Option one would be to wait until I was fully healed and then restart the run in the Peak District, where I'd finished my last day of running. The issue with that option was that I had no idea how long the recovery would take, and we would have to rejig everything in the schedule from that point on. The route, the open running stages, the Girlguiding talks — all of it would have to be shifted back. Even entertaining that thought made my brain hurt.

Option two was just to miss out a chunk of the running route. I'd cancel the public running stages until I could run again, but would still keep moving along the route via other means and give the Girlguiding talks. Then, when I was ready to run again, I would just drop back into the schedule and carry on. Much as I didn't like the idea of not running every single mile of the route I'd planned, it was the most logistically sensible option. I had hoped I'd be able to run an unbroken line from Shetland to London, but I'd had to miss out a few miles here and there between stages when the timings didn't work out, so that plan was already scuppered. Although I was still hopeful I could make the 100-marathon distance, I hadn't registered to break any world records, and there were no rules as such — so, if there was a gap in the route, it didn't matter unless it mattered to me. And I decided that it didn't. That eased the pressure somewhat. Choosing option two meant that I wouldn't let any of the girls down and I could run again whenever I was able to, although I hoped that would be sooner rather than later.

As it turned out, the greatest challenge of this adventure wasn't the running. It was not being able to run at all. I've always found sitting still to be far more difficult than moving — because the chatter in your mind is louder when you're still. On the plus side, I had Jamie by my side to help calm my buzzy brain. To intrusive thoughts of 'What if my foot never gets better?' Jamie would reply, 'It will.' And when I said to him, 'What about if this is the end of the run? What if it stays bad for months and then it's winter — I won't run through winter, I can't,' he replied, 'Anna, you've run over one thousand miles in your bare feet. I think even if you stopped here, it's pretty amazing.' If my dark thoughts were kites in the wind which wanted to fly off, get all tangled up and do some catastrophising, then Jamie kept them tethered to the ground. They could fly, but only so far. They never got out of my grasp. I just watched them flap erratically in the breeze, while I worked out what to do.

After a week by my side, Jamie left to go home. The pain in my foot had subsided and, with the help of a sterile needle and some TCP, I'd managed to squeeze almost all of the pus out of the wound (much to Jamie's delight). I could now just about walk on it with only a slight limp — all of which was progress.

With some motion restored, I got back to standing up for long periods of time, and that meant I could deliver talks to the girls again. So, I continued the onward journey from Manchester to Liverpool via train, to visit a group of girls at the Royal Philharmonic Hall. I'd had to cancel visits to several groups over the past week, which was the right decision but gutting, nonetheless. To think that girls who had followed the journey since Shetland had patiently waited for me to make it to their unit and then I'd not shown up — that broke my heart.

A local leader called Hannah collected me from Liverpool train station and ferried me to the hall for the talk. On the way there, I wondered how I could stand in front of these girls and encourage them to be brave, now and in the future, when I was feeling completely the opposite. But I resolved that it's easy to be brave when things are going well. Real bravery doesn't come in the form of standing triumphant on a mountain top, your hair blowing out behind you in the breeze. It is much messier than that and far less dramatic. Real bravery happens in the micro-moments of life. In the quiet places that no one else sees. In the valleys filled with shadow, between the mountain tops. It is ugly and wriggle-in-your-skin uncomfortable and there is no one or nothing else to trust in those moments except yourself. So, when the girls asked me why I had a bandage on my foot, I told them. And when they asked me what I was going to do, I said that I didn't know yet. But I promised them that I would find a way to keep going, just as soon as I could.

The Isle of Man & Northern Ireland

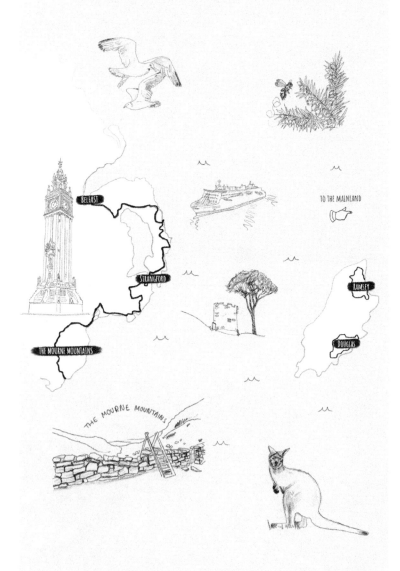

BELFAST

STRANGFORD

THE MOURNE MOUNTAINS

TO THE MAINLAND

RAMSEY

DOUGLAS

THE MOURNE MOUNTAINS

19

Running Rehab

There are wild wallabies living on the Isle of Man. I'll pause for a moment to let that piece of information sink in. Wild. Wallabies. Animals native to Australia and Tasmania living on a rocky outcrop in the middle of the Irish Sea. I'd like to believe that they took it upon themselves to hop aboard a first-class flight from the land down under (enjoying nibbles and champers along the way), but the truth is that a pair of them escaped from a wildlife park in the north-west of the Isle of Man back in 1965. Armed with nothing but a newfound freedom and a devil-may-care attitude, the wallabies began to breed and, with no predators to stop their population growth, there are now believed to be more than 160 of them living there, roaming wild and free.

I tell you all of this because, after visiting the girls in Liverpool, I took a ferry to the Isle of Man. My foot had continued to heal, albeit slowly. Walking became easier and I managed to do a five-minute tester run along the cool paving slabs of Liverpool docks. I followed that with a 10-minute run the following day, and then I got buck-wild and ran for 20 whole minutes. It was the strangest thing to be moving again after eight days of no running at all — it felt as if someone had swapped my right leg from the knee down with a stranger's. To run 1,000 miles and then to suddenly stop, well, my body barely knew what to do with itself when I broke into a run — the muscles felt all wonky and out of place. But slowly, slowly, I coaxed the foot back into action.

Originally, I'd planned to do a lap of the Isle of Man, running the Raad ny Foillan, or the Way of the Gull, a 100-mile footpath that traces the coast. But with my foot still in recovery mode, that plan went out the window. Instead, I would use the visit to do some rehab and get myself back into shape for the coming weeks. I was pleased that I'd made the decision to visit the island rather than head straight to Northern Ireland, but I couldn't help but arrive in a distracted state of mind. I was feeling far more positive about the foot situation and had gone from wondering if it would ever heal to knowing that it would. . . given time. I just didn't know how much time that would be. But there was nothing I could do about it except take things day by day.

At the ferry terminal in Douglas, I was greeted by my host Mark. As we drove away from the terminal car park, he asked me whether I was intending to run up any hills while I was on the island.

'Oh, is the Isle of Man hilly?' was my reply.

'Are you joking?' He laughed.

As it turns out, the Isle of Man is one big pile of hilliness. It's hilly around the edges and there's one even bigger hill in the middle of it, which locals refer to as 'the mountain'. How great that mound of earth must feel to be known as simply the Mountain. It must be like being Adele. Or Beyoncé. Or Oprah. I'll confess, I didn't know much about the Isle of Man before visiting. I knew that the famous cyclist Mark Cavendish was born there, that the island held a TT race each year and, as a cat lover, I knew it had some connection with the Manx cat — which is a kitty without a tail, miaow — but beyond that, I had no idea what to expect.

Mark and his partner, Nikki, were the perfect people to stay with that week. Their house was spacious and had a chilled vibe. It was a detached old mill, with a big garden and views out onto the horizon. They gave me a tour, showed me to my room on the top floor and finished up with a walk-through of the kitchen, which included a special snack drawer and strict instructions to 'help myself'. All in all, Mark said to make myself at home. So, that's just what I did.

I would sit in the living room on my laptop, watching rain trickle down the large windowpanes overlooking the garden. I tried not to think about my foot, but my mind drifted to it often. I wanted to be more present, so I kept apologising to Mark and Nikki for being a terrible guest, and then wondering if I should stop apologising. Because it's really very annoying when someone apologises constantly. But I wanted them to know that I wasn't myself and that I was sorry that I didn't have more energy to give them. The hole in my foot had sucked it all out of me.

Over the next few days, Mark showed me around the island.

ANNA MCNUFF

He took me up to see the Motor Museum where he volunteered, which housed over 500 cars and bikes — some of them very rare and all of them very cool. We drove along winding roads, over 'the Mountain' and along clifftops as I gazed out of the window at the luscious landscape. Seas of heather — maroon in some places, purple in others — stretched out across wind-swept moors and reminded me of the wildness of the Scot-tish Highlands. Hillsides tumbled steeply into the sea and, where the land was shallower, there were stretches of golden sandy beach, secluded pebble coves and quaint fishing villages flanked by sharp granite-topped peaks that made me think of the Lake District. All of which made sense because the island was once connected to Scotland and Cumbria before melting glaciers caused sea levels to rise and cut it off from the main-land some 10,000 years ago.

During my week on the island, I would sometimes wake up to find Mark's home surrounded by fog. The locals called this the Cloak of Manann. Manann is a character from Irish mythology — a warrior king who is best known as the god of the sea. Manannán mac Lir (the Little Son of the Sea) uses the fog as a cloak of invisibility to disguise his home and the dwell-ings of others, to keep them safe from harm. I had wished many times on the journey that I had a cloak like Manann's to make me invisible when I wanted to be, and I now wondered if he might let me borrow it until my foot had healed.

In between the sightseeing with Mark and trying Manann's cloak on for size, I gave a talk to a group of local Guides, and gradually, I set myself running goals. On one day, I did a

5-mile round trip to a coffee shop in the capital of Douglas — because it was always nice to be running fuelled by coffee. The following day, I ran 5 miles again, and all went swimmingly, but the morning after that, my foot flared up. Of course, I took it well. I'm joking. I didn't. I gathered up all of my adventure toys and threw them, nay launched them, out of the pram. I was frustrated. My recovery was so stop-start that it was officially driving me nuts. I felt like it was unfair. I'd 'behaved myself' and sat still for what felt like an eternity and, in return, the foot was supposed to be getting steadily better, not getting better and then worse again. I was done with waiting for it to heal. I was done with being patient.

While I was busy being angry at the situation, I got a message from my mum. She was checking in on how I was, ahead of her and my dad coming to visit me in Northern Ireland the following week. Given that mums are prone to catastrophising, her casual check-in was very cool of her. She was doing a great job at holding back on the certainty that I would get septicaemia and lose my whole foot as a result of the infected cut. But then again, Mum always surprises me. She mixes her motherly worry with an ability to transform into the most wonderful life coach. I mean, she actually is a qualified life coach, but she never needed a qualification for that. She has always been the greatest coach in my life. When Mum is in her coaching flow, it's like talking to a wiser, more experienced, more objective version of myself. And what a valuable tool that is when you can no longer trust your own thoughts.

Mum has always been one to push on through pain and

discomfort herself, so as I was struggling to dance that fine line between whether to rest or push on, I knew that her advice would be priceless. I thought about messaging her back, but I hit the call button instead.

'Hiya, petal, you okay?'

'Hiya, Mum. Umm. Not really. I'm going bananas here. . . I know it's going to take time, but my foot still really hurts. And it's been ten days now.'

'Okay, how does it look?'

'It looks much better.'

'Better every day? Or is it getting better then worse?'

'No, it's looking better every day', I said. 'But the pain is still the same as last week. I wanted to be running properly by now. I did do some five milers and it was okay. I mean painful, but okay. And I was going to go for a run again t0day, but now I'm even in pain walking on the carpet.'

'Right.'

'And so now I'm worried that means I'm going to make it worse by running on it and. . . well. I don't know. I'm just so confused. I'm not sure whether I should back off and rest it again or whether I've gone soft.'

'Anna! You have not gone soft.'

'I know, but you know what I mean. . .' I said, and there was a long pause. My confidence had taken a battering. I didn't know if I could trust my decisions anymore.

'Anna — so you've just run twice on your recently injured foot, which is more than you've done in a few weeks. Is that right?'

'Yes. . . I know, bu—'

'And it sounds to me like you've done everything you can to make the foot better. It looks better. It's getting better?'

'It is,' I said. There was another pause, then Mum softened her tone.

'Then all that's left to get better, Anna, is your mind.'

That was it. Tears collected in the corners of my eyes. Mum had hit the nail on the head. She was right. I knew it myself, deep down — the one thing that was usually my greatest source of strength, my mind, had started to betray me. I was tired of constantly having to think myself well again and, as a result, I'd given in to the whispers of doubt. Mum had helped me to the realisation that it wasn't my foot that was the problem anymore. It was my head. That was a tough pill to swallow. I fell silent.

'Are you okay?' she asked.

'Yes. . . it's just, you're right. I know it's likely my head that's holding me back, but I'm so tired of it.'

'Anna. . . this is your body, remember. You are in control of how it registers pain, and I suspect that your foot has been in pain for a very long time and it's now just remembering that pain. If it looks better, then it probably is better.'

'Mmm hmm.'

'Time to buck up and crack on then?' Mum joked, and I laughed.

I chatted to Mum for another 10 minutes. We talked about visualisation techniques and things I could do before I went to sleep at night that would help me to heal.

'Feeling better now, pet?'

'Yes, thank you. That's helped. I'll give running a go this afternoon with my new brain in and see how I go.'

'Sounds good. And besides — you'd better be properly back on your feet by the time we get over to Northern Ireland because I want to do some running!'

'Alright then, Mum. I promise to be moving again by then so you can get your training in!' I rolled my eyes.

'Great — your dad doesn't care, he's going to sit in coffee shops, but I'm up for an adventure!' she added.

I hung up and felt so grateful for a mum like mine. Someone who can remind you that you are stronger than you realise. When I was feeling weak, which I was that day, Mum was my strength. She was able to collect up those parts of me that had become buried somewhere beneath the mess and pain of the last 10 days and float them to the surface.

Over the next few days on the Isle of Man, I did exactly what Mum and I had agreed. I decided that if my foot was going to be in pain, then so be it. It was just pain. I ran another 5 miles, then 7 miles, and then, on the final day, I headed up to Ramsey in the north and ran on a section of the Raad ny

Foillan. Even though I hadn't been able to run the whole path, I was stoked to get a taster of it, at least. When not on the trail itself, I was running on quiet country roads and it felt fantastic to be stretching out my legs. I enjoyed the feeling of my soles pounding on the tarmac once again — even if there was a touch of pain in each stride, I grew comfortable with that discomfort. I greeted it like an old friend, one I had got to know better over the past week. By the time I'd finished exploring the area around Ramsey, I'd covered a tidy 10 miles and I was elated! Dear God, how good it felt to be running into double digits again.

The following morning, I hugged Mark and Nikki goodbye. I thanked them for their patience and kindness, for acting as my tour guides and for access to their bottomless snack drawer, then I boarded a ferry bound for Northern Ireland. As I pulled away from the shore, I finally felt like I had made peace with the injury. It had taken two and a half weeks of riding a mental and physical roller coaster, but the injury no longer dominated my mind. Since Stockport, it had felt like such a heavy burden, as if each day I was lifting an atlas stone to just even make it through 24 hours with my sanity intact. But now that stone had shrunk to the size of a pebble. I could pick it up, appreciate its importance and even its beauty and place it in my backpack. And there it would stay, always a part of the adventure, always a part of me. But very much in the past.

20

A Visit from the Mothership

My ferry was three hours late arriving in Belfast. It was a long and slow journey over rough seas and it was surreal to step out of the arrivals terminal and see Mama and Papa McNuff standing in the car park of the terminal. Two faces so familiar in unfamiliar surroundings. Moments later, I was locked in a tight squeeze with my mum, which was followed swiftly by an equally tight hug with my dad — the cumulative effect of which made my whole body breathe a sigh of relief. I'd been trying my best to keep it together for the past two weeks since I'd waved goodbye to Jamie in Manchester. Truth be told, I'd failed at holding it all together many times since leaving Shetland. The hugs from my folks grounded me. Whatever happened from that moment on, whether I was able to run the miles I hoped to in Northern Ireland or not, didn't matter. The important thing was that I'd be getting some quality hang-time with two people I loved.

After leaving the ferry terminal, we three slipped easily back into family life. I found comfort in the normality of slightly fraught parent-child and parent-to-parent exchanges and couldn't help but smile when Mum spent 10 minutes trying to navigate us out of a Belfast car park using Google maps on her phone. Dad took the micky out of her at intervals and I complained about feeling car sick (on account of going round many car park roundabouts). It was reminiscent of so many 90s family holidays — we could have been anywhere in Europe; the only thing that was missing were my brothers.

Sitting in the back of the car, I felt like a kid. I was amazed at how, aged 34, it was still possible to feel like a child. But I suppose that never really leaves you, no matter how old you get. All any of us want is to be loved and feel safe, after all. And, strangely, being in the back of a hire car with my parents having a barney in a car park in Belfast did just that.

After many more wrong turns and a few more navigational 'discussions', we made a brief stop at a campground south of Belfast to visit a group of Brownies. Twenty of them ran laps around a large field in bare feet, before I told stories around a campfire while they sat on gnarled tree stumps and snuggled up in fleecy blankets. They oohed and aahed at descriptions of the scenery I'd run through so far and urrrrghed! at the tale of the dead rabbit. As the sun began to set, my folks and I waved the Brownies goodbye and made our way to a rented apartment (our base camp for the following few days), just outside the coastal town of Bangor. It was a spacious flat with a large bay window on the first floor and I knew that Mum would enjoy sitting at the window and watching the boats bob around in the bay. We were alike in that way. Having a good vantage point from which to watch the world go by was a favourite pastime for the both of us.

The following morning, we were up and at 'em — ready to head into the centre of Belfast for the first public running stage in two weeks. I knew that if I could make it the full 15 miles I had planned for the day then I'd finally get back on schedule. I was a jangle of nerves and excitement, but Mum was even more excited than me. She'd been in her running gear since the moment she got out of bed (I had some suspicions that she might have slept in it) and let out a loud 'Whooop!' every time I mentioned going running. She too was coming back from injury, having torn the anterior cruciate ligament (ACL) in her knee in a skiing accident 18 months earlier. She'd chosen not to have an operation to repair the ligament and so, after a lot of lunging exercises and some hard work to rehab the knee, she was elated to be back on her feet and running. Mum was doing 5 miles at home, so she planned to join me for small portions at the start of each day and have Dad pick her up whenever her knee gave out.

Although I ate huge amounts during and after running, my morning routine involved only having a light breakfast. It didn't sit well to have too much lolling around in my stomach at the start of the day and, since I hadn't actually been doing much running over the past few weeks, my appetite had decreased. I should have known better than to attempt a light breakfast in the presence of Sue McNuff, however. Mum is the world's greatest fan of a hearty morning meal — so much so that she should be breakfast's global ambassador. She was therefore horrified that I was intending to eat 'just' toast and Marmite for the most important meal of the day. She staged a one-woman sit-in and insisted that I eat some 'real food' (muesli) before I was allowed to leave the apartment.

With both of our bellies full of muesli, we made it to The Albert Clock Memorial by Belfast Harbour at 11 a.m.. I wasn't sure how many people would turn up for the running stage, if any. I'd been deliberately quiet on social media for the previous week. Ordinarily, in the lead-up to an open running stage, I'd be restating when and where I was starting from and actively encouraging people to join in, but I hadn't done that for Belfast — largely because I didn't mind the idea of slipping quietly through Northern Ireland while I built the miles back up.

There was one man waiting at the clock tower when we arrived, standing in the shadow of its ornately carved, sandy-coloured stone. He was my height, around 5 feet 10, with a shaved head and a short grey beard. He was wearing dark sunglasses, a blue running top, black shorts and bright green trainers and had a small hydration pack on his back. All in all, he looked like a serious runner — as if he'd been plucked from the Ultra-Trail du Mont-Blanc and dropped in the middle of Belfast. I immediately felt a fizz of nerves in my belly. What if this man was going to be disappointed with our speed? What if I had to cut the stage short if my foot was too sore? But from the moment I said hello, I realised I needn't have worried at all. He oozed a laid-back vibe which, when accompanied by a strong Northern Irish accent, put me immediately at ease. This man was as cool as a cucumber. Cooler, in fact. We chatted for a few minutes before getting ready to hit the road. I explained that I was rehabbing my foot and that we were hoping to cover 15 miles to Newtownards, but I'd be playing it by ear.

'Whatever you want to do, that's grand by me,' the man smiled.

'Great. Thank you. Oh, and this is my mum,' I said, opening my arms and presenting my mum to him as if she was a Paul Daniel's magic trick and I was Debbie McGee.

'Hello, Anna's mum,' said the man.

'Okay, let's g— Oh! I need to know one thing. . .' I said.

'What's that?'

'What's your name?'

'Oh, I'm Darr'n.'

'Darr'n?' I repeated in a Northern Irish accent, smiling.

'I guess that'd be Darren to a Londoner like me,' Mum chipped in, adding extra London twang.

'It would, but you can call me Darr'n,' he smiled.

'Brilliant. Right then, Darr'n, you ready to rock?'

'Absolutely.'

And we were off, hotfooting it through the backstreets of Belfast before joining a traffic-free cycle trail. The trail was just about the most perfect surface I could have asked for that day. The tarmac was smooth, there were no cars to think about, no curb-hopping to do and the navigation consisted of my favourite type of directions: 'straight, straight, straight'. It was my kind of route and we settled quickly into a steady pace as we weaved through the suburbs of Belfast, pausing briefly at C. S. Lewis Square — named after Belfast's most famous author — where there are bronze statues of several characters from The Lion, the Witch and the Wardrobe. There was Mr Tumnus, the White Witch and a few others dotted around, but the statue of Aslan the lion was my favourite. He looked so regal and his bronze mane was spectacular, exploding from his head like a dozen rays of bright, bronzy sunshine. I had always liked Aslan in the Narnia books. He seemed so wise and noble. Under his statue, the inscription read: 'Aslan — the embodiment of all that is good.'

'Isn't that lovely?' I mused to Mum, who was standing next to me and was now inspecting the statue too.

'Hmm. I don't know.'

'What do you mean, you don't know?'

'Well, his head looks a bit small for a male lion,' she said.

'Mum! Are you questioning Aslan's integrity?'

'No. I'm just questioning his proportions,' she said, matter-of-factly.

We left C. S. Lewis Square (some of us more satisfied with the proportions of the statues than others) and continued on the trail. Considering only one person had turned up for the run, Darren was the perfect guy for the job. My mum loves to chat and she loves to run. So, it follows that she likes to chat while running, and Darren was a chatty fella. Mum and I took it in turns to run by his side and get to know him a little better.

'I'm on a run streak at the moment,' he said.

'A run what?' I asked.

'A streak,' he said, and I eyed him more closely. From what I knew about streaking, it involved being nakey-nakey, and Darren didn't look naked to me. Unless he was wearing a hologram of clothes.

'What's a streak?'

'Oh. It's where you try to run every day, for as long as you can.'

'Every day?'

'Yep.'

'How far?'

'Oh, it doesn't matter. . . but my days are usually three miles. Some people just do half a mile. It's less about the distance and more about just getting out and moving, you know? It's good for the head in that way, gives a focus.'

'I bet it is. Do you ever have days when you think "nah — I can't be arsed"?'

'Yup, I've had those days — but you've just got to get out there anyway. . . otherwise the whole streak is ruined.'

'So what day of. . . er. . . streaking are you on?'

'Oh. . . wait now. . . this would be day one, seven, one, four.'

'What? One thousand, seven hundred and fourteen?!'

'Yes.'

'You've run every day for one thousand, seven hundred and fourteen days?'

'I have.'

'Bloody hell, Darren! That's impressive.'

'Says the woman running around the country barefoot. . .'

'Yeah, but I've taken days off!'

'You're right. You're such a softie, Anna,' he smiled.

I was impressed by Darren's commitment, and I liked the idea of 'streaking'. Especially if it didn't need to be about distance. Surely even on days when you feel like poo on a stick you could manage a half-mile run? I could see how streaking could become a constant in a person's life, something to anchor each day, a reason to leave the house, a really healthy habit. And it was nice to have those to balance out all the naughty ones.

In between time spent talking with Darren, I would drop back to check in on how the still-healing foot wound was feeling, and I'd let Mum pick up the chat baton. Before we'd left the apartment that morning, Mum had repeatedly said to me, 'Whatever you do, Anna, it's probably best not to bring up politics today.' Well, 7 miles into the run, as we passed the Stormont Estate, I could swear that I heard mum quizzing Darren about the history and politics of Northern Ireland.

We followed the trail and its luscious tarmac all the way

to the town of Comber, which Darren told me should be pronounced 'CUMMER'. He also said that it should be shouted as aggressively as possible, to get the accent just right. As we were running through the town, we happened to see my dad, who was sitting in a coffee shop by a large window, reading a paper. We knocked on the window and then gate-crashed his peace and quiet to take a short lunch break, before hitting the road again.

Now, I'm not sure at exactly what point Mum's plan to 'only join me for a few miles' went out the window, but it did.

After 15 miles of running, all three of us made our way into the town of Newtownards, or just 'ARDS' (which Darren told me should be said with as equal vigour as CUMMER). It felt amazing to be back on the road — meeting locals again, seeing new sights and, this time, doing all of that with Mum in tow. It was a near-perfect way to properly restart the adventure.

After our day out with Darren, Mum and I hit the road again the next day. With no more open running stages or any meeting points to make, Mum was forced to slot into my usual routine, which meant starting running after midday. As a morning person, the late start drove Mum round the bend. She would bounce around the apartment like a cooped-up puppy dawg, repeatedly asking 'Ready now?' every 10 minutes, until I finally relented and opened the door to let her outside.

We didn't find any more traffic-free trails on the second day, but we ran side by side on quiet country lanes, heading east from Ards onto the Ards Peninsula and then turning south to follow the coast. We plodded through tiny towns and small fishing ports and, well, truly put the world to rights. We giggled as we took it in turns to duck into the bushes for roadside wees, marvelled at stately country homes and talked the hind legs off many donkeys (which we stopped to pet in the fields). Through all of that, I realised that there are times when Mum is my mum and there are times when she is my friend. I like that she is a mum first and foremost, and a friend second, but when she cuts loose in friendship mode, she is the most energetic friend I have.

Mum's not only a great chatter, but she's also a solid run partner too — a leggy 5 ft 10, her running strides are smooth and long. She had Adventure Pace nailed within the first day and it was like having a pacemaker on the road next to me, swinging her arms as she went. Most days she wore a bright green T-shirt that said 'One. . . Two. . . Three. . . GO!' on the back. That made me smile because it pretty much summed her up. Except you could probably leave out the one, two, three and just skip straight to the GO! Some days, Mum had more GO than I could handle and, in the afternoons, when my foot got sore, I struggled to keep pace. So, in a bid to slow Mum down and distract me from the foot pain, I put her to work on capturing some video footage and taught her how to use my fancy GoPro camera — which naturally resulted in a lot of footage of her nostrils and her shouting 'Anna! Which way do I face it?'

While Mum and I ran, Dad continued to whizz off to

nearby coffee shops and hang out in those for the day. There, he'd speak to the locals, catch up on some work or read the paper, doing what it is that dads do best when they sit in coffee shops. I was envious in some ways. Oh, how I longed to sit in a coffee shop and read the paper (well, the travel section at least). Being on an adventure and sitting in coffee shops were my two states of happiness. I truly was a by-product of my parents in that respect. I bonded with Mum through running and with Dad over a shared loved of a decent flat white. So, he humoured me by providing updates on where he'd managed to find the best one in Northern Ireland so far.

After two days on the run together, Mum had done two full 15-milers by my side, which came as a surprise after her saying that she'd only come along for 'a few miles each day'. On the third morning, she woke up and confessed that she was feeling sore, so she was just going to join me until halfway, which was around 8 miles.

At the halfway marker, we stopped for lunch in Portavogie. Well, I had lunch, Mum opted for a giant latte (she wasn't as big on lunches as she was on breakfasts). I have a photo of her from that day, all smiles and sweat-encrusted face. Dad had driven down the coast to join us and so Mum had been reunited with her reading glasses, and she was beaming out from behind them. She looked very youthful. Whether it was the power of the Irish Sea air or the size of the latte, I'll never know, but as we got up from lunch, Mum took a deep breath and made an announcement.

'I'm coming with you.'

'What?'

'This afternoon. I'm coming with you. I can't leave you out there alone,' she said, and I laughed.

'Mum, I hate to break it to you, but I've been out there "alone" since the Shetland Islands. I think I'll be alright.'

'Yes, but, well. . . I'm here to give you company and it seems silly. There's only eight miles left.'

'But is your knee sore?'

'Yes, but it'll be okay. I'll just need to warm it up. It'll cope with a few more miles.'

And so, at approximately 3.17 p.m., two McNuff women could be seen hobbling out of the car park of The New Quays restaurant in Portavogie. We took off out of town, each of us limping on different legs. Mum was insisting that her knee just needed to 'get used to it', and I was insisting that I just needed to 'desensitise' my foot into action. We were both moving our arms as much as we could to will our legs onwards. At that moment, my dad drove by, beeping the horn and waving. What on earth must we have looked like? Two hobbling runners, both swinging our arms like lunatics, willing parts of our body into submission. It was a one-of-a-kind moment and a neat memory for the family album.

At the small town of Portaferry, the mini adventure with my folks drew to a close. From there, they'd be driving to the airport to make their way home and I'd be getting a ferry across

Strangford Lough, to continue running down the east coast. Mum had been such a good sport. She'd certainly stepped up to retain her legendary status over the course of the past week. First the pep talk on the Isle of Man, and now we'd had fun on the run — proper girl time out on the road together. She'd covered 46 miles over three days which, considering the last time she ran more than 15 miles was when training for the London Marathon in 1996, was an impressive feat. That's the power of some good chat for you. Or maybe that's just the power of my mum.

***

After my parents left, I found a sweet state of flow. My foot was sore, but no more than it had been when I'd arrived in Northern Ireland, and, best of all, I was actually enjoying running again. In fact, I was bloomin' loving it. I became addicted to the sweet satisfaction of my bare feet pushing off the tarmac. I could feel each and every part of each foot as they made contact with the ground. The ball of my foot would land lightly, followed swiftly by the heel — then, when I could feel the full cool of the tarmac, I'd roll slightly forward and push off from the pad beneath my toes. Land, roll, push off. Land, roll, push off. Swoosh. Swoosh. Swoosh. The tarmac was smooth so there were no nasty surprises underfoot and, rather than sapping it from me, it felt like the road was actually gifting me energy. I couldn't remember the last time that had happened. I had missed this. I had missed the feeling of being in motion, with some puff in my lungs and not a care in the world.

I swooshed onwards, down quiet country back roads, past neat hedgerows, clusters of shady woodland and small farms. Every now and then, a car or the local postie would rumble on by, but other than that, I was alone. At each crossroad, I would stop briefly and contemplate whether I liked the look of that road with the low hanging branches straight ahead or the one to my right with moss in the middle of it. After a breath or two, I'd take off again. Back to the swooshing. Back in the rhythm, back in the groove, at last. On some days, I even used the network of back roads to run routes that were longer than I needed to. I was having a whale of a time and anything I could do to get my body used to averaging 20+ mile days again was much needed if there was any chance of me still making the 100-marathon target by mid-November.

I continued to follow the coastline south for the next few days, through small fishing villages and over the rocky clifftops of County Down. I was stopped by passers-by every now and then, and my favourite exchange was with a farmer near Killough. He was driving a muddied, blue Land Rover and stopped it in the middle of the road. And I mean, right in the middle of the road. He then rolled down his window.

'And where are you off to in those bare feet of yours?' he asked.

'London,' I replied.

'Are you now?'

'I am.'

'Well now, I've got t' be hearing about this,' he said, turning off the engine and getting out, still with the car in the middle of the road. The farmer and I then had a 10-minute chat. He didn't seem bothered about holding anyone up and nonchalantly waved at other cars to go around him while we talked. I liked his relaxed approach to life (and the rules of the road) and I aimed to take a little bit of his attitude with me for the remaining months of the run.

After the chat with the farmer, I padded onwards, over the boardwalk alongside the Ballybannan River at Dundrum, through the heather-fringed dunes of Murlough Nature Reserve and then along the golden sands of Newcastle Beach — where the mighty Mourne Mountains loomed large on the horizon. I spent a day running in the mist of the Mourne Mountains themselves and, at Kilkeel, my time in Northern Ireland came to a close. It had been nothing short of spectacular — the bonding time with my parents, the beautiful scenery, the small villages, the friendly people — all of it. I'd notched up 100 miles in Northern Ireland, putting the 'running' total up to 1,185 miles and, for the first time in weeks, I felt like I was back in the game. From Kilkeel, I'd be making a quick detour down to Dublin to catch a ferry to North Wales, where I'd restart the journey on the British mainland. I broke my silence on social media and put up a post with a big picture of my face and a thumbs-up. The caption read: 'I'm back on the road and back up to speed at last! You Welshies better get the kettle on and that Bara Brith buttered because I'm-a-comin for you!'

Wales & the Midlands

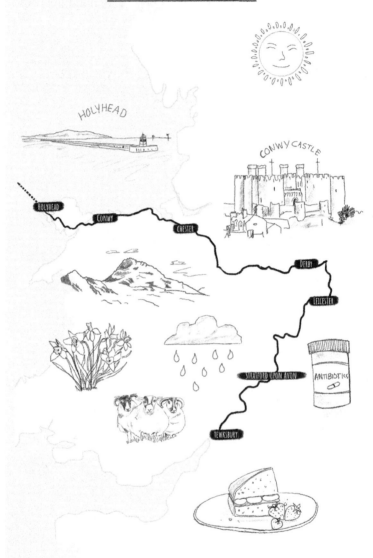

21

Back in the Game!

I've got a whole lot of love for Wales. It's somewhere I go back to time and time again for mini adventures and, over the years, every time I visit, I come home with a giant grin plastered across my face. I had high hopes for my run across its north coast, but I didn't know anyone on Anglesey in the north-west. So, when I encountered a logistical hiccup and was stuck for someone to transport my main kit bag from Holyhead ferry port, I had a few anxious nights of sleep. With all the miles and time lost to the foot infection, I couldn't afford to lose another day of running. If I couldn't find someone to take up the bag baton as I got off the ferry, then I'd have to stay put to sort it out, which would lose me yet more time. I needn't have worried — a local Guide leader called Angela came to the rescue. Angela (who should really have worn her underpants on the outside of her clothing from that day on) completed a 90-minute round trip to the ferry port to collect the bag and drop it with a host further along my route.

With my kit bag taken care of, I headed east and I loosely followed the coast. I ran along cycle paths and grassy trails as well as small back country roads with strips of grass down the middle. I stopped at lone corner shops in tiny towns and, from the limited supplies on offer there, engineered a new mid-run snack. I'd buy a banana and a packet of caramel chocolate Rolos. I would put one Rolo on the banana, take a bite, then get out a new Rolo for the next bite. And so on, until the banana was gone and there was only one Rolo left in the pack. Which, of course, I then gave to the person in the vicinity whom I loved the most — myself. This new snack would henceforth be known as the Roloana. It was the perfect injection of sugary, fruity goodness to fuel my afternoons and was a nibble to rival the usual favourites of sausage rolls, cheese and milkshakes.

On my fourth day of running across Wales, I was joined by a very special guest — one Tori James. In 2007, Tori became the first Welsh woman to climb Everest. She was only 25 at the time, which also made her the youngest British woman to have made it to the top of the highest mountain in the world.

I'd first been introduced to Tori through a friend of a friend, and for our first 'mate date', we'd embarked on a mini adventure together in the Brecon Beacons — running along Offa's Dyke before dropping down the valley into a bothy on the shore of the Grwyne Fawr reservoir. I remember being nervous the first time I met Tori because, well, she was nails. She did things that required precision and expedition-specific training. I ran along trails that were already marked on a map. And still, I got lost, ate chocolate and dished out hugs to unsuspecting strangers en route. If adventurers were Disney characters from Up, then Tori was Russell the wilderness explorer and I was the dog who gets distracted by squirrels.

Tori has red-brown hair, dark brown eyes and a pearly white complexion. She is a neat mix of friendly and matter of fact, and someone I would always trust to know what to do in a crisis. Although Tori lived way off my running route, in Cardiff, she was keen to join at some point as I journeyed through. Not only were we long overdue a catch-up, but she had also recently been appointed as the president of Girlguiding Cymru (Wales), so she made the long trip to the north coast to intercept me as I ran across the country.

I met Tori, her two-year-old son, Max, and a small group of supporters at the clock tower on Bangor high street at 11 a.m. At first, it seemed I had a fair few people who were going to run with me from Bangor, but I soon realised that the majority were there just to wave me off. The only ones who would be joining in for an 18-mile journey to Conwy were Tori (on her bike, with Max on the back) and another woman called Tabitha (also on her bike). Tabitha had found out about the run the night before and said I was the perfect excuse for the easy ride she had scheduled on her training programme. I loved the idea of running in a bike sandwich — with Tori and Tabitha as the bread and me as the filling. At this stage in the journey, I craved anything that was new and different because difference led to my other favourite D word: distraction. And distraction was often what I needed to get me through the next hour, the next day, the next week and, eventually, to London.

There were the usual rounds of photos, chats and hugs before we lifted Max into his seat over the back wheel of Tori's bike and got ready to hit the road.

'I'm not sure how far we're going to be able to come with you,' said Tori as she strapped Max in. 'I'd love to go the whole hog, but Max might have other ideas.'

'Of course. However long you can come for is fab,' I said, and I meant it.

Motherhood in itself is a feat — to attempt to cajole a two-year-old into an 18-mile adventure was admirable. With Max now safely atop his bicycle throne, I thought it was high time I checked in with the man himself, to see how he was feeling about the day. I crouched down so that I was eye level with him in the seat.

'Are you ready for an adventure, Max?'

'Yeaaah,' he said, slowly, looking down and fiddling with his seat strap.

'Do you think it's going to be fun?' I asked.

Max screwed up his face and thought for a moment. 'Yeah,' he said again, although this time more quietly.

'And do you know that we're going to see a castle at the end?'

'Castle?' He looked up.

'Yes. A BIG castle!'

'Hmmm. Mummy!' Max said, pointing at Tori's back.

'Yes, that is your mummy and she's wonderful, isn't she?'

'Yeah,' Max said again, before letting out a giggle.

Tori honked her bike horn, Max squealed, we waved goodbye to the others who had gathered at the Bangor clock tower — and we were off. I took the first few strides over the smooth cobbles of Bangor high street, surrounded by honks and cheers as Tori and Tabitha's wheels made their first revolutions on a journey towards Conwy Castle.

After weaving through the outskirts of Bangor, we started down a quiet, traffic-free bike trail. Tabitha was a fantastic addition to the group because she brought with her some local route-finding knowledge, which meant that Tori and I didn't have to look at a map. Tab-Nav was all over it.

We all rode along and chatted, wheeling and padding over a tarmacked bike trail scattered with twigs and leaves. As I nattered away with Tori, Max seemed to be enjoying himself. He interrupted us with his own chat every now and then, shouting things like 'tree!' and 'stream!' whenever there was an exciting new landmark on the trail. This is brilliant, I thought. Tori was going to get a day out on the bike, we were going to have a chance to catch up, and Max seemed happy too. . .

'Okay, want to get out now, Mummy,' said Max. Tori looked at me and I smiled. We'd made it 2 miles.

'Okay, Maxy, we'll get out soon,' she told him.

We carried on for another few minutes and Max reabsorbed himself in the surroundings. 'Tree! Tree!' he shouted, which was a sure sign that all would be forgotten and that he was ready to get lost in the adventure. . .

'Okay, want to get out now, Mummy. . .' he said.

Tori and I stayed silent and looked at one another.

'Mummy? Mummy? Mummy! Out now,' he repeated, and this time it was more of a demand than a request.

'Oh, I'm so sorry about this. We might have to head back soon,' Tori said.

And that was the cue I needed. I went into distraction overdrive, giving it one last go to see if we could get Max excited enough about his surroundings so that he would forget all about the idea of wanting 'out' of his seat. Selfishly, I wanted to have Tori with me for as much of the day as I could, but it would also be lovely for her to get a day out on the bike.

Somehow, the distraction tactic worked and Max settled into the journey. A change in scenery helped too, as the route took us out of the forest and onto quiet open roads lined with hedges and past rolling green fields. After being alongside the fields for a while, there were fewer things for Max to point at. Concerned that we might lose his attention, we switched to snack-based incentives. Tori would power up a hill on the bike and pull in at a patch of blackberries, making sure Max's seat was close enough that he could reach for them. : I'd follow quickly behind, picking extra blackberries to hold in my hand as I ran, then deliver to him on the move whenever there was a bush shortage at the roadside. If we grew concerned that there may be a snack shortage, we could send Tabitha ahead to seek out exactly where the best bushes were. It was a military operation and a conveyer belt of berry wonderment for the little fella.

Although all was going swell in toddlerville, we thought
it best not to push our luck, so we decided to stop halfway
through the day's run at a small seaside town and let Max
out for a run around. As we turned off the main route and
detoured towards the Beach Pavilion Cafe on the seafront, I
tried repeatedly to pronounce the name of the place we were
going to.

'Klanfekkin?' I said.

'Try again,' Tori laughed.

'Klanferchan?'

'Nope!'

'Klanfairlacha?'

'Say it with me. . . Klan — Fair — vechun.'

'Klanfairvechun.'

Nailed it.

At Llanfairfechan, we propped up the bikes next to a large
picnic table at the Pavilion Cafe and I was feeling grateful that
Max had given us all an excuse for a wriggle break. I was having one of those days where I needed some solid food in my
belly and Llanfairfechan was a beautiful spot for a lunch stop.
Rows of wooden groynes ran out to the sea along a beach that
turned from grey pebbles closer to the shore into toffee-colour-
ed sand at the water's edge. Alongside the beach, a stone promenade led away from the cafe and towards a collection of houses.

Behind the houses, a large shelf of rock cut across a cold blue sky and plunged steeply into the sea. There were clusters of trees at its base with more seaside homes snuggled in between. Tabitha went inside to get started on her food order, while Tori and I enjoyed the view a little longer.

'It's beautiful, isn't it?' I said to Tori.

'It is. And I've never been here before.'

'Really?'

'Really.'

I was dead chuffed that Tori had been able to come out and see a new bit of her own backyard with me. I'd always hoped the run might do that — give people an excuse to make time and space to explore little pockets of the unfamiliar, close to home.

For lunch at Llanfairfechan, I ordered beans on toast, a milkshake and a coffee. I thought briefly about having cheese on top of my beans on toast — because that would have made it just about perfect — but decided the milkshake had probably shoved enough fat into my body for it to be dealing with that afternoon. Max did a few laps of the cafe with Tori and then refuelled his toddler tank by wolfing down a cheese sandwich. Sandwich demolished, he got down from the picnic table and stood next to it, looking around.

'I'm jus' going to go round here now, Mummy, 'kay?' he pointed towards the back of the cafe and began toddling off towards it.

'Uh, Max. . . Max. . .' Tori called as Max continued to toddle away from the table.

'It's okay, I've got him,' I laughed, getting up and chasing after him. Together, Max and I completed another couple of laps of the cafe, before heading down some stone steps onto the pebble beach to play with the seagulls.

The seagull-watching at Llanfairfechan clearly exhausted Max because, within a mile of leaving the lunch stop, he was fast asleep on the back of the bike, head bobbing from side to side as Tori, Tabitha and I continued along winding lanes which skirted the coast. Max woke up an hour later, just in time to announce that he was hungry again. Tori said she was feeling peckish too, so she handed Max a packet of Mini Cheddars from her bumbag. I watched as Max munched on a few Cheddars. He was up for sharing his snacks with his mum, so Tori began stretching her hand behind her while she rode. Max would then place a cheddar into her outstretched palm for her to eat. At first, I marvelled at such a wonderful display of snack passing. Tori had Max well-trained — what two-year-old could be your on-bike snack support crew with such ease? It was then I noticed that Max was licking the cheese flavour off each Cheddar before handing a moist biscuit to Tori. Licky Cheddars. Yummy.

The final hill before Conwy was one hell of a steep one — close to a 20% incline. Tabitha was as fit as a fiddle and made light work of the climb, but I was huffing and puffing away on my two feet and I knew I would have still struggled to get up it on a normal bike, let alone one with a two-year-old on the back. But there was no stopping Tori. She got up out of the saddle, pulled on the handlebars to heave the bike onwards and upwards and shoved harder on the pedals.

'Mummy strong!' shouted Max, raising his arms in the air as the bike kicked up in front of him.

'Yes, Mummy strong,' I shouted back, raising my arms in the air too.

'Mummy go!' Max shouted louder still, and pointed towards Tori's back.

On the final mile into Conwy, we took a quiet route which skirted the marina. There wasn't a scrap of wind so the water was glass-like — flecked with turquoise and sparkling in the afternoon sunshine. When we rounded the final bend and Conwy Castle came into view, I let out a little whoop. I was definitely more excited to see it than Max was in the end. It really is the most spectacular medieval masterpiece — plenty of turrets, framed beautifully by the Telford Suspension Bridge in front of it and the green-grey crags of Snowdonia National Park rising behind it. Setting eyes on the castle was a serene end to what had been a perfect day on the road. Tabitha had enjoyed a relaxed training ride; Tori had made it the whole 18 miles with Max; and I'd hung out with a friend and been entertained by a toddler's antics in the process.

I knew that one day, I wanted to be a mum too. I'd been taking notes, watching Max and Tori all day. From what I could gather, motherhood was all about two things: being able to maintain a steady flow of snacks at all times and somehow keeping the wheels turning, no matter how steep the climb. I could only hope that if and when I did have a kiddy, I'd be a STRONG MUMMY like Tori — willing to risk toddler tantrums and naptime disasters for the sake of a day of adventure.

After the day out with Max, Tori and Tabitha, I continued to run east across the country and enjoyed the start of a September Indian summer. Temperatures were in the mid-twenties, the skies were bright and clear and there were miles and miles of coastline with beautiful promenades, coffee shops and long stretches of sandy beach to run along. I was impressed with how my foot was holding up too. There was a flap of skin around the area where the infection had been and it had been clinging on for a while. I hadn't wanted to pull it off because it was protecting the old wound and the softer skin beneath it. But after Conwy, that flap of skin made a bid for freedom. It was all dangly and waving at me. I didn't know quite what to do with the flap when it detached itself after dinner one evening, so I gave it a little tug, then popped it in the kitchen bin at my host's house. Aren't I just the loveliest guest? It felt very satisfying and like it was the final piece of the puzzle for my foot to fully heal.

My foot was playing ball, the weather was top-bombin' and local runners were coming out in their droves to run by my side. I was flying high and, after all the attention the run had got in Sheffield, I felt comfortable talking to the press again.

A few days after arriving in Wales I was contacted by

BBC Wales, asking if they could do a piece on the run. They filmed an interview by the seaside and then took footage of me running off with a fandango of brightly clad runners for another day along the coast towards Prestatyn. The interview was shared on the BBC regional news and also their Facebook page — where it was watched by almost 2 million people. That was a whole lot of eyes on the run, which you would think would always be a fantastic thing. But publicity is a double-edged sword. When something you're doing reaches more people, there will be huge waves of support, but the hollow behind those waves can be filled with negativity. I suspected there may be some less-than-nice remarks on the BBC article yet, after a few days of smooth running under sunny skies, I felt strong enough to read them:

She'll need new knees and a hip replacement before age 50. Barmy.

What a moron this woman is. Will the NHS be footing the bill?

Another extreme endurance event with no benefit to mankind.

Daft and pointless.

And my favourite one:
Oh, for God's sake. Get a real job like the rest of us.

I won't lie — it really stung to read the comments. Largely because I would never try to tear another person down, so I'll never understand what there is to gain from turning nasty thoughts into nasty words written on a screen. Of course, I shouldn't have taken it personally. I know it's more about them than me — but when you're exhausted and you're trying your best, you take it personally. And if you're reading comments about you or something you care about, there's a tendency to only focus on the bad ones. Thankfully, amid the venomous remarks, there were many positive ones to balance them out, and every now and then, someone would really leap in to defend the run. And when they did, they did it with great gusto (and a lot more words):

I would like to say that, as a Girlguiding leader myself, the effect she is having on our girls is very inspirational. Whilst outwardly it seems she is 'only running' she is also out there speaking to girls in Rainbows all the way up to Rangers. She is telling these girls to be strong, to stand up for what they believe in, that they can be the things they aspire to be. That is very inspirational, especially for the girls who are less confident, those who come from turbulent backgrounds, who feel they can never escape and those who feel like they won't ever be what they want to be. I have girls in my units who have listened to Anna and I have seen the light go on in their head and see the realisation that they can be brave, they can make a change — it might be hard work, but they CAN do it. Please don't take what Anna is doing as 'only running' or 'self-punishment'. She is doing this for Girlguiding and all those girls in units across the country. — Steph Walker

Well, reading that got me all choked up. Perhaps I wouldn't read comments on articles in the future, but as no-nonsense life guru Seth Godin says: You cannot be all things to all people. I have spent my life trying not to be vanilla. Because vanilla is nice 'n' all, but it won't set the world alight. So, there was some kind of triumph in the fact that there were people out there who really seemed to hate what I was doing. In some roundabout way, they made me even more determined to make London. Because I wasn't doing it for them, for the people who didn't get it. I was doing it for the ones who did.

22

Washed Away

I was back in England and back running. It was strange to cross the border into England and think back to the last time I was there, some three weeks earlier at Liverpool. I was like a comet that had slingshotted into space and come back around. I'd collided with some debris en route and bits of me had fallen off (or got left in a kitchen bin) but now I was well and truly back in the atmosphere.

The reintroduction to England started with a 20-mile public running stage from Chester to Nantwich. It was Chester Pride weekend, so I made a last-minute change of meeting point to avoid the roads that were closed for the parade in the city centre. I was already running late (as was tradition) but I took an extra five minutes to paint some rainbows on my face and affix gemstones to the outsides of my eyes. I took a quick picture before I left the hotel room and posted it on social media. 'Love is love' read the caption. Because ain't that the truth.

I wasn't sure whether everyone would have got the memo about the new canal-side meeting point, so when I saw a group of 30 runners waiting at the bottom of the stone steps, I smiled so hard that the rainbows on my cheeks almost touched my forehead.

'Mooornin' everyone!' I shouted as I walked down the steps.

The group spun round to face me and let out a loud cheer. Despite being 1,350 miles into the run, I still always arrived at each public running stage wondering if I would live up to the expectations people had of me. In one sense, I didn't have the energy to be anything other than myself, but I also hoped, for the sake of the time and effort that runners had put into supporting me, that me just being me was enough for them. It was that kind of cheery reaction to my arrival that put me at ease. Some of the other runners had got into the pride theme too, with rainbows scattered here and there, and there were a few kids who had decided to come dressed in unicorn onesies. Because if you can't rock up for a run dressed as a unicorn when you're six years old, when can you?

It was canals for the win as I followed the Shropshire Union over the next few days, heading south-east on a dreamy mixture of grass and mud. It was now late September, and the moment I left the banks of the canal at Market Drayton, it was as if someone at the British Weather HQ flipped a switch. 'Okay, team. . . that'll do. That's enough of the dry stuff. Crack open the rain, turn it up to full blast and make it POUR.' And pour it did. Gone was the Indian summer I'd enjoyed while running across North Wales. It rained, and it rained, and it rained. It rained cats and dogs (and elephants too). It rained so much that the roads were flooded — which would either mean that I had to backtrack to avoid a complete road closure and run extra miles or wade through knee-height murky water to make it across the flooded area. The wading made me nervous because the wound on my foot had only just about healed. I couldn't see what was beneath my feet in the sloppy brown water, and the water likely contained all kinds of cow and sheep poo which had run off the surrounding farms. I was pretty sure that watery shite wasn't the best thing to expose recently healed foot infections to but, still, onwards through the watery poo I ran.

Throughout the downpours, I did my best to stay chipper. I was focused on one mile at a time and tried not to get 'angry' at the weather. I say I tried. I still got angry from time to time, letting out swear words or a frustrated wail when I came across yet another flooded road, but there was nothing I could do about it. When the weather is crap, I find it best not to think too much about precisely how crap it is. So, I turned my brain off for a while and just kept moving forwards.

The days that followed were long and miserable. I was soaked to the skin within the first hour of running every day and my teeth were chattering by the early afternoon. In a bid to stay warm, I opted to keep moving as much as possible and not to take a break at a cafe or pub like I usually would. Above all, I was adamant I was going to make it to the next public running stage in Nottingham, on time, as promised.

I ploughed on with the plan for some hefty daily mileage, pushing it up and up, doing 20+ miles most days and, on one day, completing a 26-miler — my biggest yet.

After a few days of rain-running, I noticed that I was struggling to get out of bed in the morning. Even if I got 10 hours of sleep, I woke up feeling like I'd only had three. I was also permanently ravenous. I was a perpetually hungry bear anyway, but now nothing seemed to fill my belly cavern.

One evening, I was headed for a Girlguiding talk in Uttoxeter. I was only 2 miles out from the Girlguiding HQ and I knew that there'd be tea and cake when I got there (there always was) but I was starving and starting to get the shakes. My legs turned to jelly, my belly rumbled, and I felt like I couldn't run another step unless I ate something. I passed a garden centre with a cafe and bounded up the side of the gravel driveway to the large, glass sliding doors. The place was deserted and the cafe area was roped off, but I found a shop assistant crouching behind a collection of garden gnomes, tending to some plants. The assistant said it was close to closing time so the cafe was shut, but they had a few things on the shelves next to the till that I could buy. I scanned the items on the shelf. Short of eating a cactus, the only option for a snack was a large baton of fruit cake. It was enormous — one of those loaves you'd take over to your nanna's house to share with the whole family. Well. Of course, I bought it. I got three paces outside the store before I ripped off the packaging, opened my mouth as wide as it would go and took a massive bite. I told myself I'd just have a few chomps and then put the rest in my pack for the following day. But five bites later, I'd eaten half the loaf, and five bites after that, there was just a lone raisin and a cherry in my dirty palm.

'Anna. You animal,' I said aloud, feeling disgusted.

I looked around to see if the man inside the store had watched me behave as if I hadn't eaten in weeks. He hadn't, thank goodness, so I popped the last cherry in my mouth and ran off again.

The following morning, I woke up in a host's house just outside Derby with a throbbing headache and a sore throat. It felt like I'd attempted to swallow a bag of golf balls overnight and they'd got stuck. I poked the glands just behind my jaw and they were swollen and bruised. Oh, dear. In hindsight, I should have taken note of my grogginess in the mornings, and I should have thought more about the fact that my body was constantly craving fuel, but I was so blinkered in the mission to stay on schedule that I didn't. It'd been a whirlwind of a journey since leaving Northern Ireland. A hectic talk schedule, cold, wet weather and lots of miles were, of course, all of the ingredients for a disaster pie.

I rolled out of bed, went to the mirror in the bathroom and shone the torch light from my phone into my mouth. There were white spots on my tonsils. I heaved a deep sigh. 'For God's sake,' I said, trudging, bleary-eyed down the stairs to my hosts.

'Hi. . . Darcy,' I rasped. 'I'm not going to be running today — I think I've got tonsillitis.'

I'd had tonsillitis more times than I cared to remember

and I knew the signs of it well. Ever since I was a kid, whenever I was rundown I'd get tonsillitis. After inspecting my throat again, I felt too dreadful to think about anything except sleep, so I went back to bed for a few hours and then headed to a local drop-in clinic. I told the doctor that I had tonsillitis and the look on his face said, 'Oh, here we go. Another wannabe doctor with a self-diagnosis.' That was until he took a look down my throat and recoiled in disgust. He wrote a prescription right away and I started my second course of antibiotics in as many weeks. If there was one thing I didn't need when on an adventure where my body was already rundown, it was a set of drugs that lowered my immune system.

I crawled back into bed at Darcy's and sent Abby two messages. The first one said that I was going to try to go through with the running stage set for the following day. I'd only just got back on the road after the foot injury, and I'd cancelled so many public running stages already. As soon as I sent the message, I knew I'd made a mistake. What was I doing? I'd just been told I had tonsillitis. I quickly came to my senses and sent Abby another message.

On reflection, doing tomorrow's run stage would be silly. Can we cancel it please? So gutted! Can you let them know I've got tonsillitis? I'm going to take three full days of rest to see if I can get my bod and golf-ball throat back on track!

No probs. I'll let the runners know now, and post in the Facebook group too.

That night I slept for 18 hours straight. I then spent the following few days grappling with the sensation that I was 'losing time' by being stationary. . . again. In those days, I tried to stay upbeat. Some hours I succeeded, and others I failed. Sometimes I was at one with the situation. Because if I could come back from the foot injury, then what was a little tonsillitis to contend with? But there were other hours when I let myself think too much. I doubted my ability to overcome the challenge that the tonsillitis had laid at my door. In those hours, I felt passive. Submissive to the adventure and all its twists and turns. As if I were a boxer who'd made it to the third round and the blows were coming thick and fast. Foot infection. Left hook. Tonsillitis. Right hook. I was too exhausted to sit up and wipe the blood from my face and even think about fighting back. I just let the punches rain down.

I put the enforced days of rest in the Midlands to good use by giving myself a stern talking to. The truth was, without a support crew or professional help and advice on the road, I was my own coach, nutritionist, physio and manager. In those roles, it seemed I was very keen to make sure that everyone else was okay and got what they needed, but I needed to do a better job at looking after myself. If I was going to have any chance of making the 100-marathon distance, I couldn't afford any more time off to illness or injury. So, I held an emergency meeting with my support crew (me) and made a new set of self-care rules:

Rule 1: If the weather was bad, I should reduce the mileage.

Rule 2: When I arrived at a Girlguiding talk after finishing a day's run, I should take at least 15 minutes to myself. To drink a hot cup of tea, take stock of the day, clean my feet and put on some warm and dry clothes. Even if I had to seem impolite and lock myself into the bogs to do it.

Rule 3: I had to be asleep by 9 p.m., and I should do absolutely anything to make sure I got at least 10 hours of shut eye. Even if that meant pulling on my big girl pants and asking my host if I could let myself out of their house and lock the door behind me after they'd gone to work in the morning.

These all felt like selfish things to do. But, ultimately, if I didn't swing them into action then I'd put the whole run in jeopardy, and the biggest good I could do was to keep moving and keep talking to the girls. Oh, and how could I forget. . .

Rule 4: I should definitely eat more broccoli. Broccoli solves many problems.

After a couple of days of rest, the white spots in my throat had disappeared and I was ready to hit the road again. I still felt ropey, but I reasoned that as long as I told everyone I was unwell (so there wasn't pressure to make miles or go fast) then I could just keep moving forwards as steadily as I pleased.

A 15-strong group of local runners turned up to join me at Nottingham and, as we ran out of the city, I felt surprisingly positive. I was in the midst of dodging yet another adventure curveball and the runners of Nottingham had showed up to help me do it.

I'd love to tell you a wonderful tale of my first day back on the road post-tonsillitis, but of all the things I can remember about running south from Nottingham, it was the overwhelming smell of chicken farms. If you've ever smelt a chicken farm, you'll know what I'm talking about. For those who have yet to experience the delights, it's like cow manure but with a sharper acidic tinge — it's a whiff that stings the nostrils and ends with subtle notes of rotten egg. I'm not selling the north Midlands as a destination for running, am I? I promise, it was very nice. There were green hills and country roads, and the runners were so very kind and chatty. But it really did smell a lot like chickens.

Over the following week, the days continued to be wet and sloppy, but it didn't put people off coming out to join in with the run, and I was thankful for a deluge of cheery runners and a string of local hosts. One evening, near Leicester, I stayed with a woman called Claire and her family, which included two fabulous cats (who am I kidding? All cats are fabulous). As we were all curled up post-dinner, watching Strictly Come Dancing on the telly-box, Claire confessed that it had been out of her comfort zone to offer to host me that night.

'Really?' I said.

'Really. I almost didn't send the email,' she replied.

It had never even crossed my mind that hosting a stranger would be an uncomfortable thing to do. But, of course, it is. When you let someone into your home you open yourself up, in every sense. I was reminded that comfort zones were about so much more than physical challenges. I had run well and truly out of mine on this adventure and, in letting me into her home, Claire had stepped just as far out of hers.

On one day, there was a special guest appearance by a woman named Heather, who came out with a fortieth birthday helium balloon attached to her hip. I couldn't quite believe that she'd chosen to run with me, in the rain, on a landmark birthday, rather than stay at home and drink wine or have a nice bath. But she said it was the 'best birthday ever!' and smiled more than I thought it was humanely possibly to smile while running.

At Coventry, I was joined by a friend called Sally Orange, who likes to run marathons around the world dressed as pieces of fruit. In fact, Sally is the only person in the world to have run a marathon on every continent in fancy dress, and, more specifically, dressed as fruit. As ex-military and someone with first-hand experience of depression and anxiety, she uses the runs to raise funds and awareness of mental ill health. Sally is a wonderful person to do a running race with because whenever she's asked what time she's going for in her marathons, she replies: 'I'm going for the time of my life!' Amen to that. In years gone by, she's run the London Marathon dressed as a strawberry, a marathon in Afghanistan as a banana, one in New Zealand as a kiwi fruit, Argentina as a bunch of grapes, and she even transformed herself into a pear for 26.2 miles on Antarctica. The day she joined me for a running stage in Coventry, she brightened my day by coming dressed as an apple. I felt dreadful when I unwrapped a slice of apple cake that my host had given me and took a big bite in front of her.

Fully juiced up from Sally's company, the stage from So-lihull to Stratford-upon-Avon saw the return of canal-side running and, of equal importance, canal-side pub stops. I chatted with two sisters, George and Charlotte, about a dream they had of completing a long ultrarun together one day. We finished the 22-mile rainy stage at Stratford-upon-Avon and the sisters nipped off to collect a surprise Victoria sponge cake they'd baked for me. Attached to the foil-covered cake was a tag that read: 'For awesome Anna. Who deserves to eat cake more than anyone else. You are INCREDIBLE.' I was touched by the sponge prezzie as I bundled into a car, headed for a Girlguiding talk at Pershore with the cake on my lap. I tried to keep the two layers of thick jam and cream sponge together when we rounded corners and did all I could to resist falling face first forwards into it and eating my way out.

That night, I was dropped off at a farm and glamping site run by a local couple who'd offered to take me in. I was de-lighted that the couple hadn't made pudding so I could share the Victoria sponge (big thanks to George and Charlotte for making me seem like the best guest EVER). After a cosy family dinner in a farmhouse kitchen (complete with dogs asleep in the corner), I made my way through a field, under a mixture of torchlight and moonlight, to a large yurt. I sat on a giant double bed opposite a toasty wood burner and popped the last two antibiotic pills into my mouth. After swallowing them down, I flopped back onto the mattress and stared up at a line of prayer flags hanging from the ceiling. With a belly full of dinner and Victoria sponge, legs aching from the 138 miles covered since Nottingham and cheeks aching from smiling, I felt relieved. With 1,354 miles of the journey down, I was managing to just about keep the runaway train on the rails, all I could think of now was that I was about to run into a very special area of the country — my adopted home city of Gloucester.

BAREFOOT BRITAIN

The West Country

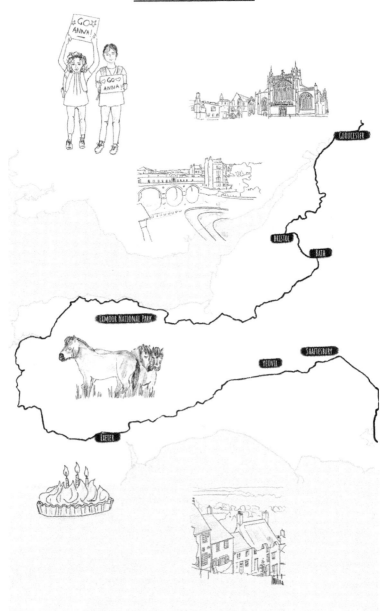

GLOUCESTER

BRISTOL

BATH

EXMOOR National Park

SHAFTESBURY

YEOVIL

EXETER

23

Glaaaawwwster!

Home is a complicated word. Over years of vagabonding, I've thought a lot about what it really means. Is a home a house? Is it where you were born? Is it where you've spent most of your life? I've recently come to the conclusion that home is none of these things. Home is a feeling. It's a place where you feel secure, like the best version of yourself, at peace and at ease.

My home is ever-changing. Sometimes, I feel at home when I'm at my parents' house in south-west London, which is where I grew up. I feel strangely at home whenever I'm in New Zealand. And, as Jamie and I have often managed our relationship while thousands of miles apart, then home is whenever we're together — wherever in the world that might be. All of that said, over the past few years, home in Britain has become the West Country city of Gloucester.

Gloucester is the perfect size for a city. With a population of 120,000 people, it has all of the things you might need, but it's still quiet enough. I like that it's bustling in the daytime but the streets are deserted if you walk home from the city centre at 11 p.m. at night. I also like that Gloucester is rough around the edges. Beyond the newly renovated docks area and the recently restored cathedral, it's got crumbling buildings, dirty chicken shops and seedy pubs that smell of must and urine. Of course, it has real problems too, which I don't like — an over-spilling job centre, homelessness and drug addicts. Plus, there's the man in the high street who shouts obscenities at you as you walk past. But Gloucester is a down-to-earth place. There's a realness to it, and real places have real people, with real problems.

At the end of my first day of running in the county of Gloucestershire, I was collected by Jamie. It was lovely to see him standing there, in a pub car park, wearing skinny jeans and a puffer coat. In fact, it was so lovely that it freaked me out. I spent the car journey back to our place in quiet contemplation, wondering if I'd made a huge mistake. Was it a terrible idea to have organised a route which took me through my home city, when I still had a whole month left to go until the finish line?

It was easy enough to keep running when I didn't have to think about what I was missing at home. I'd deliberately avoided coming home at any point during the run for that very reason — to keep it at arm's length. Ordinarily, normality grates on me. I am allergic to anything that feels too run-of-the-mill. But, at that point in the journey, I craved it. I more than craved it; I ached for it. And I was worried that if I let that glimpse of normal life back in, if I let myself relax, let myself feel safe and comfortable, if I collapsed onto a giant sofa in a familiar living room, I would never want to leave. It now seemed that the real danger for the adventure wasn't about getting cut feet, avoiding tonsillitis or dodging traffic. It was spending the night curled up on the sofa at home with The Graham Norton Show on the telly and the smell of Jamie cooking me up his trademark McDonald Thai green curry on the stove in the kitchen.

Despite my fears that Jamie's Thai green curry would render me immobile, the following morning, I dragged my tired legs and buzzy mind to Tewkesbury to run the 21 miles into Gloucester city itself. There was a large crowd of runners gathered on the stone paving slabs just in front of Tewkesbury Abbey. They were a welcome distraction from a brain in overdrive and, when I stepped out of the car to a round of cheering and clapping, I grinned like the Cheshire Cat. Well, a Gloucestershire cat. Then and there, I decided to leave all my concerns about getting too comfortable behind.

'Less thinking, more moving,' I muttered, as I strode towards the group.

I spotted a few familiar faces in the crowd — some local runners I recognised, a good friend from university who lived just down the road in Stroud and GB Paralympian Mel Nicholls. I knew Mel from the adventure world. After retiring from wheelchair racing with the British squad, she'd taken to doing long endurance events on her hand bike. After months of running with people I'd never met before, to have so many familiar faces joining me that day felt surreal, and I was touched that they'd all given up their Saturdays to come out and play.

As we'd had a lot of sign-ups for the Tewkesbury to Gloucester stage, Logistics Queen Abby had lined up a chief navigator for the occasion. It was something we'd started to implement whenever I had big groups joining in for the public running stages, so I could focus on chatting to the runners and not worry about where we were going. For this stage, a woman called Clare had volunteered for the role and she had taken it on in style. She'd not only decided to lead us from the saddle of her bike, as opposed to on foot (which I thought was genius), but she had also gone to the length of wearing a pair of 'Pants of Perspective' — a set of magic leggings that feature heavily in another book I've written about running the length of New Zealand. Clare's legs looked resplendent in the morning sunshine outside the abbey, adorned in a rainbow, a star-spangled sky and a unicorn having a fight with a robot.

'Okay, everyone, are you ready?' I shouted to the group as I fastened the clips on my backpack into position and got my camera out to film the start of the stage.

'Yeeaaahhh!' came the cheer from the crowd behind me.

'Then it's time for us to run to. . . three. . . two. . . one. . . GLAAAWWWWWSSSSTTTEEEEERRRR!' I bellowed at the top of my lungs in my best West Country drawl.

'GLAAAAWWWWSSSTTTTTEERRRRR!' the crowd echoed behind me, and we were off, my bare feet slap, slap, slapping on the flag stones of the Tewkesbury streets, the noise of shuffling trainers and excited chatter around me.

Once out of town, we got straight into the groove on

some proper West Country roads — my bare feet squelching through mud and cow dung as we ran along quiet lanes peppered with hay, past tractors rumbling slowly towards farms and houses selling duck eggs on stalls in their front gardens. Although I was running in the middle of a fandango of 20, I knew that over 100 people had signed up to come and join in at some point during that stage. Sure enough, a few miles later, the first new group of runners appeared. They emerged from a nondescript side road and merged seamlessly with the group — the way cars do from slip lanes onto the motorway. A few miles later, a couple more runners joined in and, before long, we were a 40-strong neon convoy, picking up new and brightly dressed runners every few miles or so. Despite the ever-growing group size, Clare continued to do a stellar job in her role as chief navigational officer and stayed as cool as a cucumber, brightly clad unicorn legs spinning, whizzing up and down the group on her bike, making sure everyone knew where to go.

As the group grew, we did our best to stick to back roads so that we were away from the traffic, but there were a few sections where we had no choice but to run down the side of a major road. Uneasy as this made me feel, there was a real power in running in such a big group. Everyone was brightly dressed, so we could be easily seen, and the cars were forced to wait. We held up our fair share of traffic, which I'm sure would have annoyed some drivers going about their usual Saturday business, but most of them were friendly — tooting and honking their horns when they had a chance to pass the group. One woman even wound down her car window as she drove slowly alongside me.

'Do you want these? They're my son's but he says you can have them,' she shouted, dangling a pair of white trainers out of the window.

'Oh! No. I'm fine, thank you.'

'She's doing a barefoot run!' shouted another runner behind me.

'Are you?' The woman looked baffled.

'Yes. It's on purpose. But thanks so much for the shoe offer. And thanks to your son too.' I nodded at her teenager in the back.

'Oh! No problem. I thought you'd lost your shoes or something. And in that case are you okay for everything else? I mean, do you need anything? Water? Food?' she smiled.

'Ah, that's so kind. I'm all good, thanks. We're headed to Gloucester, so not far to go now,' I replied. And with that, the woman wound up the window, gave us all a beep and drove on by. West Country folk — how lovely they are.

Just when I thought the atmosphere in the group couldn't get any more party-like, I spotted a new group of runners at a roundabout on the outskirts of Cheltenham. There were 10 of them, jumping up and down and waving, all wearing bright tutus. The tutu gang hitched itself to the back of the main group, and on we went, rolling across the soft grass of Cheltenham Racecourse and alongside the old steam railway line. Choo-choo!

'This is definitely the biggest group I've had run with me so far!' I announced as we hit the Honeybourne Line — an old trainline turned cycle trail which leads to Cheltenham Spa railway station.

'We're reaching critical mass!' someone shouted from behind me.

And they were right. We weren't just a wave of runners, we were a tsunami — the thunderous roar of trainers on tarmac around me, excited chatter and puffs and pants — the whoops and cheers growing at every junction. At one point, I found myself smack bang in the middle of the group. In front of me were a stream of coloured T-shirts bobbing along the trail, and the same again behind. It was like being in my own mini marathon. A completely self-organised, unofficial gathering of strangers, with everyone from kids to oldies and several runners with dogs too.

As we left the Honeybourne Line and took a side road near the train station, I realised where we were.

'Hang on, guys! Hold up!' I yelled.

It wasn't easy trying to bring such a large group to a halt, especially not when I was in the middle of it as opposed to at the front, but eventually, the message was passed down the line like Chinese whispers and everyone stopped.

'What's up, Anna? Are you alright?' said Chief Navigator Clare, a look of concern on her face.

'Yeah, I'm fine, it's just. . . my friend lives there,' I said, pointing across the road.

'Well, do you want to go and say hello?'

'Yeah, actually, I do. Do you mind?' I said, now addressing the whole group. I mean this was their Saturday, after all. And they had come out to run, not for me to stop at random houses and say hello to friends.

I hadn't seen my friend Helen, her hubby, Andrew, and their kids, Max and Bo, since way before starting the run. I knew they'd been loosely following on social media, but they would have had no idea that I'd be running past their door that day. And in reality, I hadn't had any idea until I was actually running past their door either. I gave three hard raps on the grey front door and buzzed the bell for good measure. I pressed my face up against the glass of the porch door and waited for 30 seconds, but there was no reply. Which was a shame. It would have been a lovely surprise. I turned around to leave and then. . .

'What the?! McNuff!'

I swung back around to see the door was open and in it stood my friend Helen.

'Hello! I was, you know. . . in the area. . . in my bare feet and thought I'd pop by,' I said casually.

'You nutter! You actually have no shoes on. I mean, I knew you would, it's just hard to believe. Max, Bo! Get out here. The mad McNuff is here!'

I gave Helen a giant hug and, being the kind woman she

is, she invited me in for tea and cake. She actually invited the other runners too, but it seemed too much to pile 50 of us into her house and, besides, I needed to get a wriggle on. There was a news crew waiting to film the arrival in Gloucester and we were already behind time. I dished out a few more hugs to Helen, Andrew and the kids before bounding off back out of their driveway and joining the fandango of runners again. I thanked them for their patience in waiting for me, and we set off for the final 10 miles to Gloucester.

Before the pit stop at Helen's, I'd been starting to flag and my legs had begun to feel jelly-like. But the brief hug 'n' hello with Helen and her fam had put a real spring in my step. Mostly because I knew that they didn't really care if I ran 100 marathons in my bare feet or not. They would still welcome me at their door and invite me in for tea and cake anyway. It always pays to have friends like that.

Since leaving Tewkesbury, we'd passed a few people standing at the side of the road with homemade signs — they often had drawings of bare feet on them and read either 'Barefoot Britain' or 'Go, Anna!' But as I ran around the side of Gloucestershire Airport and crossed a local park, the roadside support went next level. There was a group of Brownies and Rainbows with their parents, waiting in a field with an array of signs. The kids, aged between five and ten years old, began jumping up and down and pointing at me as I approached, and so I did the same, making sure they knew I was just as excited to see them as they were me. One of the signs was at least 2 metres wide and was appropriate for waving so close to the airport as it looked like a set of plane wings. The young girl who was holding it was doing her best not to take flight in the breeze. I stopped briefly to deliver some high-fives to all the sign bearers and their families and inspect their signs, complimenting them on the use of colour and spattering of glitter.

'The girls would love to run with you for a bit, if that's okay?' said the dad of one of the Brownies.

'Of course that's okay. The more the merrier,' I smiled. One of the younger girls balled her hand into a fist and said 'Yesss!' and another started dancing on the spot.

'On one condition though girls?'

'Yes?' said the older Brownie.

'You keep the pace steady and make sure we can keep up with you?' I said, looking serious.

'Okay. I can do that,' said the dancing girl, furrowing her brow and looking equally serious in her reply. And we were off — now an even larger group with some mini adventurers in tow.

I'd expected the girls to join in for a hundred metres or so, but they ran along with us for half a mile before heading back to the park. I had a feeling they would have kept going all the way to Gloucester if their parents had let them.

It was approaching 3 p.m. as we neared the city centre and some of the runners who'd been with me since Tewkesbury began to struggle. Twenty-one miles was a long way to run on any day, but even more so for those who were attempting that kind of distance for the first time. I was doing my best to cheer on the stragglers and keeping them updated on just how far there was to go. Well, okay, I was shaving half a mile off whatever distance there was left, because you can always cling on for half a mile longer than you think you can.

As we made it to the pedestrianised section of Gloucester city centre, time moved in slow motion. I passed The New Inn Hotel — a fifteenth-century pub with a cobblestone courtyard and picnic tables and wooden barrels out the front. That was familiar, as was everything else on the high street. . . the bargain 99p stores, the card shop, the two chain coffee shops, the hairdresser's and, above all of that, the Tudor buildings, with white walls bulging through black beams, like the belly of an old man who'd just eaten too much roast dinner.

Beyond the crossroads, we passed the historic G. A. Baker & Son jeweller's, an Edwardian store front which has been preserved from a bygone era. Baker's clock juts out from above the shop, and beneath that are five life-size characters, each standing in front of a bell — an Irishwoman, an Englishman, a Scotsman and a Welshwoman, with Father Time in the middle. I'd always found the figures to be beautiful, if a little creepy, and if any store front summed up the journey I'd been on so far, Baker & Son's was it.

It was strange to think that the last time I'd been on the high street was four months ago. Before all of this barefoot madness had even begun. It was as if two parallel worlds were colliding — like the me of the present was running, barefoot, past the hopeful, naive version of myself who was readying herself to leave the city all those months ago. So much had changed in that time, yet everything still looked the same. I tried to work out what it all meant, to pin those thoughts down and get a closer look at them, but there was so much going on around me that they were plucked from my grasp before I had the chance — carried off like dandelion seeds on the breeze.

The city centre was busy and some people seemed to know who I was and what I was doing.

'It's Anna! Go, Anna!' they shouted.

'Well done, barefoot lady!' said someone else.

And there were, of course, many others who had no idea why there was a tall woman with a fuchsia 'fro, in bare feet, leading 50 runners down the high street like the Pied Piper. But they were kind enough to clap and cheer anyway.

At the end of Southgate Street, we reached a familiar zebra crossing. I bounded over it and started down the stone steps which led to Gloucester Quays — a separate area of the city, where the Gloucester and Sharpness Canal meets the River Severn and ends in a set of beautifully renovated shipping warehouses.

'Almost there!' yelled a runner next to me, as we crossed over old tram tracks on the floor and passed a metal pulley cart.

'Glaaaawwwsssster!' shouted another.

'Almost home,' I whispered, mostly to myself, but it was

also a message to my weary legs. And now I could feel a lump in my throat. The support from the runners had been phenomenal, and even though I called Gloucester 'home', I was still an adopted child to the city. The thought that I might be supported and celebrated as if I were one of 'them' filled me with gratitude and a sense of belonging.

As I entered into the shadow of the Victoria and Britannia Warehouses and ran alongside the water, seagulls swooped overhead, squawking above the thunder of trainer hooves on stone paving slabs. The squawks were a familiar sound and one I'd missed since being away (even if I didn't miss the gulls dive-bombing my lunch or taking a dump on me from time to time). An eruption of cheers and claps drew my attention from the gulls, and I heard the crowd before I saw them.

At the other end of the docks, supporters had gathered in an open square that was often used for concerts and food festivals. The crowd had made a neat finish line chute, a few people deep at the sides, which ended with a wall of cheering and waving bodies. When I saw them, I couldn't believe it. They couldn't all be here for me? Could they? There were some three hundred of them. I didn't even know that many people in Gloucester. I was dumbstruck and all I could say as my legs carried me closer to the crowd was 'Thank you! Thank you! Oh wow. . . Thank youuu!'

The feeling of running into a crowd of people that size, knowing that they've gathered for you, is overwhelming. It's a mixture of embarrassment, gratitude and joy. My heart rate picked up and I was flooded with warmth, as if I'd just been given a giant hug by the universe. I spotted Jamie's mum, Ann, at one end of the crowd — she was going wild, waving and clapping and jumping around on the spot. Jamie's brother Lee and his missus Chantel were making equally as much noise, and then next to them was Jamie — doing what he does best and working the crowd into a frenzy. It was lovely to see him and it was equally lovely to see the strawberry milkshake he was holding in his hand. The boy knew me too well. I threw my arms in the air for the final few strides and the crowd roared in reply. I gave Jamie a kiss and collected my milkshake, then turned around to welcome in the rest of the runners. I knew that some of them were exhausted — many had gone way beyond anything they'd ever run before — but looking at their smiling faces you wouldn't have known it at all. They had all done themselves proud, and Gloucester had done me proud. I couldn't have asked for a better welcome home.

That evening, I had just about come down from my runner's high when I peeled off my sweaty kit and clambered into the bath. I took a long, relaxing soak and stayed in until my fingertips wrinkled and the water turned cold. I didn't even do any admin in the bath. I just stared at the ceiling and thought back over the events of the past 24 hours.

How could I have ever thought I'd regret running through home? The level of support from Gloucestershire runners and those showing up to wave signs had been mind-blowing. It was beyond anything I could have imagined, and it made me feel more connected to the city than ever before. There's a Spanish word, querencia, which doesn't translate directly into English, but it refers to a special type of home. A querencia is a place from which we are able to draw strength. It's where we feel nourished, grounded and inspired. A querencia is everything you could ever want in a home because the actual location doesn't matter — it's dictated by a feeling. It's often used to describe the place in a ring where a bull will go to summon the energy for its next charge. And, at the end of my days in Gloucester, I had found that energy. It was time to resume the charge for London.

24

'Why Are You Bonkers?'

After leaving Gloucester, I loosely followed the Cotswold Way, and any fears I had about not being able to find the will to leave the city were quick to disappear —squished into the tarmac beneath my cowpat-infused footprints as I weaved my way south. The rain of the past few weeks had subsided, but the aftermath of flooding was still everywhere. When on the trail, I waded through sections of waterlogged quagmire, mud and grit, and even whole tree branches were strewn across the roads. Tiptoeing around debris made for slow progress, but I was running alone, so I could take my sweet time. I paused at junctions, inspecting small white signs on weather-beaten iron posts, and chopped and changed the route at will. I listened to wind whistle through the trees and the surge in my legs that said 'that-a-way', and off I went.

I padded through small villages with triangle-shaped greens in the centre of them, past chocolate-box homes made from sandy-coloured Cotswold stone, topped with thatched roofs. I found old red telephone boxes tucked away in long-for-gotten corners, which now either housed a defibrillator or had been stuffed with books and converted into a mini local library with instructions that read: 'Take a book you'd like and leave one you've loved.' Every village I passed through seemed to have a church or a pub, or both. And much as I was neither a big drinker nor a religious soul, I liked the fact that even these small places had a gathering point. Somewhere to connect, to come together.

I had forgotten (but was soon reminded) that the Cotswolds are hilly. I should know that. I live right next to the Cotswolds, but I'd never run over so many of the hills in such a short space of time. Up and down I went. Round, along and up some more, slogging through forests to the crest of a ridge before plunging back down into the green-sloped valley below. At the end of each day my legs ached, and my feet were caked in mud — some of it still fresh and sloppy, other bits dry and crusty. It was spattered up the backs of my calves, had collected in the creases on my palms, and my legs and torso were covered in muddy handprints. And yet, I was content — enjoying exploring tiny pockets of the country I had no idea existed, even though they were just down the road from where I lived.

When I made it to Hawkesbury Upton, I discovered that a woman named Louise had hijacked the town sign, decorating it with bunting and sweets and placing a cardboard sign over the top of the original one that read: 'Welcome Anna McNuff Superstar!' Even though she'd been waiting for me since 7 a.m. and I ran through the village at 3 p.m., she was somehow still smiling. I was taken aback by Louise's decorating effort and that she'd managed to rally other villagers into cheering me on too, but I shouldn't have been surprised. If there was one thing I'd learned I could rely on in Britain it was a sense of community. We all need the support of a community, whatever form that takes, like we need food and water. The Barefoot Britain community was now strung out across the country, from Shetland to London, and online too, and I was still in awe of the power of it. The people within it inspired me every day. With their faith in how truly 'Great' their own corner of Britain was. With their faith in the run. With their faith in me.

A large chunk of that community had come from the Girlguiding network, and before I ran out of Gloucestershire, I had one final visit to make. I backtracked north to Dursley, where 100 young girls had gathered at Dursley school for an evening of adventure tales. While I was still keeping to the rule of taking a few minutes of me-time at the end of a day, whenever I finished a day's run and headed off to give a talk, I always initially wondered quite how I was going to summon the energy to do it. I was exhausted 99.9% of the time, but by this point in the journey, I was also on autopilot. So, I stayed in cruise-control from finishing running, right to the talk, and never let myself think about how tired I was until the talk was done.

Within 10 minutes of starting my spiel at Dursley, I was into my stride. Any feelings of exhaustion disappeared in a puff of smoke, replaced by laughs and cheers from the girls in the audience. Together, we created a tornado of energy. I threw some at them, they hurled it back, and it multiplied until there was no world beyond the one in that room. The girls were now in my adventures with me — I took them to

South America, to New Zealand, and across the USA on a bike called Boudica. Then, I told them a partially finished tale about a very long barefoot run and, at the end of the talk, there was time for a round of questions. I always love taking questions from kids, more so than adults, because you never quite know what's going to come out of their mouths.

There was the usual barrage of queries about what I'd stepped in along the way, why I had chosen to run barefoot and what my favourite adventure was so far. At the very end of the Q & A session, a girl in the front row stuck up her hand. She couldn't have been more than eight years old.

'Yes. . . and what's your question?' I asked.

'Um. . . Anna. . . I was wondering. . .' the girl said, swirling her mousy-brown, shoulder-length hair with one finger.

'Yes?'

'Why are you bonkers?' She was straight-faced with un-blinking blue eyes. There were giggles from the audience and the girl looked around, nervously. I stifled a laugh. But then I realised, it was a deadly serious question. I thought for a moment.

'That's a very good question. Do you think I'm bonkers?' I asked, and the girl nodded in reply.

'Why is that?'

'Because. . . umm. . . everyone wears shoes and you're doing a loooong barefoot run,' she replied, still twiddling her hair.

357

'I am. And, yes, that does make me a bit bonkers, but do you know what I think?'

'What?'

'That it's good to be bonkers. Because bonkers is different. And being different is a wonderful thing. If you always do what other people do then you might end up in a very crowded place, and that can feel a bit suffocating. Do you know what I mean by "suffocating"?'

The girl nodded in reply.

'But. . . if you do something different then you might end up, say, at the top of a mountain, or on a barefoot run, and then there's lots of space. Space to breathe and to be yourself. Does that make sense?'

The girl nodded again.

'Do you think you might be a bit bonkers?' I asked.

'Yes,' whispered the girl, smiling.

'Fantastic. Then you need to stay that way,' I said, raising my voice so that the whole room could hear. Then I leaned in close, looked the girl in the eye and lowered my voice to a whisper. 'Do you promise to stay bonkers?'

'I promise,' she whispered back.

***

As I left Gloucestershire and tracked east across Somerset over the following week, Rain returned to southern Britain and it brought its best friend, Gusty Wind, to the party. It was mid-October and the sun was now setting at 6 p.m., a far cry from the 11 p.m. sunsets in Shetland. With my tendency to start running later in the day, I was now often finishing at dusk. On one particular day, I had underestimated the time it would take to cover 22 miles, or rather, I had overestimated my speed, and I arrived in the city of Wells after dark. As I scampered along the pavement, guided by the beam of my head-torch, squinting to make sure I didn't step on anything sharp, I chastised myself for not starting the run sooner. I made a resolution to leave earlier in the day from then on, to be sure that my tootsies were tucked up, long before sundown.

A few days into the journey across Somerset, I had a fandango of six join me for the run out of Bridgwater. We met in light drizzle at a local park and, in a break from the norm, three out of the six runners were men. Even more strange was that two of the men were called Chris. To help me tell them apart, one of them had kindly grown a beard. Non-bearded Chris was a local to the area and an ultrarunner, so I had high hopes that he would help with navigation during the 23-mile stage to the north coast of Devon. Bearded Chris was from much further afield — he had made a 300-mile round trip to join in the stage. Which did make me wonder if he had grown the beard in the time it had taken him to drive to Bridgwater that morning. Bearded Chris was to be awarded the trophy for the furthest travelled so far by anyone joining in a public running stage.

The unusual 50/50 male–female split in the group made for some neat energy and the vibe was fun and relaxed as we took off from town. Conversation flowed easily as everyone got to know one another, and soon, we were out of the suburbs, running on grey roads, under grey skies, but with sunshine in our hearts. Somerset had mostly been flat so far, but as we approached the border of the county, the hills were back. . . with a vengeance. For once, I actually knew I was going to be running upwards (and downwards) ahead of the day and, to my surprise, I was looking forward to going over the Quantocks. Sometimes, it was nice to have a mini challenge within the bigger challenge — a shift in focus to break up the monotony.

As we made our way steadily towards the foot of the hills, we ran through open fields lined with hedgerows. It rained on and off for much of the morning and, when the fields ended, we entered into dark, dank woodland. The pace of the group slowed as we started up the first climb and the chatter between us died down too. In the darkness of the wood, I became acutely aware of how quiet it was. There was no traffic on the road and all I could hear was the sound of rain pattering on the leaves of the trees. The air was brisk and all around us the woods were filled with mist, which was rolling gently from between the trees and spilling across the road — the way that dry ice might do onto a stage. Moss clung to spindly, barren branches which reached up and over our heads, forming a latticed roof, blocking the sunlight and making the woods seem darker still. Gnarled, knobbly roots, slick from the drizzle, spread across the forest floor and disappeared beneath piles of rusty-brown leaves. In the mist, the colours of the forest were muted. Except for leaves, everything else was greyscale. Inky-black trunks and charcoal branches cut silhouettes against a backdrop of silvery-white. All in all, there was a real eeriness to the place. I felt like I was running through the set of a dystopian fairy tale. I looked left and right as I padded onwards, wondering when Little Red Riding Hood was going to peek out from behind one of the trunks and beckon me to follow her through the mist to Grandmother's house.

I couldn't move as quickly up the climbs as I would have done on the flat and so it wasn't only the surroundings that were giving me the chills — my toes had the chills too. The slower pace meant there were fewer strides per minute, and less pounding on my tootsies to remind them to stay awake. Plus, the wind had picked up and it was blowing across the tops of them. Even the tufts of punk-rocker hair on my big toes didn't offer any protection. I did my best to stay immersed in chat with the bunch of high-spirited runners, but the higher we went, the colder my feet got, and the less I talked. As we continued onto the top of the largest climb of the day, my toes became painful and then. . . they went numb. I didn't like that at all. I was used to all kinds of sensations in my feet, but they'd never gone numb from the cold before. I was relieved when we finally reached the summit of the hill, where the woods fell away either side and we ran a few hundred metres across a clearing.

'Is this the top?' shouted bearded Chris.

'Yeap! This is it,' I said, checking the map. 'Let's get down quick. I'm worried my feet are going to fall off!'

'But. . . we've got to stop here,' said non-bearded Chris.

'Stop? Why?' I asked, thinking that I really didn't want to stop anywhere except a pub on a cold, wet day like today, least of all at the top of an exposed hill.

'This is Dead Woman's Ditch.'

'Dead Woman's Ditch?'

'Yeah — it's super creepy! Look.' He pointed to a sign-post. 'Apparently, there was a murder here in the seventeen hundreds.'

I later learned the true extent of the Somerset scandal, which was that, in 1735, a woman named Jane from a nearby village had been murdered up on this moor by her husband, John. John was popular with the community and had taken to dating Jane and they had slept together. All of that should be well and good, except John had a dark secret — he was in love with another woman in the village called Ann, whom he intended to marry. Societal pressure forced John to marry Jane, which he resented. So, one night, having loaded up on local cider, John took Jane to the top of the hill in the Quan-tocks and killed her. It's rumoured that if you go up to Dead Woman's Ditch at night you'll hear Jane's screams. But worse than that, you'll hear a male voice too — the ghost of John, who was arrested for her murder and slung into jail. He is still angry after all these years that Jane came between him and his true love, Ann. He'll come out of the darkness and try to chase you away, so that no one else learns of what he did that fateful night.

I looked around at the three other women in the group. My heart had now turned as cold as my toes. But then I realised that if what Chris had said was true, then this was a memorable place, and memorable places needed photographic evidence for posterity. And besides, one of the rules of running at Adventure Pace was that you should stop to take photos of local landmarks. And this was a landmark, sort of.

'Hannah, Sophie, Kat — fancy playing dead with me for a moment?'

There were hesitant nods from the women, who despite being soaked to the bone and cold too, were up for posing with the sign. The boys acted as directors of photography as we did our best to channel our inner zombies and hung off the sign in a variety of positions, faces like the living dead — tongues out, eyes wide. The resulting photo was a marvel. It's one of my favourites from the trip, in fact. Not only because it was a unique and creepy place in the British countryside, but because the ladies had really gone for it. Their faces were spectacularly contorted and the result was a gruesome picture. If ever I were asked to suggest corpses for acting roles, I now knew where to come.

I looked around and thought about what we'd just done. Did we just take the micky out of that woman's death? A stiff wind blew across the top of the hill and the trees around us rattled.

'Let's get out of here! This place is giving me the willies,' I said.

'Me too,' said Sophie

'Me three,' said Kat.

Day-of-the-Dead photoshoot complete, we tanked it down the other side of the hill. Twenty minutes later, my cold toes and I were cosied up next to a roaring fire at The Carew Arms. I'd ordered a plate of ham, egg and chips and, around me, each member of the group was now tucking gleefully into their own late pub lunch. I'll admit that I took longer than was necessary to go through my usual process of ceremoniously dunking each fluffy chip into the yolk of the egg before eating it. Rain had started to rattle against the windowpanes and it now looked properly windy outside. I was trying to delay going out into the cold for as long as I could. But there is only so long a plate of ham, egg and chips can last and, before long, it was time for all of us to pry ourselves away from the comfort of the fire and forge onwards in the rain, towards the north coast of Devon.

25

Rocks in my Pockets

The day I left Minehead, my feet were sore. They'd ached and tingled through the night and I hoped that they'd calm down by the morning, but when I took the first few steps onto the road, it felt as if the skin on my soles had been burned. Running over the Quantocks in icy rain had clearly aggravated my tootsies. Even though I knew I still had dozens of layers of hard skin built up on my feet, they felt paper thin, as if my soles were made of tissue paper. I knew I'd face more cold weather before I finished the run in mid-November and that made me wonder how I'd cope on the days ahead. But I tried not to wonder too long. Wondering only seemed to lead to worrying, after all.

I ran away from Minehead on a mixture of trail and road until I reached Selworthy Beacon, then I chose to follow the South West Coastal Path from there. The coastal path was a longer route and I suspected it would be slower going than the road, but I was entering the fringes of Exmoor National Park — a place I knew and loved, and where I wanted to feel the earth beneath my feet. I took care to pick a line along the trail that avoided any sharp rocks, dancing along the soft grass at the edge or hopping between patches of flat, dry mud and seeking out large rocks with smooth flat tops. The cool of the sandstone felt wonderful on my sore feet — like applying an ice pack to a throbbing muscle — and as I pushed off from each smooth stone, I looked eagerly for the next one.

Alone in Exmoor, I felt at peace. I was happy to be there because Exmoor has always been a happy place for me. I've visited the park countless times, and each time I do, I am transported to another world. And that truly is the only way to describe Exmoor — otherworldly. The boggy moorland which dominates much of the park is harsh, windswept and wild. In between those moors are hidden valleys, tumbling rivers and secluded woods. The landscape is rugged and raw, with wildflowers and forests that make it seem like a part of the Scottish Highlands has been lifted and shifted down to the coast of North Devon. Exmoor is a very special place, indeed.

A mile on from Selworthy Beacon, I passed an Exmoor pony scratching her chin on a wooden signpost and I stopped to say hello. She was a beautiful chestnut-brown with a honey-coloured belly and a black mane. Her nose was stout, with a stripe of cream close to the nostrils, which made it look as if she'd been drinking from a pail of cream.

'Hello pony, what are you up to today?' I asked.

The pony didn't say anything in reply, but she paused her chin-scratching session for a moment and stared at me. She flicked her long black tail and shook her mane, before returning to the signpost scratch-a-thon. Oh, to be an Exmoor pony,

I thought.

I turned away from the pony and looked out across the Bristol Channel. The Welsh coastline was some 28 miles across the water and mostly a blur, but I could see a few patches of light and, by looking at the map, I worked out that those lights would be Barry Island to the east and Porthcawl to the west. I inhaled deeply and then let my breath flow out across the water. Much as I'd tried to let it go, I was still harbouring concerns about my sore feet, and how they'd cope with the impending cold weather. As a result, it had felt noisy in my mind for much of the morning. But in that moment, all was quiet and still. I turned away from the twinkling lights of Wales and took off along the cliffs.

For the next couple of miles, I stayed up high, stopping briefly to look back on where I'd come from and take in the scenery every now and then. In the distance, along the coast, fields rolled off towards the horizon like a neatly laid patchwork quilt, dark hedges acting as the stitching between squares of bright green. Gorse lined the edges of the trail, its yellow flowers like pockets of sunshine, and all around me the bracken leaves were turning to golds and browns — starting to wilt as they lay down for winter. Small clusters of wild mushrooms had gathered in shady patches by the side of the trail and fingers of moss crept out from beneath the long grass — sometimes forming a mossy mound and other times partially covering a piece of sandstone. I liked to run on the moss where I could because it was the dreamiest of surfaces, like a mini springboard beneath my feet. In between the gorse and moss, white wildflowers were scattered here and there — little explosions of light against a backdrop of green and brown.

There was no doubt that choosing to follow the coastal trail was wonderful for the scenery, but jeepers it was slow going. Far slower than I'd expected. After leaving the clifftops, I spent a significant amount of time on my arse — slipping down slopes and squelching around in muddy forests. Just shy of Bossington, I emerged from the forest as a mud monster, then pushed on to Porlock, where I stopped briefly to inhale a strawberry milkshake and sausage roll. I was in such a rush to keep moving that I didn't even sit down to eat and drink, choosing instead to inhale my goodies while standing outside. It was unusual that I didn't at least take a small break to eat, but I was feeling supercharged by the energy in the park, propelled onward by a force that wasn't my own. Perhaps it was because I knew I had a challenge on my hands. I hadn't looked ahead to check exactly how many hills I would need to run over to make it to Lynmouth, but I had a feeling that the figure would equate to: LOADS. I had 23 miles to run that day, and doing it before dark would be impossible if I didn't get a wriggle on.

When I reached the Worthy Combe Toll Road, I stopped briefly at a white wooden gate to read a crumbling cream sign with black lettering:

No responsibility attaches to the owner of this road for any carnage or injury suffered by any person using this road, from any cause whatsoever whether due to said owner's negligence, nonfeasance, or misfeasance or to the state of the road or anything near the road or overhanging the same or otherwise, and all persons using the road do so entirely at their own risk.

Wowsers. I had no idea what nonfeasance or misfeasance meant, but I was bang up for finding out. Close by it was another, smaller sign, which said that the road was only for cars and cyclists, and that people on foot should take the nearby coastal trail. But I reasoned that a) this sign was smaller, and b) I was on a very long journey; therefore, I could flex the rules. I pushed £1 into a metal box, stepped through the gate and started up a steep climb.

I always love journeying along old roads because I like to imagine what it might have been like to travel that way hundreds of years ago. And that was especially true on the Worthy Combe Toll Road, which is surrounded by an ancient woodland. Some trees towered towards the sky, but others were stouter — their roots all twisted and gnarled, with nobbles on the trunks like the knuckles on the hands of a weather-beaten fisherman. I could see why only light vehicles were allowed to use the road because the tarmac was patchy and had crumbled completely in many places. It was littered with leaves and small pieces of rock, dislodged from an old stone wall which ran alongside it. Every now and then, I'd pass a small branch of a tree that had fallen to the ground, presumably broken off by a storm at some point. The branches had settled in the middle of the road and were now encased in bright green moss — like snakes frozen in time, mid-slither across the track.

At the summit of the climb, I ran out from the woodland and squinted in bright sunlight as the landscape opened out into moorland. I stopped to look back down the road. I'd slogged upwards for 30 minutes and the sea now seemed a long way off. I could see a headland jutting out into the water beyond Bossington and, although it was warm day, a fine mist was floating across the moor. Droplets of moisture clung to the hairs on my forearms and made them glisten. I paused briefly at a T-junction where the toll road came to an end at the main road across the park. I spied a trail opposite the junction and took one last look back at the sea behind me. I was sad to be leaving the coast behind for the rest of the day, but I was sure there'd be more spectacular scenery ahead of me. And so, with dirt on my soles and wonder in my heart, I took off along the trail.

Even though I'd visited Exmoor before, I had barely scratched the surface on those visits and so there was a real sense of the unknown, a syncopated beat which I welcomed with open arms after the humdrum of country roads and miles of tarmac. Running along the banks of the East Lyn River, I felt closer to the landscape. Like I was no longer just looking out on it — I was a part of it. As if there was a deep connection between Exmoor and me. I passed the odd small stone house, but otherwise I didn't see a soul all afternoon, listening only to the sound of my feet moving over the earth and the rush of the river to my right.

That afternoon, something shifted in me in the Doone Valley, and I ran without fear or doubt. I was confident when moving over difficult sections of trail and I felt like I was making great progress. That was until I checked the map at 4 p.m. and reality reared its head. I'd covered 19 miles, there were still 4 miles left to make to Lynmouth. . . and sunset was fast approaching.

There was nothing for it but to pick up the pace and follow the road for the final few miles. It wasn't a decision I made lightly; although I had a headtorch in my pack, I had no high-vis gear on. If any cars came by in the dark, I'd be a sitting duck. A shot of adrenaline pulsed through my veins — I needed to make it to town, and it had to be fast. I took off like a woman possessed, pushing harder and harder, forcing my legs to move quicker than they wanted to, sucking in lungfuls of thick, soupy air.

A mist descended on the valley and, as dusk fell, the trees around me seemed to make more sound than usual. I pricked up my ears and strained my eyes through the darkness. Probably time to put that headtorch on now, I thought, stopping to pull it out of my pack and affix it to my head. It grew darker still, and now I could see the droplets of my breath on the air in the beam of the headtorch. I moved my feet faster and faster. Two miles to go. I ran, and I ran, and I ran. I ran as if I were being chased and my life depended on it. Now addicted to my newfound speed, I ran as if I couldn't stop even if I tried. Intoxicated by a cocktail of adrenaline and endorphins, my body took over. I was drenched in sweat and caked in mud, but my mind was crystal-clear. I was full-blown feral. I felt liberated. I felt powerful. I felt wild. And I liked it.

***

'Yes, deary, what can I get you?' asked the woman behind the counter. I was standing in a quaint tearoom in Lynmouth, surrounded by gingham tablecloths and eyeing a row of home-made jams.

'A pot of tea and a cheese and ham sandwich, please. Does it come with crisps?' I asked. Which was an important question. Because, of course, I had high hopes of putting the crisps in the sandwich and it just wouldn't be the same without them.

'It does,' the woman smiled, then wrote down the order on a small pad of paper.

'Great, thank you.'

'On a bike ride, are you?' She gestured to my running leggings, which were still spattered with mud from the previous day.

'Oh, I'm not on a bike. . .'

'No bike? Ah, in that case, you're walking the coastal path.' She raised a knowing finger in the air before punching in some numbers into the heavy grey keypad of an old-fashioned till.

'I'm actually running,' I mumbled and the drawer of the till popped open with a ping!

'Running?!' The woman looked confused. 'Well, you're

definitely going to need those crisps then. I'll pop you some extras on the plate,' she smiled.

I decided not to add into the mix that I was actually running in my bare feet; seeing as today was a rest day, my feet were tucked up in shoes, so she needn't know any different.

As expected, I felt like I'd been run over by a bus the morning I'd woken up in Lynmouth. After the wild 'n' speedy run into town, my feet and legs had throbbed and ached overnight. When I push my muscles too far, and I mean way too far, I often feel sick in the hours afterwards. But the sickness isn't in my stomach — it's like my legs want to throw up, except they can't. So, short of chundering from my kneecaps, I just ride out the waves of nausea. It's the strangest feeling, but that's the only way to describe it. I slept through breakfast and did some trigger-point therapy on my quads and hamstrings (which made me feel equally vom-tastic) before spending a lazy day in town, catching up on admin, wandering between tearooms and coffee shops and drinking many, many milkshakes.

Lynmouth was the perfect place to take a day of rest. Situated at the estuary of the east and west Lyn rivers, it's a haven of tranquillity. If you're travelling by car, there's only one way in and one way out — the road ends at the sea. That makes the town feel entirely separate from the rest of the world, somehow — as if you have stepped through a gateway to a secret garden where forest-covered hillsides tumble into the cold blue sea.

Left to my own devices, with no host or other runners, I was in a reflective mood, so I took a stroll through town just as the sun was beginning to set. I ambled alongside the estuary and looked back on the small stone bridge that spans it. Quaint, white-washed homes were dotted around the centre of town, with larger ones up in the hills. Above the buildings, the cliffs were alive with colour — yellows, reds and greens exploding like fireworks above exposed grey rock which plunged steeply into the sea. I wandered on, past lines of lobster pots piled up against a grey stone wall, to Rhenish Tower, a tall, stone building with a beacon at the top which was once used to guide mariners into the harbour. As the sun dipped closer to the line of the horizon and low hanging wisps of white cloud turned to tangerine, I continued on through town and out along the shore. I watched a couple of brave souls who had gone for an evening surf, wetsuit-clad, bobbing between gently rolling waves, just two black dots on an indigo sea. There was a nip in the air, so I snuggled deeper into my duffel coat and walked back towards the edge of town to sit on a bench and watch the pebbles on Blacklands Beach bathe in the last rays of sunlight.

I was grateful to sit on that bench and let the cogs in my brain turn because I had something on my mind. On other journeys in America, South America and New Zealand, I'd had a lot of time disconnected from the world. . . from phone signal, from Wi-Fi. This journey had been different, and deliberately so, but in recent weeks, amid all of the commotion, I'd found it difficult to think clearly. To tune in with how I was feeling — about life, about the run, about the remaining five weeks until the finish. Things often seem 'fine' when life is all go, go, go, but it's only when you stop that reality jumps up and gives you a cheeky slap around the chops. That's what happened when I was stationary in Lynmouth.

I'd been feeling the slow creep of melancholy for a week or so now. It wasn't unusual for me to feel low at that time of the year. I often struggle in early autumn, when the days get shorter and a long winter looms ahead of me. I know its official title is Seasonal Affective Disorder (SAD). It's depression in some form — I feel it as a dull ache in my bones and a leaden weight on my body. In fact, the best way to describe it is that it feels as if I have rocks in my pockets and I am lying on the bed of an ocean. I can see the surface above my head, I can see the sunlight sparkling up there. I can see the people whizzing to and fro in their boats, having fun. But I stay on the bottom for a few weeks of the year because I don't have the energy to swim to the surface. And besides, it's quiet down here on the bedrock. It's just me and the fishes, and no one expects anything of me.

Of course, I know it's brighter up there. A few times, I convince myself that swimming to the surface is what I should do. Because we are taught that we must always be happy, if we can. So, out of duty and gratitude for this beautiful life, I kick frantically and propel myself to where the cold, deep water meets the air. I feel the sun on my face for a brief moment as I break the surface, and I inhale a lungful of fresh salty air, but it's no good. Soon, the weight of the rocks in my pockets pull me gently back down to the bottom. And there I stay, for a while. Until the rocks dissolve and become light enough to allow me to float back to join the rest of the world.

As is the case with slumps, the fix is never instant. So, I indulged in mine for a while. I wallowed in it. I allowed myself to feel all the feels and to just be sad. Sometimes, I was sad about specific things, like missing Jamie, my family and wondering whether I would make the 100-marathon target after all, and other times. . . I was sad for no reason at all. But I continued to get up, to run and to keep moving as if I was on autopilot and slowly, slowly the rocks in my pockets began to dissolve.

It helped that autumn was in full swing because, despite the yearly slump it brings, there's something comforting about it. If ever you need proof that the world is continually turning beneath your feet, autumn, with its kaleidoscope of reds and yellows, delivers just that. After Lynmouth, I stopped regularly to take pictures of piles of coppery leaves gathered in patches at the sides of the roads. Although I liked the bright ones, my favourites were the brown leaves with small dots of green still visible — little mavericks, resisting the end of the summer, defiant in their spots. And so, thanks to autumn and the funky leaves, my mood brightened. . . just a smidge.

Near Instow, I enjoyed a day of running along the Tarka Trail. It was my birthday, and I ran under sunshine and thunderstorms. Best of all, one of my best friends, Faye, had managed to chase me down on the trail. She rode her bike with her dog, Molly, sitting on her shoulders and delivered a home-baked lemon meringue pie. If a Jack Russell riding high on a 6 ft 1 redhead carrying a pie can't cheer you up, I don't know what will. Faye even brought me a spoon. Not a knife to cut the pie and share it. Just one big spoon. For me. Now, that's a true friend. And my mood, now infused with lemon meringue and dog hair, brightened. . . just a smidge.

Throughout Devon, as I headed south towards Dartmoor National Park, I continued to be taken in by kind hosts who fed me and let me lay about on their sofas in the evening watching Strictly Come Dancing, not saying much at all. I carried on giving talks and when the girls asked me whether the adventure was always AWESOME, I treated them like adults. I spoke to them openly and honestly about the reality of a long adventure on the road. I said I was very tired, but that, so long as there weren't any more foot-related disasters, I was determined to make London. And through all of that, my mood brightened. . . just a smidge. Lastly, and most importantly, I re-pinked my hair. What was once a curly faded 'fro became magenta and bright again. And for the first time in weeks, that's how I now felt inside too.

26

Island-hopping

I am never one to do battle with Mother Nature. I have learned over the years that it's a fight you cannot win. But on the fringes of Dartmoor, I began a new battle with the daylight hours. Gone were the times when I could start running at midday and finish at 7 p.m.. Now with only eight hours of sunlight to play with, I was forced to adjust my run routine to finish the miles before it got dark. One morning, at Okehampton, I kicked my butt into gear and asked my host to drop me off to begin the day at 9 a.m.. As soon as I set off, I knew I'd made a mistake. In the shadow of the hedgerows, the sun hadn't yet touched the small country lanes and the ground was carpeted with a light frost. Within 10 minutes, the soles of my feet were stinging and my toes were numb. Every now and then, I would stop and clutch them in my hand in a bid to warm them up. If I had cold hands, I would usually tuck them under my armpits to get the blood back into them. But I was at least seven years of intensive yoga away from being able to get my feet up to my pits, so I settled for holding one foot at a time in my hands instead, and that did the trick.

Every now and then, I hit a patch of tarmac where the

sun had sneaked through the hedge. I would stand in the rays of morning light and revel in the warmth. It was still freezing but, in contrast to the rest of the road, that scrap of sun-kissed tarmac felt like underfloor heating. I'd savour the warmth, allowing myself a few seconds standing in one spot before taking a deep breath and ploughing on. By 11 a.m. the roads had warmed up enough so as not to be uncomfortable and the life returned to my toes. It was a fine line I was now treading in bare feet. Start too late and I'd finish in the dark. Start too early and I'd have numb toes.

With no solution to the dilemma but to keep on trucking onwards, I went past thatched cottages and old stone stately homes, through Hinton St George, Chard and Yeovil — more miles, more talks and more kind hosts. Now I was out of my funk, the miles passed more easily. I pushed the daily mileage up and was running 23 or 24 miles most days, and one week I clocked up 177 miles — the biggest distance yet. I had to take stock and marvel at the human body at that point. I'd hoped mine was capable of bashing out big miles like that, but the fitness and the strength had built so slowly, I'd barely noticed it. I'd come a long way since those uncomfortable 7 miles from Skaw Beach in Shetland. My body was now a machine. I was in awe of its unrelenting ability to propel me onwards.

It was around this time that I began to look back on the past four and a half months of running. I became addicted to looking at my tracker map each night and took a sick satisfaction from noting that the mini me on the map of Great Britain had moved just a little bit further each day. The finish line in

London still seemed a long way off, but I enjoyed reminiscing all the same. In the evenings, I'd flick back through my social media feed, looking at pictures of me in the Highlands, my bare feet, the cuts, the scenery. . . I'd read what I'd written in the captions and think 'who is that person?' It didn't feel like me. I mean, I knew it was me, but I felt detached from her, somehow. As if it were all some kind of bizarre dream in which I was participating. Had I really run all that way? Surely, I couldn't still be doing this? But the words and pictures written by my own hand told me otherwise.

One evening, when I was looking at the map of my route, reality hit home. I knew it already, really, but I hadn't wanted to face it. Perhaps it had even contributed to my low mood over the past few weeks. I'd covered 1,800 miles in the four and a half months since leaving Shetland, but I now only had one month left before reaching the finish line date I'd set myself in London on 17 November. It didn't take a maths genius to work out that running another 820 miles in just four weeks would be a tall order. It would mean averaging 27 miles per day, every day, with no days of rest. Much as I spend a lot of time with my head in the clouds, I had to be realistic — that kind of daily mileage was cray cray. I'd ground myself to the bone getting this far; finding the juice to run even further each day. . . it just wasn't going to happen. Maybe I could just carry on running through winter, rejig the schedule again? I thought. But that would be madness.

In my heart, I already knew what I wanted to do. The foot infection, the tonsillitis, it had all tipped things just the wrong side of possible. I wanted to let the 100-marathon target go. To say my goodbyes, light a little flame beneath it and watch it float on up into the air like a Chinese lantern. I was gutted, but the whole point of the run was to share the reality of it with the girls. And if that meant I had to admit that I had fallen short, then so be it. Instead, I would just run as far as I could in the month I had left and see how many miles I could cover.

***

Now, it's at this point that I have to confess. . . when I was planning the route for the run, I got bored towards the end of the process. The route was based on places I wanted to see, where there were cool trails and where I could visit the Girl Guiding members, but as I laid out the plan for running along the south coast and up into London, I could feel myself thinking, 'Yada, yada, yada. . .'

Not that the UK's south coast is in any way boring — it is far from that. It is stunning. But as it's the closest coastline to where I spent 30 years of my life (London), I have visited the south coast often. I knew I had to be excited about the journey in order to keep me motivated because excitement was a key weapon in my armoury. And maintaining that excitement would be especially important as I neared the end of the journey when I would be weary. So, even before I began the run, I knew the route needed some spice. A little chilli oil on my

Great Britain pizza. Some zing! Something to restoke the fire for the final few weeks to the finish. So, I had decided I would dilly-dally around offshore for a few days, visiting the Channel Islands of Guernsey and Jersey on my way from Poole to London.

I say 'on my way' — the islands are not really on the way at all. In fact, they are very much out of the way — some 207 miles off the coast in the English Channel. They are much closer to France than they are to Britain. But these are minor details. The major details were that, having visited both islands before, I remembered them to be full of lush sandy beaches, beautiful coves and aquamarine seas. I also had a vague recollection about there being lots of small, quiet back roads and delicious ice cream. Perfect for a lady on a barefoot mission.

I spent two days on Guernsey and learned many things while there. I learned that their postboxes are the same shape and style as on mainland Britain, except they are blue not red (Mind. Blown.). I discovered that there is a 35-mph speed limit across the whole island and on certain roads called ruettes tranquilles there is a 15-mph speed limit and pedestrians, horses and bikes have priority over cars. Knowing that slower forms of transport were welcome on the Guernsey lanes gave me a new lease of life and I clocked up my longest day of running yet — 27 miles of wiggling around the coast. Cha-ching! Which, considering the island is just 9 miles long, meant that I covered most of it in just one day.

Guernsey's big sister, Jersey, is a larger island and hillier too. The last time I'd been to Jersey (in the summer) it was scorching hot and the white sandy beaches of St Aubin and St Brelade's Bay made it feel like the Caribbean. Naturally, I expected the same Caribbean climate on the barefoot journey, but I had forgotten it was autumn. Instead of the bright sunshine I was hoping for, it tipped with rain for the two days. A group of eight of us started in light drizzle and finished in the pouring rain. I couldn't stop for more than two minutes when running because my toes became cold and painful but even in the cold and rain, Jersey was still gorgeous.

I was especially touched that among the group were a family of four, who were on holiday from Durham. The parents somehow managed to get their teenage boys to join in with the whole 23-mile stage, and not only that — the boys did it all barefoot. I was super-impressed, although I wasn't sure how they were feeling throughout the run (they didn't say too much).

We finished on the golden sand of St Aubin's Bay, across the road from the Grand Jersey Hotel and Spa. We were eager to take shelter as a group and, despite it being a posh establishment, the hotel welcomed a puddle of smelly, sopping runners who wanted nothing more than to relax in their plush leather chairs (soaking them in the process) and to drink hot chocolate and beer in the 'champagne lounge'.

I rounded off my time on Jersey with a live appearance on the ITV Jersey evening news and couldn't have been more chuffed with the whirlwind trip to the Channel Islands. All in all, it had felt longer than four days. And no matter how many people had told me I was mad for choosing a route that included the islands, I was so glad I did. Not only because I was eager to explore these hidden pockets of Britain, but also because being away from the mainland somehow made me feel like I had crossed over into another dimension, a parallel universe. Yes, the people in Jersey and Guernsey were still coming out to run with me; yes, I was still giving talks to local Girlguiding units; and, yes, I was still doing media interviews — but, somehow, it seemed less pressured. At over 2,000 miles through the journey, it felt like I had pressed pause on the 'real' part of the run. I was just playing instead. Even though it was cold and raining, the good company, fantastic tootsie surfaces and the magic blue postboxes recharged me to the max. By the time I boarded the ferry back to mainland Britain, I was a battery running at full again.

BAREFOOT BRITAIN

THE FINISH!

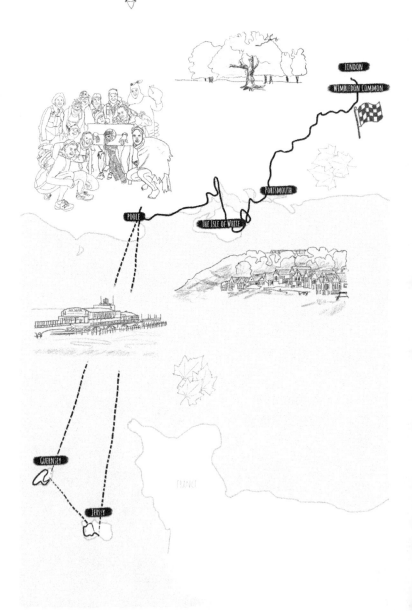

LONDON

WIMBLEDON COMMON

PORTSMOUTH

POOLE

THE ISLE OF WHITE

GUERNSEY

JERSEY

FRANCE

27

Mike, Lobster of the
South Seas

It was 11 p.m. when I sailed into the calm of Poole Harbour. I'd got seasick on the crossing, so I waited until the last possible moment to move and was one of the final passengers off the ferry. As everyone filtered away from the terminal in cars or were collected by friends and family, I made my way inside. There were three workers in the terminal building, packing up and getting ready to shut up shop for the night. I lay down on a row of seats, shut my eyes and waited for my next host to arrive. I was just about to nod off when the door burst open. In stepped a woman holding a tiny red and white megaphone to her lips.

'Taxi for McNuff. . . crch. . . Taxi for McNuff!' she shouted, looking around the room as if she were searching for me in a crowd of imaginary people.

'Yes, please,' I mumbled, raising a limp arm. I sat up on the row of chairs, then wobbled to my feet. 'Hello, Super Sue, how are you?'

'I'm good. But. . . oh — you look a bit pale. Let's get you home.'

I'd first met Sue Barrett, aka Super Sue, four years earlier. After getting back from a long and adventuresome run through New Zealand, I'd cofounded a women's adventure community called Adventure Queens. It started off as a way to offer no-frills tips and advice to women who wanted to go wild camping but didn't know where to start. Then the idea grew (gloriously unshaven, hairy) legs and ran away with itself. At the time of writing, Adventure Queens is a community of over 10,000, run by a team of 40 volunteers, with local groups all around Britain and abroad.

In the first year of running the community, we gave out a grant — a pot of cash and kit — to send someone on a life-changing adventure. Adventure had changed my life, after all, so I thought it would be pure magic if we could do the same thing for someone else. We were overrun with applications for the grant from women from all walks of life — each of them with very personal reasons for wanting to go adventurin' — but there was something about one of the applications that really caught my eye. It had been submitted by one Sue Barrett.

Sue was 55 years old and planning to run, cycle and swim along the spine of the Alps through eight European countries. She wrote:

I want to see eight countries from the top of their Alpine peaks, I want to stay in those little mountain huts and share stories with new people and I want to see if I can move my body 1,300 miles under my own steam.

Sue was at a real crossroads in her life, having worked in primary education for 30+ years and now facing redundancy. A mum of two (now grown-up) girls, she'd also been caring for her elderly parents for several years alongside work and everything else. The time had now come to do something for herself, and that thing was an adventure:

I want to keep my mind and body as strong as possible for as long as possible and to inspire and encourage my children to keep active and challenge themselves. I've run a marathon and done a sprint triathlon and I want to try to go a bit further. And, well. . . I haven't had a gap year yet and I thought it's about time I did. Everyone should have one, shouldn't they?

I couldn't agree more that Sue deserved a gap year. She deserved to be on a freakin' gap year for the rest of her life. I had no idea what it must be like to not only have given over your life to raising your kids, but then to also be caring for your parents. It was clear that Sue put the needs of others before her own, and I wanted to help her put herself first, for once. There was a part of the application form where we asked how long the adventure would take and Sue's reply was:

If I took the idea of 'Around the Alps in 80 days' as a theme, then 80 days hopefully. . . however, if I took the 'Menopausal Mum in the Mountains' approach and I get really hot then I could be a little while longer. . .

It helped that Sue had a cracking sense of humour, and at 55, she was the oldest applicant for the grant — there was something extra special about that. She had the power to inspire a whole other generation of women.

So, we gave Sue some spondoolies. We loaded her up with a few pieces of advice and sorted her out some kit. And in the summer of 2018, she spent three months running and cycling 1,300 miles along the Via Alpina trail — starting in Slovenia before passing through Italy, Austria, Germany, Liechtenstein, Switzerland, France and finishing in Monaco. And so, Sue became Super Sue. Although, really, she was already extremely super — she didn't need a big mountainous adventure to make her that way.

Over the course of watching Sue's adventure unfold, I became fond of her. She was kind, funny and hard as nails beneath it all. In the years that had passed since her Alpine excursions, I'd kept tabs on her adventures in between my own. So, when I found out she'd volunteered to host me while I was on the barefoot run, I was over the moon.

Super Sue lives on the edge of the New Forest in Hampshire. She was well-placed to act as a 'home base' on the south coast for several nights before and after I did my route jiggery-pokery to the Channel Islands. She'd offered to drive me back and forth to catch ferries, to be my taxi to Girlguiding talks in the evenings on the mainland and, of course, join me for a few stints of jogging herself. Although she reminded me on several occasions that she would be running with her shoes on. I said that was okay. Super she was, stupid she was not.

I'd been looking forward to the stay with Sue since the journey began. Largely because I had a feeling that Sue's company would be just what I needed to steel myself for the final three weeks to the finish line, and also because I knew that I could collapse and be completely myself in her company. That said, I hadn't allowed myself to think too much about the visit in the lead-up, for fear I might not make it that far. So, I'd parked it in a quiet corner of my mind, and only when I was a few days away did I actually believe I'd be staying with her. When I messaged her to check in, her reply to me read: 'Can't wait to see you. I'm ready for anything! Let me know what you need and I'll do whatever.'

I'd been to Sue's home before so there was something lovely about walking through the door and knowing the layout already. And it really did feel like a 'home base' because of that. In the bedroom downstairs, she had laid out a box full of snack bars, fruit, energy drinks and rehydration sachets. I gobbled my way through half of the box quickly, only to find she would restock it when I was out running during the day. Super Sue's B & B was the best place to be for the perpetually hungry runner.

On 31 October, after a few days of being looked after by Super Sue, I readied myself to leave the house for a day of running out of Poole. It was a public running stage and in the usual pre-event email that went out to those signed up, I'd announced that the stage would be in Halloween fancy dress.

Or rather, I would be in Halloween fancy dress, and anyone else who felt the urge to join me in the realm of the spirits was more than welcome. Sue had taken the reins of the costume design — she'd simply raised one finger in the air and said, 'Leave it with me, McNuff. I'm on it.'

Sure enough, that morning, I opened one of the drawers in the guest room at Sue's to discover I had a choice of two costumes: a skeleton or a pumpkin. I was feeling more skeletal than root-vegetable-like that day, so I pulled on a black poncho with a skeleton printed on it and paired it with a white tutu. I'm not sure skeletons technically wear tutus, but hey, this is the twenty-first century. That skeleton could darn well be anything it wanted to be and perhaps my skeleton indulged in ballet in the underworld on its days off.

Super Sue drove me to meet a group of runners on a wet and windy Poole seafront, outside the RNLI Lifeboat Museum. I spent the car journey there slathering white face paint on while I chatted to Sue. I was in a great mood that morning. It felt good to be back on the mainland. It was now also only two and a half weeks until the finish in London, and it really had begun to feel like I was on the final leg. I hadn't allowed myself to think about arriving back on the mainland for the final time. . . because it was tantalisingly close to the finish. But now there I was. Tantalisingly close to the finish.

I'd just finished smearing white face paint into the little curve around my nostrils —making sure my whole schnozz was coated in white — when we stopped at a set of traffic lights, and I spotted a young boy and two adults on the cycle path next to the road. One of the adults was holding on to the back seat of the bike and it was clear that this was the first time the kid was riding without stabilisers. Doing anything for the first time always warrants praise, so I wound down the window and shouted to the boy: 'You're doing amazing! Well done. Super impressive!' The kid looked at me and grinned but his grin quickly turned to a look of confusion and both the women started laughing. It was then I remembered that my face was painted white. The poor child. Some random woman with a white face and pink hair had just shouted at him from a car window. If he wasn't scared of ghosts and ghouls on Halloween already, he would be now.

Having successfully fulfilled my skeleton duties by frightening a small child en route to the start, Super Sue parked the car and we made our way to the Poole seafront. I'd expected one or two people to join me in dressing up for Halloween, but when I caught sight of the group for the first time, I couldn't quite believe my eyes. There were 20 people, and the majority were in fancy dress. It was a cold morning on the south coast and the wind was biting, so many had opted to layer their chosen outfit over the usual brightly coloured running gear. There was a woman dressed as a bat, with small purple bat wings poking out the top of her head, a woman in a zombie mask, two young boys with skeleton face paint on, another full skeleton, a woman dressed as a corpse bride (complete with fake blood) and her corpse dog too, who was dressed in a dark, ragged overcoat, as if he had been resurrected from the underworld. And then there was a man named Mike, who had come dressed as that classic Halloween creature: a lobster. Yes, you read that right, a lobster. He was in full red-lobster attire, complete with giant claws for his hands and squiggly antenna things poking out of his lobster headpiece. Given that it was freezing that day, I had a feeling that Mike would be the one staying the warmest. Sensible lobster.

'Well, would you look at you lot!' I shouted, and a cheer went up from the group.

We set off along the seafront and I settled into what I hoped would be an easy morning of running; that day's run was to be a 25-mile saunter along the seashore from Poole to Bournemouth, before ducking inland via Highcliffe-on-Sea and on to finish the day at the sailing mecca of Lymington.

Within the first few paces, the two young boys dressed as skeletons, who I found out were five and seven years old, appeared at my side. They were full of energy, as young boys are, darting to and fro, doing extra metres whenever they could. How I envied that energy. Both of them were running in Astro-turf football boots — football-specific trainers with studded rubber soles. As I grew up playing football, I recognised them immediately and something about the two boys reminded me of my own two brothers.

'Anna! Anna!' shouted the older of the two, running backwards as he spoke to me (which he did with little effort). 'My name's Ben!'

'Oh, nice to meet you, Ben. You're a very awesome skeleton.'

'Thanks. You're a good Skeleton too. . . This is my brother, Jack,' he said, pointing at the younger boy.

'Hi Jack,' I said, waving at the younger boy, who smiled in reply.

'You know our uncle!'

'Do I now? And who's that?'

'It's Uncle Al. Al Humphreys. He's an adventurer. Our dad's his brother,' the boy said, pointing behind me to a man in board shorts and a bobble hat. I turned to look back and the man offered up a smile and a wave.

'Ahh! I do know your uncle. He's very cool. Does he take you out on adventures?'

'Sometimes. . . Anna! Anna!' shouted Ben again, as if I'd stopped listening, but I hadn't at all.

I smiled. 'Yes, Ben?'

'Did I tell you that I once held a fish?'

'No, you didn't,' I said.

'Well, I did, and then. . . do you know what?'

'What?'

'It pooped in my hand!' he shouted, bursting into laughter.

'Poo in the hand!' echoed Jack, laughing too. And now I was laughing as well. If there was any nugget of information I needed to get me through that day's run, it was two skeletons telling me about the time a fish did a poo in their palm.

The important conversation over with, Ben then darted off to a nearby tree, leaping in the air to slap one of the leaves on a low-hanging branch.

'Yes! Did it!' he shouted as Jack followed suit, leaping into the air and just managing to touch the edge of the leaves with his fingertips. 'Yes! Did it too!' he shouted.

For the next few miles, the skeleton boys became my own personal cheer squad, and the 'Skeleton Squad' was formed. They cheered when we reached some sand which spilled out over onto the pavement. They cheered when we ran over grass. They even cheered when we stopped to use some Portaloos on the seafront.

'Yeaaaah! TOILET BREAK!' Jack shouted.

'Wahoooooo!' said Ben, raising his arms in the air.

Once we made it out of Poole itself, we dropped back onto the coast and ran along the seafront beneath Canford Cliffs. The sand on Canford Beach is a long, slim stretch of golden-white. There wasn't much sun breaking through the clouds, so the sea was grey-blue and navy in deeper patches. We ran on past rows of grey-brick beach huts painted in blue, yellow and white; each hut had its own number above the door. The cliffs above the huts were biscuit-coloured with streaks of white running through them like layers of cream in the middle of a Victoria sponge. Stout bushes overhung from the top of the cliffs, some of them clinging on bravely to the rock face itself. The trees at the base of the cliff had started to turn ahead of winter — their leaves a mix of gold and orange, and in front of them was long grass that lined the edge of the walkway.

I knew the weather forecast for the day was stormy and, as we hit the coast, the wind picked up around us and rain blew through in patches, but it didn't seem to bother the group. In fact, no matter how bad the weather got, it wouldn't have bothered me because I knew that, from Canford Cliffs onwards, it was a 9-mile run along a fully pedestrianised promenade. Nine miles of traffic-free, beachside running. Ahhh.

As soon as we made it beachside, I relaxed. I didn't need to think about navigation for a while, or traffic, or anything at all really. I chose to run on the paved promenade because that's where most of the runners in their shoes wanted to be, but if things got too tough, I could just hop onto the beach beside it. I didn't even mind that we were running into a stonking headwind — it was going to be a good day and I was determined nothing would change that.

By late morning, my bond had tightened with the Skeleton Squad boys — we'd developed a secret Skeleton Squad handshake and everything. The boys were intending to run as far as Boscombe Pier, which was 8 miles into the day. Impressive for a five- and seven-year-old, I thought. As they neared the end of their time with me, their dad slipped his shoes off and the boys soon followed suit. Ben looked like he could go forever, shoes or no shoes, but Jack started to get tired and lag behind. We cheered him on at intervals and waited for him to catch up on the final section, only for him to start sprinting. He was off! His dad couldn't even keep up with him. Take THAT for a turn of skeletal speed.

We paused at Boscombe Pier to wave goodbye to the Humphreys family, as well as a few other ghosts and ghouls who were going to drop out from the stage there too.

'Hey, Anna, Anna!'

'Yeah, what is it?' I said, turning to Ben.

'Next time you're on the telly, make sure you tell them about the SKELETON SQUAD, okay?' And I was delighted that he did the Skeleton Squad secret handshake movement as he said it.

'Okay. I promise. Skeleton Squad FOREVER,' I said.

'Yeah. FOREVER,' Jack and Ben repeated back to me.

After leaving the boys at the pier, we continued to follow the shore, running along the beach at Boscombe, then Southbourne, and then getting the Mudeford ferry across the estuary of the River Mude.

That afternoon, as we tipped over 16 miles, I spent some time chatting to Mike the Halloween Lobster. Mike was a cool dude, with brown hair, tattoos on his arms, and wearing running sandals. Although a novice runner, Mike had bypassed running in trainers. He said sandals felt better.

It was nice to have the chance to chat to Mike as this was the second running stage he'd joined me on. He'd run a wet and windy 7 miles with me the previous week from Wimborne to Poole, and I knew that his longest run before that was 3 miles. So, the fact that we were now at 16 miles and he hadn't tapped out was impressive. I asked him about why he'd recently taken up running and he explained that he suffered with depression and anxiety, and that running was his way of coping with it. 'I find it really helps, with my head, I mean. Even a little run, it'll change my mood for the rest of the day. Momentum is everything, it's really scary where the mind can go when it's left to stagnate, so I think it's always best to keep moving,' he said. And I couldn't agree more.

I often feel that way — there's something mystical about the power of running, the act of being in motion under your own steam. It alleviates worry. It restores a sense of feeling in control, and best of all, it puts you in the present. A present where, perhaps, the world isn't so complicated after all. Maybe it's just as simple as putting one foot in front of the other and keeping moving as best you can.

Despite the joy that running brought to Mike, by 18 miles I could see he was struggling. His legs were stiff, his head was stooped, his shoulders were slumped forwards, and he was staring at the heels of the runner in front of him as he shuffled down the road. The reality was, he could bow out from the stage whenever he wanted to. Anyone could. We'd passed countless bus stops, a train station, and other runners had been collected or turned back when they'd had enough. Mike was clearly in pain, but it was also clear that he wanted to keep going.

'How you doing, lobster man?' I asked, running alongside

him.

'Mmm hmm,' he said, raising a brief smile.

'You're doing amazing,' I said.

'Thanks, Anna.'

'Hey, everyone — we've just passed eighteen miles!' I shouted to the group, and there was a loud cheer. 'Better still, Mike the Lobster has made it eighteen miles!' There was an even louder cheer.

As the afternoon wore on and the shadows of the trees and hedgerows grew long, I grew tired too. But with every mile that passed, I couldn't help but shift the focus from my own weariness to feeling proud of Mike. I barely knew him at all, but I was proud. Because he was smashing it. There were still 10 people left in the group and everyone now knew what Mike was doing and just how hard he was going to push himself to finish the stage. I flitted between letting Mike be for a while (because there is nothing more annoying than having to talk when you feel like you are dying) and every now and then shouting, 'How ya doin', Mike?' He'd shout back, 'Okay!' and I'd holler at the group, 'Yeah, Mike — he's one inspirational Lobster, maaaaaannn!' in a southern Californian accent. Then the whole group would cheer and Mike would raise his lobster claws into the air, celebrating for a brief moment before returning his gaze straight ahead of him and clambering back into the shell-shaped hurt locker.

At 5 p.m. the sun set, and the group ran down Lymington

high street in the darkness. My feet were sore and everyone was weary, but the finish line was approaching. The power of the Skeleton Squad boys and all of the other ghosts and ghouls who had run by my side had carried me through and there was a buzz in the air. The kind of electric energy that comes from having put in a day of hard graft but knowing that you can soon bring your weary body to a halt. At the end of the high street, the flat paving slabs turned into small cobbles, and I had to concentrate hard so as not to fall over as we ran down a small hill to finish up the day on the Lymington harbour front. Mike was delighted. He looked a mess, a hot mess thanks to his lobster suit, but he was beaming.

'Look what you did, Anna!' he said, as I pulled him in for a congratulatory hug.

'Look what I did? Mike, are you kidding? You did that. I couldn't make you run twenty-five miles. I couldn't make anyone run twenty-five miles. That was all you up in there.'

'Me and the lobster,' he said.

'Yeah, actually, if we're thanking anyone, it should be the lobster.'

'Anna?' Mike said.

'Yeap?'

'Can I ask you one more thing? It's really important.'

'Of course — fire away,' I said, and Mike knelt down on the ground. He pulled a marker pen out of his back pocket and laid a piece of his costume on the ground.

'Would you sign my claw?' he asked, and I smiled.

'Mike, Inspirational Lobster of the South Seas, it would be an honour to sign your claw.'

And so, on a cobbled street in the south of Great Britain, I knelt down in the darkness and signed the claw of Mike the Inspirational Lobster. I was exhausted too, but Mike's struggle had helped me keep things in perspective.

Mike's journey that day, both mental and physical, made me think back to the times when I'd gone further or faster than expected, and how those moments had played such a massive part in what I believed I was capable of from that point on. A rowing race where the odds were stacked against me. A 2-km ergometer test. An Ironman. The time I ran 60 miles (when I'd only ever run 15 before). I'd gone into all of these things hoping for the best but never in a million years expecting my body to go as far or as fast as it did.

You can never predict quite when those moments might happen, and it's some kind of alchemy. Even in hindsight you can't quite put your finger on which elements made it such a success. All you can do is put yourself out there often enough for there to be an opportunity for everything to slot into place. That day on the south coast, Mike had put himself out there. And, as it turns out, all he needed was an excuse to go for a run, a pair of sandals and a lobster outfit.

28

The Mind Fog

I had high hopes that the excitement from Halloween would stay with me for the remaining 10 days of running to London. But soon, my exhaustion began to eat away at the Halloween joy, and this time it felt worse than ever. I'd noticed that my body ached more than usual and I woke up each morning feeling like I was suffering from some kind of flu. It would take the first 5 miles to get the blood pumping round my system and for that fluey sensation to disappear. The ongoing fatigue was a cause for concern. I was so close to the end now. I couldn't let things go completely to pot; I needed to be careful. But I had grown weary of self-care. My morning routine of 10 minutes of yoga before I started running had gone out the window and, with next to no energy in the evenings, I was doing less and less trigger-point therapy — largely because it was painful and required psyching myself up to do it. I'd expected to be physically exhausted at this point in the run, so none of that came as a great surprise. But what was worrying me more was that a new guest had pulled up a chair at the tiredness tea party — mental exhaustion.

It started on the day I ran towards Southampton and it

descended like a fog. I felt like I was just going through the motions that morning — greeting a group of runners, taking photos, talking about the route — doing all of that while feeling like I wasn't really there. As if I was floating somewhere outside my body, watching it all happen. Even the fact that there was a guy in full Peter Pan fancy dress didn't snap me out of it. By mid-morning we were skirting the southern reaches of the New Forest National Park, right at the section where it reaches the River Solent estuary on the UK's south coast. Patches of tall trees were interspersed with open sections of moss-covered bog, and ponies were grazing here and there. We ran on and off of the road at intervals, enjoying the relief of the spongy ground and stopping to talk to a few of the ponies. The group did a fantastic job of keeping the Adventure Pace rules alive: detouring to play in kids' playgrounds, leaping from the swings, going on the roundabout, playing on the seesaw. We sung eighties power ballads at the top of our lungs, and when we left the forest we weaved through the suburbs, cutting down alleyways behind houses, running beside the fences of back gardens and popping out in quiet cul-de-sacs.

In the early afternoon, we reached a junction where I needed to make a decision: whether we should take a gravelly, traffic-free bike path or stick to running along the pavement beside a busy road.

'What do you want to do, Anna?' said one of the runners, and the group came to a halt.

Everyone was looking at me, waiting for a decision. I was

the only one who could make that call; after all, I was the only one without shoes on. I stood still for a minute, looking at the ground of the trail and then the road and then back to the trail. I was desperately trying to focus on the decision, but elements of it kept slipping from my grasp. I couldn't quite think each option through to a conclusion. I realised that one of the reasons I'd loved spending time with Super Sue over the past two weeks was that she was very good at making decisions. To have someone else make logistical calls for me, even for a brief time, had felt like a huge weight had lifted. But now I was back in the driving seat. And I was faltering. The group had now been silent for some time. . . and it was getting awkward.

'Anna? Do you want us to take the bike trail?' pressed another runner.

'I umm. Err. Oh, I don't know!' I said, throwing my arms into the air, irritated at my inability to make a decision.

In that moment, I wanted to behave like a toddler, to flop onto my stomach on the pavement and (as my mum would say) 'throw a wobbler'. I took a deep breath.

'Let's just go this way,' I said, exhaling and limply raising one arm to point in the direction of the bike path. The cracks were starting to show. I couldn't paper over them fast enough before a new one appeared.

The scariest thing about the brain fog is that it was like nothing I'd experienced before. I'd hallucinated while running for a long time in New Zealand, hearing voices in the forests, but this was different. I tried to tell myself it was a momentary strop and that the fog would soon clear, but when the bike trail re-joined the main road, my mind started up its tricks again. A dark-haired man with a five o'clock shadow wearing a cap approached the group from a side road. He was running and pushing a stroller, and so I thought, 'Oh, look, it's Jamie.' Jamie had pushed a stroller all the way across Canada, and then America. So, when I saw a dark-haired man pushing a running stroller, I assumed it was him. My brain didn't stop to question what the heck Jamie would be doing on the south coast of the UK and why he would be pushing a stroller when he was no longer running across a country. As the man made it to where the group was standing, I was confused, wondering why Jamie had a baby in the stroller.

'Hi Anna! So glad I found you. I'm Adam. And this is Lola,' he said. Of course, it wasn't Jamie at all.

Later that day, we stopped for lunch in a beautiful rustic cafe in the small town of Beaulieu. Steff's Kitchen at Fairweather's Garden Centre was a lovely place to recharge — all high ceilings and exposed wood, it had that feeling of being outside while you were inside. If there was one unexpected bonus to this adventure, it was finding wonderful cafes that I would someday come back to visit, when I had all my marbles again. Or, in the case of Fairweather's, if I needed to combine the purchase of some shrubbery with a decent meal. The 20-strong group of runners filed into the cafe behind me and split up across various tables. The cafe was busy, so I watched as they dispersed into the general public — patches of brightness, neon caps, aquamarine backpacks and fluorescent tops merging with the 'normal' people. I set up camp at a table with Super Sue along with a couple of others and then went up to the counter to order some lunch. There was an impressive cabinet displaying some very marvellous cake wedges, but I knew I needed something savoury to fuel the 11 miles left to Southampton.

'What can I get you?' said the woman behind the counter.

'I'll have a. . .' And my mind went blank. I could see a picture of the item of food I wanted to order in my mind, but I couldn't remember the words for it.

'Yes? You'd like a. . .' she pressed. I thought again. Still nothing. Crap. What was it called? I looked up at the chalk board on the wall behind the woman to see if I could spot the words that I was looking for there.

'I'd like a. . . it's fluffy. A hot thing. You put butter in it?'

'A crumpet?'

'No, not a crumpet. . . it's bigger and you put beans on it and. . .' I could see it in my head, clear as day, but I couldn't find the words. Why couldn't I find the bloody words?! This was getting embarrassing.

'It's got a skin on,' I said.

'A chicken?'

'No, not a chicken.' Although, she was doing well. If this was a game of charades, she'd have made a solid guess. Chickens were indeed fluffy and had skins.

'It's a vegetable. With a skin.'

'A jacket potato?' said the woman, now eyeing me more closely.

'Yes! A jacket potato! Sorry. I'd love a jacket potato, with beans and cheese on it, please. And can I have extra butter?'

I looked around to see if anyone had witnessed the lapse in my grasp of the English language. One of the runners was right behind me in the queue. I pulled a face at her and shrugged, and she smiled. She was cool, she'd get it, but no one else seemed to have heard — they were all too busy chatting among themselves. Phew. As a graduate in psychology and having specialised in neuroscience (did I just make myself sound intelligent there?) I know that our brains are only able to function through connectivity. Different parts 'talk' to one another, sort of like copper wires delivering internet to a home. If there aren't optimal conditions for those connections to be made then your brain feels sluggish. A bit like when you've not had enough sleep. My brain felt like that. It was clogged up and the parts of it weren't talking to one another anymore. Although I'd had help from Abby, the constant organising of talks, public running stages, route planning and the daily miles covered over five months had ground the cogs in my brain to a halt. I was so very tired of making decisions. And apparently that extended to deciding what to eat for lunch.

The following day, I was back at Super Sue's. I'd woken up to find that my ferry to the Isle of Wight was delayed on account of bad weather. Instead of spending two full days running on the island, I would now nip over for just one, weather permitting. Initially, I had thought about putting the day to good use. To run some miles in the New Forest and not take it as a rest day because I needed to keep the miles up if I was going to get as close as possible to the original 100-marathon target. But my body was like a stone. It wanted to be still, and so did my still-foggy mind. As I lay on the sofa in the living room, eating breakfast, I shouted to Sue in the kitchen.

'Sue. . . I'm thinking I might just take the day off. And just lay around here. Is that okay?'

'McNuff, you do whatever you need to do,' she called back.

'I think I need to be a slob.'

'Then a slob you must be.'

'And I also think I need to watch some Disney movies,' I continued — a comment which elicited a squeal from Sue's daughter Katy, who was sitting on the couch opposite. Katy stopped eating her breakfast and looked up.

'Did you say Disney movies?!'

'That's what I said. Aladdin is on in twenty minutes and then Mary Poppins this afternoon.'

'Mummm! Mummm! Can Anna stay forever please?!' Katy shouted into the kitchen. 'No one ever wants to watch Disney movies with me in this house!'

So, I spent the day drifting in and out of sleep on Super Sue's sofa, waking up to join in with a rousing chorus of 'A

Whole New World' and then 'Supercalifragilisticexpialido-cious'. Super Sue fed me cheese on toast and I didn't leave the house. Not even for a second. Needless to say, I crashed. Big time. Only Aladdin and Mary Poppins could save me.

29

The Naughtiest Tarmac
of Them All

Super Sue's Disney recharge day did the trick: my mind felt clearer, I was capable of making decisions again and it was finally time for me to peel myself away from her guest room and make a move towards London. The weather forecast had improved, so I completed what had been a couple of weeks of island dilly-dallying with a quick nip over to the Isle of Wight, and then met a group of runners at Portsmouth for my last day along mainland Britain's south coast. We ran under thunderous skies and were treated to spectacular full-arc rainbows throughout the day, and I remember being amazed at how, at this point in the journey, I could still be in awe of the British landscape. As the afternoon wore on, the sun peeked through the clouds in places, illuminating the leaves on the trees and making them glow. There is something so mesmerising about the mix of rain and sunshine that comes with autumn, and when we were running up high, looking down on the hills of Hampshire, I was entranced by nature's display — a confetti of copper and gold against a gunmetal sky.

Over the next few days, I followed the roads of Sussex

onwards to Surrey. Now, if someone had asked me at the start of the run where I believed would have the worst surface for running barefoot on in the whole of Great Britain, I could have come up with a few likely contenders: Glasgow, Leeds, Sheffield, Birmingham. . . all of which had their own challenges. But never in all of my days did I expect that the worst surface for a barefoot runner would be found in the leafy, wealthy county of Surrey. Two miles out of the town of Haslemere and I was in agony. I could barely keep pace with the 12-strong group of local runners who'd joined me for the day — including my cousin, which was embarrassing. I tried a few times to tell myself that my feet just needed to desensitise as usual. That was often the case, after all; they would be painful in the morning and then once the blood got flowing and my nerve endings calmed down, all would be right in the world of bare-footin' again. But my soles just wouldn't let up.

What made it worse was that I was being repeatedly passed by posh cars, running by posh houses. But there had been none of that cash splashed on the tarmac, that was for sure. It was close to the spray-and-pray naughty tarmac of Shetland, and even sharper in many places. It was, without a doubt, the naughtiest tarmac on record. I shouldn't have been so disheartened. . . but I had expected more of Surrey. I grew up there, we had history, Surrey and me, so I felt let down. Perhaps it wasn't all Surrey's fault. In any relationship there are two sides to blame, and my feet had become increasingly sore in general over the past week. The temperature was now dipping as low as 5°C on some days, which meant the wind-chill over my toes was worse than usual. And because of the cooler and wetter weather, the soles of my feet were now softer than they had been during the summer months through Scotland. Cold weather, soft soles and spiky tarmac — these were the ingredients for a misery pie and I was tucking into a big slice.

Things got easier in the afternoon; the surface changed more frequently and we were all able to nip off onto sections of trail to avoid the spiky roads. In a last-minute change of route, I decided we should have that day's halfway coffee stop in Godalming. Largely because I liked the name of the town — it sounded swanky. And that meant there might be posh artisan coffee there (possibly served with little biscuits on the side), and everyone knows that posh coffee cures all ills, sore feet included. So, the group and I were shuffling our way down Godalming high street, headed for a cafe in the centre of town when, for some reason, I looked to my right. Propped up on an outside wooden table was a small cardboard deli box which had a drawing of two bare feet on it. In felt-tip pen there were words scrawled above the feet that read: Anna McNuff! Stop here for hugs and cake. What on earth? Was I hallucinating? The rest of the group had run on so I called out to them. 'Hang on, guys, hold up a sec. There's something. . . I mean. I think we need to stop here.' I was confused. I didn't know anyone in Godalming. I hadn't even intended to be running through the town when we left Haslemere that morning. I peered in the window of the deli and a girl with brown hair wearing an apron spotted me. She threw her hands in the air in excitement and we both made our way to the door. It was then I realised I did know her! It was Vicky, a friend from way back when, who liked to do adventuresome things like stand-up paddleboarding the length of the Murray River in Australia, as you do.

'Vicky?!' I shouted.

'McNufffff! You found it!' she said, engulfing me in a hug.

'I didn't know you worked here. I mean. . . lived here? I didn't know you were in Godalming?!'

'Oh yeah. This is my job. This is our cafe. Welcome!' she beamed, throwing her arms open wide. 'We do good food, and cake.'

'Well, in that case. . . I'm not that fussed about seeing you, but the cake, you say?' I joked.

'I promise the cake is even better than me. Come in. . .'

'Are you sure, but there's. . . what. . . around twelve of us.'

'Ah, that's fine! This group by the window's about to leave. We'll squeeze you all in.'

And so, the group cosied up to one another on a long wooden table by the front window of the cafe, and soon I was surrounded by the chatter of content runners, enjoying teas, (posh) coffee, lunch and cakes. After a hearty lunch of beans on toast, Vicky brought over a ginger, blackcurrant and chocolate cake. It was a doorstop-sized slice, with the deep violet of fresh, juicy blackberries oozing from the centre of it and layers of ginger buttercream holding dark moist chocolatey sponge together. The flavour combinations blew my mind and it was the kind of cake that left your fork sticky, no matter how many times you tried to lick it clean. Surrey may have crap tarmac, but it had redeemed itself with kind people and cake.

Naughty tarmac and the Godalming Deli weren't the only surprises that Surrey was serving up. On the penultimate day of running, I got another one when I walked into Dorking Sports Centre and something, or rather someone, caught my eye. At the back of a group of 30 runners, I could have sworn I saw my mum. What's she doing here? I caught another glimpse of her before she ducked quickly behind another runner. She was looking away from me and at the ground, clearly in the hope that her not looking at me would mean that I wouldn't see her. She was like a child playing hide and seek. It didn't help that she was wearing a neon yellow long-sleeved top. I weaved through the group towards her.

'Mum? Mum?'

'Oh, bugger! Hello, petal. You weren't supposed to see me!'

'Well, you were standing right in my eyeline and, I hate to break it to you, but you're a bit hard to miss!' I tugged at her neon top.

'Oh well, you know it's my favourite running top!' she said, pulling me in for a hug. 'I thought I'd come along for a little run.'

'Brilliant. Thank you. That's made my day.' I held her

hands then gave her another squeeze.

It had been lovely to have Mum alongside me in Northern Ireland, but it felt even more special to see her that day because we were on home turf. I was just one day away from the finish line and I felt like I could really let her look after me — as if she was there to guide me safely home, like a ship coming into a harbour. Mum was my lighthouse.

A local trail running coach called Jude helped navigate us out of Dorking and onto the trails around Box Hill, but when she had to turn back, Mum took up the mantel of chief navigator. She was in her element, leading the group, not only telling everyone where to go but somehow managing to cheer them on at the same time. We ran through Epsom Downs, galloped across Epsom Racecourse and then followed roads and backstreets towards Tolworth.

Tolworth isn't really much to write home about. It's a thoroughfare where the A3 cuts through from London down to Portsmouth. But, being close to where I grew up, Tolworth has always had a special place in my heart. And so, as Tolworth Tower came into view, I felt overcome with emotion. It took me by surprise. How could a hunk of concrete and steel make me feel so much? Of course, it wasn't about the tower itself — it was more about the childhood memories it was stirring up. And, in my tired state, it all felt so vivid.

We ran by King George's playing fields, where I took part in the primary boys' football league from the age of six to eleven. There were only a couple of girls allowed to play in the league and I could still smell the mud on the pitch. I could hear the clip-clop of my footie studs on the changing-room floor and the noise from the sound of 10 games going on at once on a Saturday.

As we crossed a large roundabout at the top of Tolworth High Street and passed where Blockbuster Video used to be, I could still smell the buttered popcorn I used to cajole my parents into buying at the checkout — something to make a sleepover with friends and renting Bill and Ted's Bogus Journey (for the fifth time) on VHS even sweeter.

We ran on, past J. H. Lorimer — the shop where I used to spend all my pocket money on stickers. I could still feel the cool of a handful of coppers as I emptied them onto the till, and how my hands smelled like metal on the walk home. On we went, past the corner shop I wasn't allowed to go to because it was across a main road (but I'd sometimes go there anyway with naughty Abigail from round the corner) and on to Avondale Gymnastics Club, where I had a brief stint as an aspiring Olympic gymnast (aged 5). And, lastly, up into Berrylands — the suburb of a suburb. My home base as a nipper.

I couldn't quite put my finger on why running by these places made me feel so emotional, but bubbling beneath it all was a sense of pride. I knew that the little me from back then would approve of what big me was doing now. Because if you'd have told a six-year-old version of myself that I was going to run barefoot through Britain, she'd have looked you square in the eyes and said, 'You bet I am.' I think we all have that kind of confidence at some point, as a kid. But life, with its twists and turns, shakes it out of us. And adulthood, really, is just a long and winding journey to get back to what we once felt as a child. So that day, I realised that I was no longer just running towards Kingston. Or even running back through my memories. I was running back to myself.

30

The Finish

I opened my eyes and stared at the ceiling. Jamie was still asleep next to me and I could hear the familiar clink of cutlery and clatter of plates coming from the kitchen downstairs in my parents' house. Mum was emptying the dishwasher. This was it, I thought. It was Sunday 17 November — the last day of running. In a few hours' time, I'd be joined by a couple of hundred people for the final 7 miles of Barefoot Britain — a quick hop and a skip from Kingston upon Thames to Wimbledon Common. I tried to pin down precisely how I was feeling, but I couldn't focus. All I could think was that tomorrow I wouldn't have to run at all. Tomorrow, I could wake up and just. . . be. That filled me with a rush of relief. I quickly shoved the thought from my mind and then gave Jamie a gentle nudge. I needed a coffee to kickstart the day and Jamie was the coffee man.

The following hours were filled with all of the bedlam you might expect from the final throes of a five-and-a-half-month adventure. Of all of the public running stages we'd organised so far, this was the biggest and, in turn, that made it the most complicated. Abby had needed to contact the local council about running on the roads, we'd done our best to dodge other events that were going on in the local area that weekend and, with a big crowd, we needed to make sure that the runners got across any road junctions safely.

With 20 minutes until I needed to leave the house, we were still trying to charge radios for the volunteer marshals, I had yet to eat breakfast (which would, of course, be a 'proper' breakfast in Mum's home) and, most importantly, I needed to repaint my toenails.

Breakfast eaten and toenail-painting complete, I was finally ready to roll out. I was pulling my coat on in the hallway when Jamie breezed past me.

'I've got a surprise for you, my dear.' He gave me a kiss on the cheek and started up the stairs.

'A surprise?' I called after him.

'Yeah, for your last day. It's something really special,' he said, disappearing up the stairs. Something special? That was sweet. Jamie wasn't usually one for gifts. Nor was I. We showed our love in other ways. We rarely did birthday cards or presents because we often forgot birthdays, including our own. So, it was strange that he'd put effort into getting me a gift. Perhaps being apart over the past five and a half months had changed things? What had he got me? I wondered. Some flowers? A box of chocolates? New shoes?

'Are you ready?' Jamie called from the top of the stairs.

'I'm ready.'

'Close your eyes then,' he said, and I shut them tight.

'Okay. They're closed.'

I heard Jamie begin the journey down the stairs, the creak as he moved over the bottom step and then the shuffle of his feet on the wooden floor of the hall.

'Okay, you can open them now.'

I opened my eyes slowly and there, standing in front of me in the hall, was Jamie. He was dressed as a Brownie. More specifically, a Brownie Guide from the 1970s —sporting a short brown dress that showed most of his legs, and accessorising it with a black belt, a yellow scarf and a brown hat. I nearly wet myself with laughter.

'What the hell?'

'Well, whaddya think?' Jamie twisted from one side to another, sticking his chest out, cocking his leg and pouting.

'Where in the world did you get that?!'

'Online somewhere. I thought I'd get into the Girlguiding spirit. I told you it was special,' he beamed.

'That's special alright. . .' I went over and gave him a kiss.

'Oooh, does this mean I get my boyfriend-of-the-year badge?' Jamie smiled.

'It does. Thank you,' I said softly.

With Jamie the Brownie in tow, my parents and I bundled into the car and headed for the start of the stage at Canbury

Gardens in Kingston. A few minutes into the drive, my phone buzzed. It was a message from Jane up on Unst:

Hiya My Anna McNuff! Jane here. How're you doing, my dear? I had a big secret plan to see you at the finishing line. It was all organised — I even had my accommodation sorted. But I'm in the USA helping with my twin grandsons instead. Bother! I had SO much wanted to be the only person at both the start & the finish of your run. Thinking of you!

How lovely was that? It was a shame Jane couldn't be there, but I'd never have expected her to be. It was a long old schlep from Shetland to the outskirts of London and Jane had given me enough at the start of the adventure to earn her a lifetime of my gratitude. Jane's message got me thinking, and I wondered if there would be anyone else I'd already met on the run there today.

When we arrived at Canbury Gardens there was already a large crowd gathered by the bandstand on the banks of the River Thames. The crowd spotted me and a big cheer went up. I won't lie that it was always nice to start a run with people being so pleased to see you. Imagine if you got a cheer every time you left your home for a jog. It warmed my heart. I'm going to miss this, I thought. I spotted Abby in the crowd and made a beeline for her.

'Anna!' She threw her arms open wide and I scooped her up in a hug. Having only exchanged messages and phone calls for five and a half months, it was strange to see her in the flesh. Abby had lived every part of this run with me.

'You've got quite the crowd,' she whispered in my ear.

'I know. It's awesome. Are we all set?'

'We're all set. You just give me the nod when you're ready to rock and I'll get on the speaker and brief everyone.'

'Brilliant. I wi— Stuart?' I looked over Abby's shoulder and saw a familiar face in the crowd.

'Hellooo Anna!'

'What the? How did you?' I shook my head in disbelief. It'd been many months since I'd run with Stuart the Storyteller and we were a very long way from his home in Montrose.

'Ah, we couldn't miss your big finish now,' said Maureen, appearing by his side.

'And I see your hair's still pink!' said Stuart.

'It absolutely is. Now, have you got some stories for me today, Stuart?' I asked.

'Plenty,' he smiled.

Stuart set the ball rolling and from then on, I couldn't stop spotting familiar faces. Runners had made the journey to London from all over the country — Scotland, Leeds, Sheffield, Manchester, Wales, the Isle of Wight. . . there was even a couple from the Channel Islands. I dished out hug after hug to all of those who had made the effort to join in on the last day, including Anna Hill from Glasgow (whose St John's Wort

Oil had literally saved my soles), Hannah the Girlguiding leader from Liverpool and Super Sue — who got an extra-big squeeze. There were some people who'd come barefoot, and lots were wearing pairs of Pants of Perspective. Two women had even turned up in 'Anna fancy dress', wearing visors and bright pink wigs.

My friend Lydia, who'd once joined me on part of a long bike ride through the 50 US states, was there too, as were both my brothers. My older brother had gone all out by kitting out my nieces and nephew in T-shirts with 'Team McNuff' printed on them. 'Go, Auntie Annaaaa!' they shouted excitedly, jumping up and down on the spot. Jamie's dad and brother had also turned up and despite it being November, neither of them had their tops on — because that's just how men from Gloucester roll. All in all, I couldn't stop smiling. It was like a wedding, except everyone was in their running kits. Great Britain's Greatest Hits of People — new faces from the adventure colliding with familiar faces from years gone by.

As it approached midday, Mum did a big wolf whistle to bring the crowd to silence and Abby clambered up onto a bandstand to do the pre-run briefing. She raised a mic to her lips.

'Okay, everyone! Welcome to the final stage!' A loud cheer went up. 'A couple of things. . . Sue McNuff is our chief navigator. She's going to run at the front so that no one gets lost. Sue, can you raise your hand, please?' Abby asked, and Mum threw an arm into the air. The crowd cheered again. 'So, Sue's up the front. You can run in front of her if you want to bu—'

'Don't mess with Sue!' Jamie shouted, and the crowd laughed.

'Yes, best not to mess with Sue and just stay behind her,' Abby continued. 'And other than that, you will be running at Adventure Pace. Does everyone know what Adventure Pace is?'

'Yeeesssss!' came a chorus.

'Great. For those of you who don't — it's chat pace. So, have fun and enjoy! We'll get going in a few minutes.'

A few minutes later, I was standing beside Mum at the front of the group. I thanked everyone for being there and then started a countdown.

'Ten. . . nine. . . eight. . .'

I thought back to the start at Skaw Beach and how that had been just me — running alone along the windswept roads of Shetland, hoping that people might join in with this mad idea at some point before I reached London.

'Seven. . . six. . . five. . .'

What the hell am I going to do when this is all over? I thought. Sleep. I would sleep, that was for sure. And I'd likely have to curb my appetite. There was going to be no excuse for sitting down and smashing a whole bag of giant milk chocolate buttons in one go when I wasn't running all day. (I wasn't sure there was much excuse for it even when I was running all day.)

'Four. . . three. . . two. . . . .'

Oh no! I didn't want this to be the last run. I wanted to be surrounded by all of these lovely people a little while longer. To hang out in that sweet spot between knowing you're going to make it but not yet being done. I wasn't ready for the finish at all. But perhaps that was okay. I hadn't felt ready at the start either.

'One. . . BAREFOOT BRITAIN!'

And we were off! My brother's kids sprinted off the front of the pack straight away, roaring like caged animals and immediately breaking the 'don't run in front of Nana' rule. I set off at a steadier pace, but my heart was going at a million miles an hour and my cheeks ached, I was grinning that much. The park was alive with a fizz of positive energy, and I still couldn't get over just how many people had turned up. I swear, if you'd been looking down at earth from up in space that Sunday you'd have seen a cloud of runners' rainbow dust over Kingston upon Thames. Through the smiles, I settled into a rhythm as we followed the kids across the grass of Canbury Gardens and onto the towpath alongside the River Thames.

Over the first 10 minutes of running, good vibes and chit-chat were spread like Nutella on toast as I did my best to take selfies on the move with anyone I'd missed saying hello to before setting off. I also dished out many 'running hugs' — which is more an awkward bumping of faces, shoulders and chests than an actual hug, but the sentiment was there all the same. I then high-fived the volunteer marshals as we crossed a couple of roads and weaved through small alleyways towards Ham Common where there were clusters of roadside supporters, clapping and waving banners and British flags and ring-a-ding-a-dinging cowbells. The group powered on, along the long road to Richmond Park, up a steep hill and onto a sandy horse track through the middle of the park.

There are some noises which are innately comforting to a human being. White noise. The sounds of wind rustling through trees. Waves lapping on a shore. Well, I love the sound of a group of runners. Chatter. Intakes of breath. Laughter. The thud, thud, thud of trainers on tarmac. It calms my soul, and it did that day too. I'd been absorbed in chat since leaving Kingston, but as we reached the far side of the park, I stopped talking and listened instead. I caught snippets of conversations from those around me. People who had joined in for one stage or another were swapping stories. 'I joined in on stage seventy-eight,' puffed one runner.

'Did you? I heard that one was wet and windy,' said another.

'Oh, it was! Which stage were you?'

'Stage sixty-nine.'

'Oo err!'

It was surreal that others were thinking back over the course of the adventure, pulling at the threads of it and committing it to memory, when my mind was still mush. There was no way I could even begin to process it yet. All I knew in that moment was that it felt wonderful to know I'd created something that made other people happy.

I also had to give some credit to my feet. I looked down at them as they moved effortlessly over a mix of tarmac and trail through the park and marvelled at how far they'd come, in every sense. My soles were the thickest they'd ever been; they were leathery to the touch and could cope with back-to-back 20+ mile days without complaint. They didn't burn or tingle at night anymore, and there was no need to slather them in the once-magic St John's Wort Oil. And the tops of my feet were a wonder too. They looked strong and sun-kissed, with every tendon defined. All in all, my feet looked less afraid, somehow. Like they weren't just carrying me to the finish — they were leading me there.

On the descent at the other side of Richmond Park, we passed a herd of stags, just off to the side of the road. The group briefly came to a halt to take pictures, dozens of cameras poised in front of the majestic creatures, standing in long grass, backlit by the soft afternoon light. And then, we were off again. Tanking it towards the exit of the park and over the busy hum of the A3. Just then, I caught a flash of brown out of the corner of my eye. It was Jamie.

'How you feeling, my dear?'

'Good. I think. Happy. Sad. Something like that. I'm not sure.'

'That makes sense. . . are you going to cry?' he asked, and I laughed.

'I'm not sure. We'll see.'

What I did know is that it was all going by so fast. Too fast. There were only a couple of miles to go and I wanted so desperately to press pause.

At the start of Wimbledon Common, the group came to a stop again and I heard Mum shout from up the front: 'Okay, there's a half-marathon finishing here! So, we just need to wait for a gap to cross the course.'

We cheered on the people taking part in the half-marathon — a stream of bemused, exhausted faces, wondering why there was suddenly a large crowd of brightly clad runners clapping them across the line. Runners supporting runners. It was everything I adored about the running community of Britain.

Once the coast was clear, we took off again, across a large field and into some woodland. It was then that people started taking their shoes off. Each person would dart off from the main pack, tug free their shoes and socks and then return to the run train with naked feet. I could see at least 20 people barefoot so far. . . and there were more by the minute.

The mud came thick and fast now. Great patches of it, all boggy and wet, which got squished between my toes. It felt cool and smooth, and I loved it. Those with trainers on danced around it, but anyone in bare feet ploughed straight on through.

'Okay, everyone, just one mile to go now,' Mum shouted, and there was a loud cheer. Onwards we surged, onto a track through towering birch trees, their silver-white trunks reaching for the sky, branches adorned with fluttering drops of gold.

Half a mile to go.

I was feeling such a mix of emotions, but the overwhelming one was sadness. I had spent so many hours wishing I could stop. Stop running. Stop organising. Stop geeing myself up. Stop having to constantly find the motivation to scrape myself off the floor and get out of the door. But now, I was sad. Sad that this would all be over. That the present joy would soon become my past. I swallowed down a lump in my throat. Not yet, I thought. Not yet.

I moved to the front of the group and, as we entered Cannizaro Park, I looked back as the trail curved around a pond. The scene behind me was an explosion of colour. A long line of smiling runners in fluorescent kit — pinks, oranges, blues, greens, every colour imaginable bouncing through a landscape of brightly coloured leaves. It looked like a trail of stardust. It looked like, together, we'd set the world alight.

A new sound made me look forwards again and I heard the finish-line crowd before I saw them. Across a green field was a big group waving flags and banners. Half the crowd were adults and the other half were young girls — Brownies, Rainbows, Guides and Rangers — blowing whistles, honking horns, jumping up and down and cheering at the top of their lungs. Two young girls were holding the ends of a red and white finish-line tape and I homed in on them. The banners no longer read 'You can do it, Anna'. Instead, they read 'You did it.' I felt a lump rise in my throat and, suddenly, my mind was crystal-clear; I was finally ready for this to be over.

Fifty metres shy of the finish, the tears began to well. I'd run 2,352 miles, equivalent to the distance of 90 marathons, in bare feet. I'd fallen short of the 100-marathon target, but it didn't matter. I'd shot for the stars and landed on the moon. And there was now one heck of a party going on up on the moon. I inhaled a deep breath and time moved in slow motion as I took the last few steps. I felt a rush of elation, pride and disbelief as I threw my arms into the air and crossed the line.

Epilogue

As the Christmas lights switched on around Great Britain, I switched off. I retreated into a cocoon at my parents' home and revelled in an overwhelming sense of relief. I slept. I ate. I ate far more mince pies than anyone ever should, and then I slept some more.

I'd read a lot about how it would be unhealthy for me to go from doing so much running to doing nothing at all — that I should 'detrain' my body and ease back into a more sedentary life with some light exercise. But I didn't want to move. I couldn't move. I wanted everything to be still. My mind. My body. All of it. I craved peace and calm and quiet places.

Things still felt too loud in London, so, after a few days, Jamie and I packed our bags and escaped to the deepest, darkest depths of South Wales. We rented a cottage near Rhossili Bay on the Gower and took long walks over limestone cliffs and along the windswept golden sand. We spent our days watching waves crash onto the shore and evenings curled up under blankets by the log fire. All was calm.

Then, late one afternoon, my phone rang. It was Alice from Girlguiding.

'Anna, BBC breakfast want you on the red sofa,' she said.

'They do?'

'Yes. They'd love to feature the run.'

'When?' I asked.

'Tomorrow morning.'

'Tomorrow?!'

'I know! Sorry it's so last minute,' Alice said, and there was a pause.

'Can I have a think about it?'

'Of course.'

'It's just, I'm knackered and I—'

'Anna, I get it. You don't have to explain.'

'Okay. Thank you. I'll call you back in five?'

'Perfect, speak then.'

I hung up the phone and sat at the table, staring into space. I was surprised to have received the call-up from the BBC. There'd been a flurry of media requests after the journey had finished, but this was now a week on and interest had all but died down. I'd already spoken so much about the run and I was blown out. I looked through the doorway into the living room, where Jamie was curled up on the sofa, reading a book. He looked so cosy.

'Just one more,' I said aloud. I could always do one more interview. And I could be back on that sofa curled up myself tomorrow, I thought. I called Alice back.

'Hi Alice. Okay, we're on. What time would I need to be there?'

'Oh, brilliant — thank you! Can you make it to the studio in Manchester for six a.m.?'

I frantically loaded up a travel app. It was at least a five-hour journey via two buses and three trains from Rhossili to Manchester. I'd have to leave pronto if there was any chance of getting there on time.

'Yes, but I need to go, like now. Apparently, I've got thirteen minutes until the last bus leaves for the day. . .'

'Great, then, please. . . get on that bus! I'll send you the details later. Go, Go, Go!'

I ran upstairs, threw some clothes in a bag, explained the situation at breakneck speed to Jamie, apologised for leaving our cosy retreat and promised that I'd be back in 24 hours. Then, I stood at a roadside in rural Wales and boarded a bus headed north.

At 7 a.m. the following morning, I was sitting on the BBC red sofa chatting to Dan Walker and Louise Minchin. Thanks to the time they gave me and the interviews I'd done over the course of the journey, the Barefoot Britain story reached over 100 million people through national and international media. All of the squeezed-in chats, the patchy phone calls on the fly, the messaging while brushing my teeth (or while taking a bath) — a journey from Wales to Manchester at the drop of a hat — they were all worth it. Because they helped to spread some love and raise awareness for Girlguiding—an organisation that's doing a cracking job of holding a space for girls and young women to be their fabulous selves. And whatever those young women want to be now and when they grow up — scientist, artist, engineer, coder, writer, performer, and all of those professions that don't even exist yet — I'm down for supporting them. Especially the slightly wayward ones who have big ideas (which everyone else thinks are crazy).

When Jamie and I returned from Wales to our home in Gloucester, I finally went for a run. Running with shoes on for the first time in well over a year was strange. My feet felt heavy. As if I were in a parallel universe where gravity was tenfold. It was like running in steel-capped boots. It was liberating to not have to worry about the surface of the trail, but there was a tinge of sadness in that too — the fact that I could no longer feel the ripple of the earth beneath my feet made me feel disconnected from the landscape somehow. Like nature was an old friend, now slightly separated from me. I know I'll go barefoot from time to time in the future. When I want to feel that closeness to nature again. Although it will probably be on soft grass, squishy mud or sandy beach. You won't catch me within sniffing distance of any naughty tarmac.

In the months that followed the end of the run, I would happily talk about the why of it all. I'd be able to recall where I'd been, what I'd seen and whom I'd met, but when I had to go into any great detail about my thoughts during a day on the road, my mind went blank. In short, I knew what I had done, but I hadn't yet worked out the way I felt about it.

There's a Portuguese word, saudade, which comes close to summing it up. It's mostly used to describe a bitter-sweet longing for something you no longer have. Someone or something that brought you both pleasure and pain. There are days when I long to be back on the road — to feel as wild, free and alive as I did in those moments across the moors, on mountain passes and along deserted stretches of sandy beach. And then there are days when I never want to do anything quite so difficult ever again. (Although I'm sure I will.)

In reflecting on the journey, the biggest thing I realised is that it wasn't about me at all. Along the way, I was joined by over 2,500 runners, taken in by 127 hosts and had help from dozens of others to ferry my kit bag like a baton from Shetland all the way to London. I also consumed well over 300 sausage rolls. I'm dead chuffed with those stats. Well, not so much the sausage rolls, but you know, needs must. . .

Just like Mike the Lobster in Bournemouth and Laura in the Yorkshire Dales, at least half of the group would end up going further than they intended to, or ever had before. These runners didn't just tiptoe outside where they felt comfortable, they stomped across that line with great gusto.

And so, now, I feel a different kind of pride. Yes, I'm proud of having run a long way without shoes on and for having persevered. But I am monumentally prouder of the run itself. Of the thing that it became, independent of me. Of the movement it created and the community it brought to life. Of the fact that I set a ball rolling and the people of Britain grabbed hold of it, coated it in glitter, strung it up above a dancefloor and boogied on around it. That's what really gives me the warm fuzzies. Because there is something inexplicably beautiful about being a catalyst for other people's dreams rather than just the torchbearer of your own.

When I stood on Skaw Beach in Shetland, I thought I understood what resilience was. I thought I was pretty 'good' at it. I was especially good at trying to be strong as often as I could and handling things on my own. But I had it all wrong. We cannot possibly be strong all of the time. And while 'going it alone' has its merits, it is exhausting. I've learned that real resilience isn't about being able to always muscle through. It's having the confidence to know that, when you are feeling weak, your strength hasn't packed its bags and left for good — it's just gone on holiday for a little while. It's understanding when to back off and when to push. Ultimately, it's knowing when you have the strength to carry others and when it's time to let them carry you.

And when we do feel strong enough to take on something new, and a big idea comes a-knockin' at the door, we should never underestimate the simple power of heading out into the world, armed with nothing but a bit of puff in our lungs and some wonder in our hearts. You never know where it may lead. Or who might join in along the way. Shoes are, of course, optional.

AUTHOR NOTE

Congratulations, adventuresome human, you have reached the end! Time to put your feet up and have a nice long lie down. I know you'll be exhausted after running all that way from Shetland with me but I'd be so grateful if you could (powered by a milkshake and sausage roll) push on a little further and head over to Amazon or Good Reads right this very moment and leave a review for the book.

Even if it's just a one sentence comment, your words make a massive difference. Reviews are a huge boost to independently published authors, like me, who don't have big publishing houses to spread the word for us. It's safe to say that the more reviews up there, the more likely it is that this book will land in other people's laps.

After then, here's some ways to stay in touch:

Join my mailing list:

annamcnuff.com/McNewsletter

(No Spam, just awesomeness – that's a pinky promise)

If social media is more your kind of fandango, you can say hello here:

On Facebook: '**Anna McNuff**'

On Instagram or Twitter: **@annamcnuff**

On TikTok: **@McNuff**

Or if social media is your idea of hell, I can also be found here:

annamcnuff.com

hello@annamcnuff.com

Failing that, send me a pigeon.

THANK YOUS

A gigantic thank you to my crack-team of booky people. I'm always blown away that you continue to be up for the challenge of helping me wrangle a beastly manuscript into something I'm proud to share with the world.

To Debbie Chapman, editor extraordinaire – I'm so we pleased we had such a long debate about quite what to do when one realises that one has run out of bog roll in a public toilet. You have shown me that a knickers-down-wee-wee-waddle is not always warranted.

To Sophie Martin, fellow Mumma and toddler-chaser. Thank you for all your copyediting genius and attention to detail. For teaching me how to spell 'sprightly', for letting me keep my chatter about riding off into the sunset on a mustang, but also for encouraging me to cut things like how viaducts look like giant's legs.

To my proofreader, Alison Barnett, for taking out many, many superfluous words. Any incorrect grammar left in this book is because I have a penchant for bending the rules.

To Kim and Sally at Off Grid, for rising to the challenge of a new style of front cover (ooo errr!), for the beautifully illustrated maps and laying out the inside of the book with such finesse.

To Logistics Queen, Abby Popplestone. For all of your logistical support during the run and helping to keep the whole she-bang on track. This was an INSANE journey and I couldn't have done it without you and your cracking sense of humour.

A massive thank you to Craig Morgans, who believed so whole-heartedly in Barefoot Britain from the start and managed to get the AA Careers team on board throughout the country. Without you there wouldn't have been a Barefoot Britain series on YouTube for the girls and young women of Britain to watch – a series which I am repeatedly told makes me very 'down with the kids.'

To Christian Poole at the Running Lab for the gait analysis and invaluable advice. You changed the game and made me believe this was possible.

To Sylvia Chrisney, aka the Body Goddess, for your ongoing therapy advice from afar. And for making the schlep to Edin-burgh to treat me during the run.

To all the team at Girlguiding HQ. We only bloomin' did it! To Angelah Evans especially for getting behind the idea right off the bat. To Alice Stride for all your support during the journey and your unwavering enthusiasm throughout.

To the whole community of Girlguiding – volunteers and girls. You are a part of something hugely special, I had no idea quite how special until I did this run. Thank you for looking after me at every turn. And for the endless cups of tea. There was lots of tea.

To the runners! The hosts! The bag-ferriers. The makers of coffee and givers of gifts of cake and pizza. This manuscript was originally twice as long. TWICE as long I tell you, because I tried to include many more of you. I'm sorry I couldn't do that, but you know who you are. A deep heartfelt thank you for the time, good cheer, love and support you gave to me and the run itself. Without you, there would have been no Barefoot Britain.

To the sunshine of my life and man-shaped safety net, Jamie McDonald, for always encouraging me to raise the bar and for being there as I repeatedly melt down trying to reach it. To Storm for helping me to keep life in perspective and understanding that 'Mummy go work now'.

Lastly, to YOU. For buying this book. For supporting my journey as an independent author and allowing me into your precious brain via the medium of words. You are why I sit down to write every day.

ANNA MCNUFF:
KEYNOTE SPEAKER

Anna has delivered motivational, inspiring and entertaining talks for schools, charities and businesses around the world.

"Anna's ability to instill a sense of self-belief in those watching her speak is second to none. Honest, relatable and wonderfully down to earth."

SKY TV

"An incredibly talented speaker. Full of guts, determination, stamina and vision."

BARCLAYS BANK

"Absolutely Fantastic!"

HRH PRINCE EDWARD

"Hugely entertaining with plenty of food for thought."

GlaxoSmithKline

"Without a doubt the most energetic speaker we have ever had. Thank you for helping our team find the courage to face challenges head on."

MARS

"Anna's inspiring stories made the audience really think differently about their own personal and professional challenges."

SKODA

"What a legend! Have you considered a career in stand-up comedy?"

THE NORTH FACE

"We loved how your impact extended far beyond the stage as you took the time to speak individually with the delegates afterwards, and join us for dinner too. It was clear to everyone that you genuinely care about helping others to think differently, and do more."

EMERSON

"Refreshing, honest and wildly uplifting. Far from your average motivational speaker."

GOOGLE

For more information about booking Anna to speak:

Go to: **annamcnuff.com/speaking**

Or email **speaking@annamcnuff.com**

ALSO BY
ANNA MCNUFF

LLAMADRAMA
ANNA MCNUFF

WINNER of the Amazon Kindle Storyteller
Literary Award

"Llama Drama is simply hilarious. If anyone wants something witty and moving at the same time. Also, something empowering, then this is the one for them. I literally inhaled it."

- **Claudia Winkleman, TV Presenter and Author**

Armed with a limited grasp of Spanish and determined to meet as many llamas as possible, Anna and her friend Faye set off on a 6-month journey along the spine of the largest mountain range in the world – the Andes. Beginning in the bustling city of La Paz, the duo pedal south – through dense jungle, across pristine white salt flats and past towering volcanoes, following the path of thundering glacial rivers to the snow-tipped peaks of Patagonia.

For anyone who has ever wanted to journey through the stunning natural landscapes of South America – this story is for you.

QUESTIONS FOR
YOUR BOOK CLUB

1. By the end of the book, Anna views her journey as a success, even though she fell short of the original 100-marathon target. Is it possible for success and failure to sit side by side, within one challenge?

2. All in all, do you think the book would encourage people to give barefoot running a go, or would it make them run a mile from the idea (in shoes)?

3. Most people would say attempting something like Barefoot Britain was too risky. Before taking on a challenge, how much thought should be given over to what could go wrong?

4. Anna met a lot of quirky characters during her journey, which of them would you like to sit down and have coffee and cake with, and why?

5. The book includes plenty of vivid descriptions of wild landscapes and vibrant cities. Where in Britain did it make you want to visit the most?

6 Barefoot Britain was a roller coaster of highs and lows. Which part of the story stirred up the most emotion in you?

7. As more and more people join in with Anna's journey, the majority of these people end up running further than they ever have before. Why do you think that is? What conditions need to be in place to make us believe we can go that extra mile (or fifteen)?

8. At the end of the book Anna comments on finding the balance between knowing when to ask for help, and when to let others 'carry you for a while'. Why do you think she found it so difficult at the outset of the trip to ask for help from others?

9. If you were ever to journey the length of a country. How would you choose to do it? E.g., on foot, by bike, by car, by train?

10. What do you think played the bigger role in Anna being able to complete the challenge in the end: mental resilience, or physical resilience?

ABOUT THE AUTHOR

Anna McNuff is an adventurer, speaker, award-winning author and self-confessed mischief maker. Named by The Guardian as one of the top female adventurers of our time, she is the UK ambassador for Girlguiding, and has run, swum and cycled over 20,000 miles across the globe.

Aside from her attempt to run 100 marathons through Great Britain in bare feet, her other major journeys include cycling a beautiful pink bicycle through each and every state of the USA, cycling the spine of the Andes and running the length of New Zealand,

When not off adventuring, Anna can be found juggling motherhood with a constant desire to sneak off to a coffee shop in her home city of Gloucester and write the next book.

Printed in Great Britain
by Amazon